SHAPING MEDIEVAL LANDSCAPES

Shaping Medieval Landscapes

Settlement, Society, Environment

Tom Williamson

WIND*gather*
PRESS

Shaping Medieval Landscapes: Settlement, Society, Environment

Copyright © Tom Williamson, 2003

Firs published by: Windgather Press, 29 Bishop Road, Bollington, Macclesfield, Cheshire SK10 5NX, UK.
This edition first published by Windgather Press, 2004.

Distributed by: Central Books, 99 Wallis Road, London E9 5LN

British Library Cataloguing-in-Publication Data
A catalogue record for this book is available from the British Library

ISBN 0-9545575-8-1

Typeset and originated by Carnegie Publishing Ltd, Chatsworth Road, Lancaster
Printed and bound by Cromwell Press, Trowbridge, Wilts

Contents

Abbreviations

ERO	Essex Record Office
HRO	Hertfordshire Record Office
NRO	Norfolk Record Office
VCH	Victoria County History

Acknowledgements

This book has been many years in the making, and numerous people have – knowingly or unknowingly – contributed ideas and information. Students and former students at the Centre of East Anglian Studies have, in particular, taught me more than I have taught them: particular thanks must go to Sarah Harrison, Sarah Birtles, Sally Wilkinson, Nicola Whyte, Rosemary Hoppitt, Andrew Rogerson, Gerry Barnes, Rob Liddiard, Tim Pestell, and Jon Finch. My thanks also to Christopher Harper Bill and Jenni Tannimoto, for making life at the Centre so bearable; and to Sue Oosthuizen, for much information and advice. The staff of the Hertfordshire, Norfolk, and Suffolk Record Offices, and of the Norfolk, Suffolk, Essex, Hertfordshire and Leicestershire Archaeological Units, provided invaluable assistance and information. Special thanks are owed to Peter Liddle and Fred Hartley, for information about ridge and furrow. I would also like to thank the following: David Hall, for permission to reproduce Figure 23; Della Hooke, for Figure 41; Bruce Campbell, for Figure 51; Gary Battell, for Figures 21 and 50; the Cambridge Committee for Aerial Photography, for Figure 48; Wolverhampton Art Gallery, for Figure 45; University of Reading Institute of Agricultural History and Museum of English Rural Life, for Figure 54; Bob Silvester, for Figure 40; the Ministry of Defence, for Figure 48; Glenn Foard and Northamptonshire County Council, for Figure 24; and Brian Roberts, for Figures 5c and 18. Eric de Saumarez provided the aeroplane which made Figure 3 possible. Particular thanks to Phillip Judge, who supplied all the line drawings with his usual good humour and patience. But my greatest debt is to my family, who continue to put up with my various obsessions with the landscape; and to Christopher Taylor, for the heated discussions which led me to write this book.

List of Illustrations

Figures

FIGURE I.
'Planned countryside'
on the Essex/
Cambridgeshire
border, near Strethall:
a landscape of
rectilinear fields and
flimsy hawthorn
hedges created by
parliamentary
enclosure.

CHAPTER ONE

Debating the Open Fields

The two countrysides

A great division is scored across the landscape of lowland England, of immense importance in this country's social, economic, and environmental history. Over the long centuries it has taken a variety of forms, but today it is manifested in the contrast between what Oliver Rackham, many years ago, termed 'planned' and 'ancient' countryside. The former he described as:

> The England of big villages, few ... roads, thin hawthorn hedges, wind-swept brick farms, and ivied clumps of trees in the corners of fields: a predictable landscape of wide views, sweeping sameness, and straight lines (Rackham 1986, 5) (Figures 1 and 2).

The ancient countryside, in contrast, is

> The land of hamlets, of medieval farms in hollows of the hills, of lonely moats in the clay-lands, of immense mileages of quiet minor roads, hollow-ways, and intricate footpaths; of irregularly shaped groves and thick hedges colourful with maple, dogwood, and spindle (Rackham 1976, 17) (Figures 3 and 4).

Although, as Rackham noted, versions of these ideal types of landscape could be found in most parts of England, interdigitated in complex ways, 'planned countryside' dominates the Midland areas, running in a broad band from Northumberland to the south coast, while 'ancient countryside' is principally a feature of the regions lying to the west, and to the south east: of the south east of England and parts of East Anglia; and of the West country and the Marcher counties (Figure 5).

The planned countryside was mainly created by large-scale, planned enclosure in the period after 1700, usually achieved through parliamentary act. The hedges found in this extensive region are, for the most part, flimsy and species-poor for the simple reason that they are not very old. Prior to the great wave of enclosure in the eighteenth and nineteenth centuries, most of this had been 'champion' or open-field country. Farmers dwelt together in large villages and their land took the form of numerous small and unhedged strips, less than half an acre in extent, which were mixed together with those of their neighbours and scattered evenly throughout the territory of the vill. Farming was organised on highly communal lines, and strict rotations were

FIGURE 2.
'Planned countryside':
an early nineteenth-
century enclosure road
in Cambridgeshire.

imposed across the arable land. Strips were often grouped into two or three large fields, one of which lay fallow or uncultivated each year and was grazed in common by the village livestock – an arrangement often termed the *Midland System* by historians. These were bleak and open landscapes. Not only were hedges few in number, but woodland and pasture were also often in short supply, and in many Midland districts arable strips frequently extended to the very margins of townships. The open fields began to be enclosed – replaced by hedged fields in individual occupancy – in the late middle ages. But such was the complex intermixture of properties within them, and the strength of the communal controls over them, that enclosure was a slow and difficult

2

FIGURE 3.
'Ancient countryside': the claylands of south Norfolk from the air, showing a characteristic pattern of irregularly-shaped fields interspersed with areas of ancient woodland.

FIGURE 4.
'Ancient countryside': a sunken, winding lane bordered by substantial, species-rich hedges near Chrishall in north-west Essex.

a)

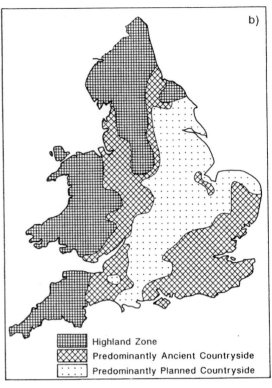

b)

Highland Zone
Predominantly Ancient Countryside
Predominantly Planned Countryside

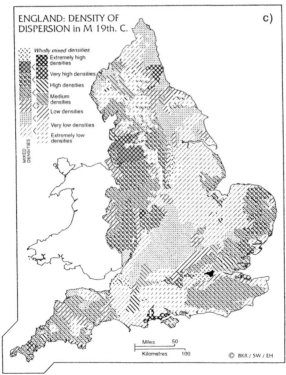

ENGLAND: DENSITY OF
DISPERSION in M 19th. C.

c)

Wholly mixed densities
Extremely high
densities
Very high densities
High densities
Medium
densities
Low densities
Very low densities
Extremely low
densities

MIXED
DENSITIES

Miles   50
Kilometres   100

© BKR / SW / EH

FIGURE 5.
Different authorities have
different definitions of the
boundary between the 'two
countrysides' but all agree that
the Midland areas of England
were characterised by more
nucleated patterns of
settlement, more regular open
field systems, and later
enclosure than the districts to
the south east or west. (a), the
boundary of Gray's 'Midland
System' (after Gray 1915); (b),
Oliver Rackham's landscape
regions (after Rackham 1986);
(c), the intensity of dispersion
as mapped by Brian Roberts
and Stuart Wrathmell, from
early nineteenth-century
Ordnance Survey maps (after
Roberts and Wrathmell 1998).
Note the low levels of
dispersion in the Midland
districts of England.

4

business. Vast areas of open arable therefore survived until the advent of parliamentary enclosure in the period after 1700.

Areas of ancient countryside, in contrast, were even in early-modern times characterised by more scattered patterns of settlement – isolated farms and small hamlets – and by more ecologically diverse landscapes. There were more hedges, and larger amounts of woodland and common land. Topographers in the sixteenth and seventeenth centuries described such landscapes as 'woodland', because of the bosky appearance presented by the numerous hedgerow trees. But enclosed fields had not always dominated these districts. In medieval times open fields had often been extensive, although they usually differed in a number of important respects from the great fields of the champion lands. Most were 'irregular' field systems, to use the jargon of historical geographers. The individual fields were often smaller and more numerous than in Midland districts (Great Gaddesden in Hertfordshire had twenty). They were associated with the various small hamlets in a township, rather than with a single nucleated village; and they were often interspersed with hedged fields in individual occupancy, and with areas of common grazing and woodland. The holdings of individuals were usually clustered in the area close to the farmstead instead of being scattered evenly throughout the area of the township or parish, equally across two or three great, unhedged fields. Often, but not always, communal controls on the practice of farming were less rigorous and pervasive than in the Midlands. Open fields of this kind were, for the most part, more easily enclosed than the 'regular' open fields of the Midlands by informal, 'piecemeal' methods – not least because there were generally only a few tenants in each part of the fields, who could therefore buy, sell, consolidate and then wall or hedge a parcel of land with comparative ease. By the seventeenth century most open fields had thus disappeared from these districts, and the division between the two kinds of landscape thus became particularly pronounced.

I have posited so far a rather simple dichotomy between the 'two country-sides', to use Rackham's term. But in reality each embraced a range of different landscapes and some districts boasted settlement patterns and field systems which exhibited intermediate characteristics. It is largely for this reason that historians and archaeologists have defined the boundaries between these two broad regions – 'planned' and 'ancient', 'woodland' and 'champion' – in a variety of ways (Figure 5). Nevertheless, such difficulties and ambiguities should not obscure the essential fact that medieval farmers in Midland areas lived in larger settlements, and organised their activities on more communal lines, than their fellows living to the south and east, or to the west.

For more than a century scholars have argued about the origins of open fields in general, and the 'champion' systems of Midland England in particular. More recently, they have pondered why some areas of England failed to develop along 'Midland' lines, ultimately becoming the irregular 'ancient countrysides' so eloquently described by Rackham. The two questions are, of course, intimately related: for any explanation for why extensive, regular open fields and nucleated villages emerged in some parts of medieval England must also account for their lack of development in others. But two things make, and have long made, this problem peculiarly intractable. Firstly, the main features of the medieval countryside briefly outlined above were all firmly in place by the time that the kind of documents that tell us about such things – surveys, court rolls, and the rest – begin to survive in some numbers, from around 1200. The less abundant documents from the twelfth century do not give us the impression that major changes to the landscape were then taking place, although as we shall see there are a few which hint at ongoing modifications. Before 1100 the documentary record grows patchier still: Domesday provides us with a vast amount of information, but says nothing directly about field systems or settlement patterns. Extensive open fields certainly existed before the Norman Conquest: a charter or land grant for Charlton in Berkshire, dated 956, thus describes how 'The said land is not surrounded on all sides by fixed limits, because on each side the acres lie next to acres' (Birch 1885, B925). Indeed, some kind of communal cultivation in intermixed strips is implied by a law of king Ine, dating from as early as the seventh century.

> If ceorls have common meadow or other deal-land to fence and some have fenced their deal, some never, and their common plough-acres or grass are eaten, go they then that own that gap and make amends to the others that have fenced their deal, for the damage that there be done (Whitelock 1955, 368).

Whether, however, open fields already existed in Saxon times in all the areas in which we later find them, and in precisely the *forms* in which we later find them, is much less clear. In the absence of detailed documentary evidence, those interested in such matters must employ other approaches, most importantly those of archaeology, or use retrogressive analysis – searching for origins in the forms, structures and distributions described in more abundant but much later documents.

In addition to this paucity of direct evidence is the puzzling question of the distribution of the 'two countrysides'. The trouble here is that it seems to exhibit little clear logic. It is not related to any very obvious aspects of the natural environment, such as climate, geology or soils. Although there is a clear tendency for areas of light, well-drained soil to be associated with nucleated settlements and champion country, the Midland system, as its name implies, is most closely associated with the Midland regions of England, a district of heavy clays. Yet other areas of superficially similar clay soils in the south east of England, in East Anglia, and in the west, are characterised by classic 'ancient countrysides': a puzzle indeed.

Nor, even more surprisingly, were these distinctions clearly mirrored in patterns of social or tenurial organisation. Throughout medieval England, agrarian society was organised under what modern historians describe as the 'manorial system', in which land was held by peasant farmers in return for rents and services paid to a manorial lord. The character of these obligations varied greatly by the thirteenth century, from place to place and with the status of the tenant. Free tenants usually only owed service at the manorial court, and rent in cash or kind. But the bond tenants – the *villeins* and cottagers who formed the majority of farmers in most open-field districts – owed labour services: in technical terms, they held their land by *service-tenancy*. For most manors included, as well as the land of the tenants, the *demesne* or home farm of the lord. Typically, this had a permanent staff of labourers, but extra villein labour – 'customary services' – were required, especially during the principal bottlenecks of the agricultural year – harvest, haymaking, and ploughing. The villeins generally held standard tenements, often called *virgates* or *bovates*, which – within any one vill – were roughly the same size, and owed the same rents and services to the lord (Harvey 1984, 7–19).

Sometimes there was one manor in a village or vill, sometimes several. Each usually had a court at which local custom relating to, among other things, the inheritance of tenements was articulated, and which thus served to recognise the property rights of those dwelling on the manor. For although in one sense the lord of the manor was its 'owner', peasants cultivators had some rights in the land and farms were inherited, passing down the family in a manner determined by local custom, and they could even – in some districts – be freely bought and sold between different members of the community. The court of the most important manor in the vill, in addition, controlled the management of the open fields, and of the meadows and pastures and other common land, making bylaws and fining miscreants (Homans 1941; Ault 1972).

Social and tenurial structures along these broad lines could be found throughout lowland England, although different regions and districts boasted their own idiosyncrasies. In some, for example, there were large numbers of free tenants, in others few. In some areas most villages had a single manor, in others they normally had two, three or more. In many areas farms passed down the generations by primogeniture (inheritance by the eldest son), but in some partible inheritance (equal division between co-heirs) was practised and in a few ultimogeniture (inheritance by the youngest son) was the norm. To a limited extent, such variations corresponded with the broad distinction between the 'two countrysides': free tenants were probably more numerous in woodland districts by the thirteenth century, partible inheritance generally more common, and the land market less restrained. But we should not exaggerate the extent of such correspondences. Many woodland areas were as highly manorialised, as we shall see, as the champion Midlands. Overall, there was little clear relationship between regional variations in settlement patterns and field systems, and patterns of social or economic organisation.

Given all this, it is hardly surprising that the origins of England's diverse medieval landscapes – and in particular, the broad contrast between the 'two countrysides' – remain issues of keen debate among historians, archaeologists, and geographers. And yet they are matters of more than antiquarian interest. There were important differences between the kinds of lifestyle enjoyed by those dwelling in large villages, surrounded by neighbours, and those living

in small hamlets and isolated farms – differences which persisted long after
the middle ages. The distinction between 'woodland' and 'champion' was a
fault line running through the social as much as the physical landscape.
And variations in patterns of settlement and fields were a significant determinant of regional economic and agrarian development well into the
eighteenth century. Above all, the differences between the 'two countrysides'
has structured the essential ecological geography of lowland England. Ancient
countryside areas are, in general, characterised by higher numbers of ancient
woods, species-rich hedges, and veteran trees, than areas of planned countryside. Little wonder, then, that the origins of open-field agriculture, and the
reasons for the marked variations in medieval landscapes and settlement
patterns, are issues which have obsessed many generations of scholars. Indeed,
any review of earlier research on this fascinating, but difficult and contentious
subject must involve – surprisingly, and almost uniquely in historical debates –
serious consideration of ideas and theories formulated as long ago as the
nineteenth century. This is because, as Robert Dodgshon perceptively remarked
in 1980, the debate

> has not been a progressive one, with each contribution adding to, or
> refining, a single line of argument. Instead, one has had a plethora of
> independent viewpoints put forward, each one tending to add uniquely
> to the debate (Dodgshon 1980, 1).

Early contributions

The earliest ideas on the origins of the open fields worth examining are those
presented by Frederick Seebohm in his *English Village Community* of 1890.
Seebohm placed at the centre of his interpretation the practice of *co-aration*,
or joint ploughing. He believed that the large, eight-ox plough employed by
early farmers was a piece of equipment too large and too costly to be owned
in its entirety by individual villagers. They therefore jointly contributed animals
to the team and, perhaps, parts to the plough itself, and the arable was shared
between them, in portions which were originally re-allotted each year but
which were eventually attached permanently to particular farms (Seebohm
1890, 120–2). He argued that both the heavy eight-ox plough, and the fully
developed three-field system, had been in existence in Roman times, and that
both were intimately associated with manorial forms of social and economic
organisation (Seebohm 1890, 409–11). Around the same time Paul Vinogradoff
proposed a more complex interpretation. Subdivided, intermixed arable arose
initially from a primitive concept of shareholding, something which was also
embodied in the tenurial structures imposed on early medieval communities.
Bovates, virgates and the rest were not simply units for assessing labour services
and other obligations. They also, and in origin mainly, denoted shares in
communal property (Vinogradoff 1892, 236; 1905, 150). The arable strips were
scattered because land in any *tun* or vill was variable in both quality and

8

accessibility: consolidated holdings might lie on soils of very different fertility, or at widely differing distance from the village. Pre-Saxon communities had, he believed, farmed enclosed fields or practised shifting agriculture, in which rights to use the land had only been temporarily allocated. Open-field farming had been introduced, together with nucleated villages, at the time of the Saxon invasions in the fifth and sixth centuries (Vinogradoff 1892, 162). Vinogradoff was by no means alone in seeing the origins of intermixed arable in primitive tribalism: similar notions were advocated around this time by a number of scholars, including G. L. Gomme and Sir Henry Maine (Gomme 1890, 191–3; Maine 1881, 65–99).

In many ways the suggestions of these nineteenth-century writers appear archaic and, in some cases, abstract and legalistic to modern eyes. Nevertheless, as we shall see two key ideas formulated in this period can help us to understand certain important aspects of early field systems: the idea that the cultivation of intermingled strips has something to do with the practice and technology of ploughing; and the idea that the dispersal of holdings, seen to varying extents in most open-field systems, had some connection with the equalisation of shares, and with the tenurial network of bovates and virgates imposed upon the landscape.

Howard Gray's *English Field Systems* was published in 1915 and determined the character of the debate on open-field origins for the next half century (Gray 1915). As Robert Dodgshon has pointed out, while earlier scholars had talked in rather general terms about medieval field systems – albeit sometimes generalising out from detailed studies of particular examples, as Seebohm did with Hitchin in Hertfordshire – Gray demonstrated that open fields displayed a range of structural variation, often restricted to particular regions, which could, indeed, be considered as distinct regional *types* of field system (Dodgshon 1980, 9). He identified six in all, and was the first scholar to recognise that the most sophisticated and developed type – comprising two or three large fields, farmed from a nucleated village – was largely restricted to the Midland areas of England – hence his term 'Midland system', which has passed into common historical parlance (Gray 1915, 108). But he also noted that within this extensive area, especially towards its western fringes, 'irregular' field systems could also be found, in which subdivided fields were organised into more than three fallowing sectors, and in which areas of enclosed fields, held in severalty, also often existed.

The other four 'systems' were geographically discrete. Gray argued that the East Anglian system, found in Norfolk and Suffolk, was similar to the Midland system in that all or most of the arable lay in intermingled strips rather than enclosed parcels. But instead of being distributed evenly throughout the territory of a township the strips of any one holding were often clustered within one area of the arable. Systems of cropping were more flexible than in the Midlands and the 'fold course' was a prominent institution. This was an area of land over which manorial lords had the exclusive right to run sheep when the fields lay fallow or before the corn in them had grown to any significant extent (Gray 1915, 349–54). The field systems of Kent were in many ways similar to those of East Anglia, but the institution of the fold course was absent (Gray 1915, 303–4). Those found in the Thames basin displayed elements of Midland, Kentish and East Anglian arrangements, and Gray considered that they were a hybrid of all three, although he nevertheless treated them as a distinct type. Lastly, across much of the north and west of Britain the 'Celtic system' prevailed. This was characterised by a settlement pattern of small hamlets (generally with less than six farms in each); relatively limited areas of cultivated land; and extensive wastes. The arable, which took the form of intermingled strips, was often divided into a permanently cropped 'infield' and a periodically cultivated 'outfield' (Gray 1915, 203–5).

Gray believed that the most important factor in the emergence of these different types of field system was ethnicity: their distribution reflected the areas settled by different racial groups, or combinations of races, during the Dark Ages. In particular, the 'Midland System' was seen by Gray as a direct importation from the Saxon homelands in northern Germany and southern Scandinavia, and its concentration here reflected the 'thorough Germanisation' of this part of England in the course of the fifth century (Gray 1915, 415). The other 'systems' were more indigenous in character, and in these the intermixture of strips resulted from the repeated division of holdings between co-heirs practising partible inheritance. In Kent and East Anglia existing Romano-British patterns of land holding had been taken over wholesale by Saxon settlers, subsequently fragmenting through the effects of partible inheritance as population rose during the Saxon period. But their later development diverged as a consequence of the Danish invasions of the ninth century, which produced a high density of free tenures, and more complex systems of manorial organisation, in East Anglia.

Gray did not suggest that agrarian arrangements had remained entirely fixed and unchanging from distant Dark Age times. In particular, he suggested that the three-field system had developed out of a two field system under the pressure of population growth. Under the latter system, half the land was under crops in any year, while under the former the figure was two thirds. Nevertheless, the roots of regional variation lay in ethnicity – in race and tribal custom. Patterns of Dark Age settlement had continued to mould the face of the countryside for more than a thousand years.

Subsequent generations of scholars have been rightly critical both of Gray's emphasis on the determining importance of Dark Age ethnic groups, and (to a lesser extent) of his concept of definable 'types' of regional field system. But it is important to note the significance of his contribution. He was the first to suggest that partible inheritance might be a major factor in the genesis of subdivided fields, drawing in particular on relatively recent Irish evidence to show how repeated division between co-heirs could, in a comparatively short time, produce complex patterns of intermingled arable strips (Gray 1915, 200–2). But equally important was his demonstration of the fact that field systems (and, indeed, settlement patterns) varied considerably from place to place across medieval England, and that to some extent such variation had a regional dimension.

Gray's emphasis on the disintegrative powers of partible inheritance meant that, by the time of the First World War, there were three principal explanations for the intermixed arable strips which were the basic building block of all open-field systems – the others being, as we have seen, co-aration and 'share holding'. The interwar years saw the promulgation of additional interpretations. In 1935 T. A. M. Bishop suggested, on the basis of Yorkshire evidence, that intermingled arable could result from the process of land clearance, or 'assarting', carried out by groups of cultivators. The newly won land was divided in the form of strips between those who had shared in the task of reclamation, and who had formerly enjoyed grazing and other rights over it (Bishop 1935). Three years later, in their book *The Open Fields*, the Orwins primarily emphasised (like Seebohm before them) the importance of co-aration in the development of intermixed arable and, indeed, the more general necessity for close co-operation amongst farmers in the supposedly wild and insecure environment of Saxon England (Orwin and Orwin 1938, 37–44). More clearly than earlier writers, however, they showed how the form of intermixed parcels as *strips* arose directly from the use of a heavy mouldboard plough, difficult to manoeuvre in small, square fields: 'the Open Fields could only have attained their final form in association with the mouldboard plough' (Orwin and Orwin 1938, 39). Throughout their book they displayed an attention to practical, agrarian matters which must have come as a refreshing change from the cultural and legalistic emphasis of most previous writers, and they often demonstrate with particular clarity the processes of change (for example, from a two- to a three-field system) rather blandly stated by others.

A few years later G. C. Homans, in his remarkable *English Villagers of the Thirteenth Century*, made in passing a number of significant contributions to the debate (Homans 1941). Homans saw, more clearly perhaps than previous contributors, the intimate connections between field systems and settlement patterns, quoting with approval a passage from the sixteenth-century topographer William Harrison:

> It is so, that our soile being divided into champaine ground and woodland, the houses of the first lie uniformelie built in everie town togither, with streets and lanes; whereas in the woodland countries (except here and there, in great market towns) they stand scattered abroad, each one dwelling in the midst of his owne occupieng (Homans 1941, 21).

While rejecting vague concepts of tribal shareholding, he nevertheless accepted that the scattering of strips in the open fields reflected the desire of cultivators to achieve 'an equality of opportunity', and to share 'proportionately in the area of the village in which good and bad soils were found – not to speak of the matters of exposure and drainage – and such sharing would necessarily mean that every holding would consist of a number of parcels scattered over the fields' (Homans 1941, 90–1). He, too, emphasised how field systems could change over time, with in particular a 'progressive' development from a two- to a three-field system. Nevertheless, he believed that many English villages and their attendant fields had their form fixed at a very early date. He was probably the first writer to emphasise how some field systems had been carefully planned, their strips laid out in a regular, recurrent sequence which mirrored the disposition of the tofts, or farm enclosures, within the village itself. Such planned arrangements often employed locational terms, such as 'towards the sun' and 'towards the shade', found in the Scandinavian practice of *solskifte*, or sun-division (Homans 1941, 83–107). These arrangements were ancient; and so too was the broader distinction between woodland and champion regions which Homans, like Gray, mainly ascribed to patterns of Dark Age settlement (Homans 1969).

Yet from the 1960s, historians and geographers began to express doubts about the extent to which the origins of the various agrarian arrangements found in medieval England could really be projected back into the dim past of the Dark Ages. In a seminal article, published in 1964, Joan Thirsk argued that the field systems encountered in early documents had often gone through a series of phases of development, and that many of the regional variations discussed by Gray and others really represented arrested stages in this process (Thirsk 1964; Thirsk 1966). The Midland System, the most developed form of open-field agriculture, was a relatively late development: most field systems of this type only came into existence in the twelfth or thirteenth century, she suggested, through the remodelling of earlier, less 'regular' arrangements.

Thirsk proposed a subtle, sophisticated model of why and how this had happened. The principal driving force was population growth, something which most scholars agreed – and still agree – continued more or less unabated from middle Saxon times through to the early fourteenth century. This first led to the proliferation of intermingled strips through partible inheritance and assarting, and subsequently to the contraction of reserves of pasture and a consequent crisis in grazing. Medieval arable farming depended on the main- tenance of sufficient livestock to provide both traction for the plough and manure for the soil. As reserves of pasture dwindled farmers were obliged to make more intensive use of the marginal grazing offered by the aftermath of the harvest, and by the fallows. But where lands lay intermingled in unhedged strips, it was hard to maximise the potential of these resources unless neigh- bouring cultivators timed their operations in concert. It would be difficult for one farmer to graze his strips as they lay fallow if adjacent lands were still under crops. Farmers were thus drawn inexorably into increased co-operation, a process which culminated in the institution of a continuous fallowing sector which occupied a half, or a third, of the land of the village.

Thirsk's article came at a time when a host of local and regional studies were being undertaken, many of the most important of which appeared in Baker and Butlin's edited volume, *Studies of Field Systems in the British Isles*, in 1973. This book vividly displayed the bewildering variety of British field systems, a range greater than Gray had ever assumed. But on the whole the contributors favoured agrarian and demographic rather than 'cultural' explanations, many implicitly or explicitly adopting some version of Thirsk's powerful model. The editors in particular followed Thirsk in seeing 'regular' or Midland style agriculture as developing out of the more 'irregular' systems, of the kinds found outside the Midland zone (Baker and Butlin 1973, 635–56).

The 1970s and 1980s and the contribution of archaeology

Until the mid 1970s the question of regional variations in the medieval landscape had largely been addressed by historians and historical geographers, and attention had principally been focused on *fields* rather than on the settlements from which they were farmed. The emergence of landscape archaeology as a distinct sub-discipline in the 1970s began to change all that. So too did an associated development – the so-called 'quantitative revolution', the explosion of field surveys and aerial reconnaissance which demonstrated that pre-medieval settlement had been much more extensive, and early population levels much higher, than an earlier generation of archaeologists had acknowledged. By the 1970s it was becoming apparent that in most areas of lowland England Romano-British (and, indeed, late prehistoric) settlements had been established on almost all soils (Taylor 1975; Cunliffe 1978). Although it also became clear that the immediate post-Roman period had seen some reduction in population levels, and some abandonment of the more marginal land, it was nevertheless evident that any explanation for the development of open-field agriculture which assumed that early medieval farmers were operating in an untouched wilderness – as implied, for example, in some of the Orwins' work – was no longer tenable. As Christopher Taylor noted in 1981:

> In many of the seminal works by geographers and historians there is still the stated or implied belief that the medieval open fields originated in a virgin landscape ... Yet if prehistoric and Roman archaeology has achieved anything in the last twenty years it is that it has proved beyond doubt that from as early as 2000 BC Britain was a well-populated country, almost totally exploited agriculturally by a sophisticated and complex society (Taylor 1981, 19).

A number of archaeologists began to use excavation and, in particular, the evidence of field-walking surveys to throw light on the origins of Midland villages – and, by implication, that of the 'champion' field systems with which they were so closely associated. A campaign of field-walking by Glenn Foard revealed that in Northamptonshire villages had not, as most previous commentators appear to have assumed, been introduced by Saxon settlers in the fifth or sixth centuries (Foard 1978). Early Saxon settlement was less extensive than Romano-British – the late and immediate post-Roman periods had seen some retreat from the heavier soils, with farms concentrating on the lighter soils of the permeable geologies. But it was just as dispersed in character, comprising a scatter of small farms and hamlets. It was only subsequently, in the course of the Saxon period, that these were abandoned as larger nucleations of settlement – villages – emerged. The precise chronology of this process was (and as we shall see, to some extent remains) a matter for debate, with Foard and Hall, working mainly in Northamptonshire, favouring a middle Saxon (i.e., eighth or ninth-century) date, and Taylor arguing for a longer chronology, extending into the late Saxon or even post-Conquest period (Foard 1978; Hall 1981, 1982; Taylor 1983). By the 1990s, a 'late' chronology was increasingly accepted by landscape historians and other students of medieval settlement (Kissock 1992).

The archaeologist David Hall was interested not only in the field-walking evidence for early medieval settlement, but also in the physical remains of the open fields, which still at this time survived over large areas of the Midlands, in the form of 'ridge and furrow' – distinctive wave-like corrugations in pasture fields representing the fossilised plough ridges of former open-field strips (Figure 6). Combining archaeological survey with documentary research – using, in particular, the evidence of late medieval surveys – Hall argued that many Midland open-field systems had originally been planned, often in the form of furlongs much longer than those which appeared on the earliest maps – the initial layouts having undergone extensive later alteration. Open fields, Hall concluded, 'do not seem to have been laid out by the early Saxons, but

FIGURE 6.
Ridge and furrow with characteristic 'reversed "S"' profile near Quainton in central Buckinghamshire.

rather later, nor do they seem to be subdivided early private holdings, but a strip system *ab initio*'. Their establishment was 'probably' associated with the 'abandonment of small scattered settlements with concomitant nucleation into villages'.

> It is likely that the laying out of open fields was substantially completed during the eighth and ninth centuries, continued pressures leading to their subdivision before the Norman Conquest (Hall 1981, 36–7).

Hall has, on the whole, been more circumspect about the reasons for this transformation of the landscape, but in 1981 cited 'increasing population, increasing demands for royal and ecclesiastical taxation, and increasing use of the heavy plough' as important causes (Hall 1981, 37).

The 1970s and 1980s also saw several important contributions from medieval historians. In a number of articles, Harold Fox accepted the broad thrust of Thirsk's essentially demographic explanation for the Midland system which, he argued, was invariably found in districts in which pasture was in short supply (Fox 1984, 121–32). It was 'an agricultural system founded on a shortage of pasture' (Fox 1984, 124). But Fox challenged Thirsk's comparatively late chronology for its adoption, her suggestion that it had only developed in the twelfth and thirteenth centuries (Fox 1981). Through a careful scrutiny of documentary evidence, especially that of early *charters* or land grants, he concluded that

> By the tenth century ... complicated systems with intermixed acre strips had developed in some townships, and it is possible that at some of these places a two- or three-field system had been or was about to be put into practice. At the end of the twelfth century there can be no doubt that the system was fully developed both in its organisation and its extent (Fox 1981, 88).

Fox also suggested that a contributory factor in the development of Midland field systems were patterns of social and economic change. A number of scholars – most notably, Glanville Jones – had recently suggested a new model for the development of early medieval territorial organisation (Jones 1971; Jones 1976; Jones 1981). In middle Saxon times, it was argued, very large estates had existed, much more extensive than later vills and manors. These had generally contained within their boundaries specialised areas, and specialised settlements, devoted to the exploitation of arable, woodland or grazing. Such large territories gradually fragmented; and as they did so, a new class of independent local lords had emerged. This fission of large estates, Fox suggested – and the consequent severance of townships from distant, ancestral grazing grounds – effectively pitchforked farmers into the kind of resource crisis described in Thirsk's model.

> The multiple estate, it can be suggested, was no seedbed for the development of a type of field system whose distinguishing feature was a rigorous integration of arable and common pasture (Fox 1981, 100).

Tenurial factors were also invoked as a major reason for regional variations in medieval field systems in a number of important articles by Bruce Campbell (Campbell 1981a). In the early Middle Ages some areas of England, as we have seen, were characterised by strong lordship – by vills in which there was only one manor, and in which all the tenants were of unfree status. Others were characterised by manorial complexity and a plethora of free tenures. Such differences were correlated, Campbell suggested, with the nature of regional field systems. Lordship was an important determinant of agrarian arrangements because 'There are several reasons for doubting whether the co-ordination and systematisation of commonfields progressed quite as smoothly, and were quite so directly related to population growth, as the Thirsk model postulates' (Campbell 1981a, 119). Campbell was doubtful whether organised peasant communities, capable of making the appropriate decisions, had even existed before the commonfield systems came into existence: 'they are as likely to have been the effect of the system, as they are to have been the cause' (Campbell 1981a, 119). Even if they had existed, it was unlikely that they would themselves have been able to bring about changes in landholding of sufficient magnitude. For this, the hand of lordship was required, if only to 'hold the ring' and act as arbiter of the new dispensation, and thus 'strong and undivided lordship would have been most favourable to the functional development of the commonfield system' (Campbell 1981a, 127). Campbell cited *inter alia* the example of north-east Norfolk, one of the most densely settled areas in medieval England. Here fields divided into strips were ubiquitous by the twelfth century but, as the area was characterised by complex manorial structures and a high density of free tenures, their form remained chaotic.

At around the same time a number of important contributions to the debate were made by the historian Robert Dodgshon, most notably in his complex, subtle book *British Field Systems: An Interpretation* (1980). This work had a broad sweep, as its title implies, dealing with developments in Wales and Scotland as well as in England. Dodgshon emphasised the conceptual distinction between subdivided fields *per se* and the various 'systems' into which these might be organised, and eschewed the kind of linear developmental sequence accepted, implicitly or explicitly, by many other writers. He noted that open fields – or at least, intermixed arable strips – could be found throughout medieval Britain, and in a range of tenurial contexts: in medieval Wales, for example, they were a feature both of settlements inhabited by bond tenants and of townships occupied by free kindreds, or *gwely* (Dodgshon 1980, 36–8, 66–74). Subdivided fields arose in part, he conjectured, from the decay of more ancient systems in which resources had been jointly held and exploited by extended families and communities, involving perhaps the periodic re-allocation of land, as still occurred into historic times in parts of early medieval Scotland. But they also developed through partible inheritance and piecemeal colonisation (Dodgshon 1980, 35–53). Far from being distinct explanations, these were all manifestations of one deeper cause: a need to define property and rights more stringently, as the amount of free land was reduced by population growth and the expansion of cultivation, and as the growth of lordship and the elaboration of feudalism required the more careful calibration of land held in return for particular services (Dodgshon 1980, 68–9). The development of intermixed holdings and the problems these posed for the organisation of farming led, in effect, to the creation of new *kinds* of farming community, composed of individuals holding their own portions of land. But the growth of lordship was also an instrumental factor in this, and especially in the emergence of the Midland system, a development which Dodgshon, following Thirsk, saw as a consequence of the need to manage stubble and fallow grazing as reserves of pasture dwindled (Dodgshon 1980, 77). Yet it was not only the growing power of lords but their proliferation which was important. The splitting of townships between different lords provided an impetus, and an opportunity, for the reorganisation of field systems along more 'regular' lines (Dodgshon 1980, 137–49).

Recent contributions

Historians, archaeologists and others continued to be fascinated by the origins of open-field agriculture, and the related question of regional variations in the medieval landscape, throughout the 1990s. Four key contributions were made to the debate which must be briefly reviewed here. One was the study of the east Midlands landscape funded by the Leverhulme Trust and carried out by Christopher Dyer, Carenza Lewis, and Patrick Mitchell-Fox, the results of which were published as the book *Village, Hamlet and Field* (Lewis *et al.* 1997 and 2001). Taking the counties of Northamptonshire, Leicestershire, Buckinghamshire and Bedfordshire, the project exhaustively examined all the available documentary, archaeological and cartographic evidence for the evolution of medieval and pre-medieval settlement. Their book introduced a number of new ideas, and included a welcome emphasis on the fact that areas of 'dispersion' could in fact be found well within the Midland belt – the distinction between 'planned' and 'ancient' countryside, in other words, should not be too tightly drawn. But the principal explanations for settlement nucleation and the emergence of the Midland System remained much as in earlier studies. Scattered early Saxon settlements, principally clustered on the lighter soils, were abandoned in the later Saxon period and replaced by nucleated villages farming extensive open fields. The main reasons for the change were rising population, subdivision and intermixture of holdings through inheritance and exchange, and dwindling supplies of pasture, which together led to a crisis in farming and recurrent disputes amongst cultivators.

> A peaceful option for a long-term resolution of their difficulties involved the inhabitants reorganising their numerous farms and hamlets into common fields where the problems of competition would be minimised. The animals of the whole community were pastured together on the land which lay fallow or awaited spring cultivation. The land was subject

to a cycle of fallowing which gave it a chance to recover some fertility (Lewis *et al.* 1997 and 2001, 199).

The change might, or might not, have involved lordly coercion, and was encouraged not only by demographic growth but also by the need to produce a marketable surplus, which could be exchanged for the wide variety of commodities increasingly available as both trade, and urban centres, expanded. The new forms of agrarian organisation and settlement 'probably spread by emulation' to all areas experiencing such a crisis. Only where population levels were relatively low, and resources of pasture extensive, did dispersed forms of settlement remain the norm. In many districts, the transformation of the landscape was completed by the time of the Norman Conquest, but elsewhere it continued into the twelfth or even thirteenth centuries (Lewis *et al.*, 1997 and 2001, 199–200).

A major challenge to the Dyer/Lewis/Mitchell-Fox thesis was, implicitly, made in an important paper published by Tony Brown and Glenn Foard in 1998 (Brown and Foard 1998). Dyer and his colleagues had discussed landscape change very much in the context of late Saxon social and economic developments, not an unreasonable procedure given their stated belief that nucleation began 'some time after 850' (Lewis *et al.* 1997 and 2001, 198). But as they also noted, archaeological fieldwork in the most thoroughly researched county – Northamptonshire – had repeatedly suggested that the process of nucleation was largely completed *before* the mid ninth century. This point was restated, with force and clarity, by Brown and Foard in a brilliant discussion of the Saxon landscape of Northamptonshire. But in a remarkable deviation from previous opinion, they also suggested that nucleation, and the laying out of regular open fields, did not in fact occur at the same time. Nucleation occurred in the seventh and eighth centuries: open fields – at least in the form in which they appear in the earliest extents and surveys – were created later, in the ninth or tenth centuries (Brown and Foard 1998, 90–2). This change was associated, in some cases, with the re-planning in more ordered form of settlements which were *already* nucleated.

Perhaps the most important recent contribution to the debate has been the work of the geographer Brian Roberts and the archaeologist Stuart Wrathmell, in mapping patterns of settlement across England for a research project sponsored by English Heritage (Roberts and Wrathmell 1998, 2000a and b). Their study, based on minute and systematic analysis of early nineteenth-century Ordnance Survey maps, confirmed the long-recognised dichotomy between 'champion' England – or the Central Province, as they prefer to call it – and the areas (or 'provinces') of more dispersed settlement lying to the south east, and to the west. But, like Dyer and his colleagues, they also emphasised that this distinction should not be too tightly drawn, for pockets of dispersion could indeed be found throughout the Midlands. The three broad 'provinces' were themselves broken down, largely on the basis of relative degrees of dispersion and nucleation, into a large number of sub-provinces: a meticulous and fascinating piece of work. But of more interest in the present context are the explanations for regional variations which Roberts and Wrathmell proposed. They pointed out, but with greater precision, a correlation noted by Oliver Rackham some fifteen years earlier: that the area of Midland England characterised by villages and extensive open fields (the 'planned countryside', the 'Central Province', call it what you will) corresponds closely with areas which not only Domesday Book, but also place names coined in middle and late Saxon times, suggest was largely devoid of woodland (Roberts and Wrathmell 2000a, 85–8; Rackham 1986, 75–8, 83). It was within this long-cleared zone that nucleated villages and extensive open fields emerged. Within the more wooded districts, in contrast, pioneer settlement was to take a more dispersed, less communal form. These are important arguments, and ones which will be afforded careful consideration in the next chapter.

One last contribution to the study of open fields needs to be mentioned here, Eric Kerridge's *The Common Fields of England*, published in 1992. This volume has been largely ignored by landscape historians, principally because it singularly fails to engage with, or even acknowledge the existence of, much of the previous research in this field – the various books and articles to which I have referred in the course of this chapter. Instead, Kerridge brought to the subject his own immense knowledge of the farming systems of early modern England, something which forms both the principal strength, and the principal weakness, of the book, which often assumes a degree of stability in patterns of agrarian organisation from the early middle ages to Tudor times which would be contested by most historians. Nevertheless, aggravating as the book often is, it makes a number of extremely important suggestions which certainly deserve far more attention than they have received from archaeologists and others.

In particular, Kerridge has important things to say about the origins of subdivided fields. Previous studies, with the notable exception of those by Robert Dodgshon, tended either to simply emphasise the effects of partible inheritance and assarting as engines for fragmentation, or avoided detailed discussion of the topic. Kerridge faces the complexity of the issue squarely. Population growth *per se*, he argued, is insufficient explanation for the development of subdivided fields, and 'it would be absurd to regard customs of partible inheritance as a major cause of common fields generally', not least because those areas in which open-field agriculture were most well-developed and firmly entrenched were precisely those in which, by the twelfth and thirteenth centuries, primogeniture was the norm (Kerridge 1992, 49). Instead, sub-divided fields arose from the proliferation of *farms*, something which was only loosely correlated with patterns of demographic change and which came about in a number of ways: 'from the division and allotment accompanying the creation of service-tenancies, the dissolution of large family holdings and inheritance, sale and purchase' (Kerridge 1992, 48). He placed particular emphasis on the transition from joint rights in land, shared by members of extended families or tribal groups, to more individualised forms of tenure;

and on 'the hutting of slaves, the planting of colonists, and the distribution to them of lands in common fields' (Kerridge 1992, 49), noting correctly that the earliest reference to open fields, in the laws of Ine, uses the word *gedelland*, shared land, land allotted in an ordered pattern to the individuals in question (Kerridge 1992, 17–21). Although Kerridge did not make the point, the suggestion that subdivided fields could arise from both the ordered allocation of land to tenants, *and* from the progressive subdivision of properties between co-heirs, receives support from the situation in medieval Wales. Here, as Dodgshon had explained in the 1980s, subdivided holdings were a feature both of bond land, *tir cyfrif,* and of that held by *gwely* tenure. Indeed, Kerridge's arguments on several points have much in common with those proposed by Dodgshon a decade earlier, and their broad emphasis chimes well with what we know about social and economic developments in middle and later Saxon times: the importance of large-scale colonisation, the decline of slavery, the transition from extended to nuclear families, and the replacement of kinship by lordship as the key articulating force in society.

Once a system of small intermixed holdings had come into existence, according to Kerridge, varying degrees of communal organisation inevitably followed. Men combined together to form common ploughs, or for the management of livestock. Kerridge placed particular emphasis on the need to maintain soil fertility, arguing that common fields came into existence as permanent cultivation replaced more primitive, shifting systems of farming. Regular folding of sheep was required to keep the arable in heart but the division of land into small, individually held farms 'was inescapably accompanied by the creation of diminutive flocks and herds that could only be well managed in common' (Kerridge 1992, 47). There are, as I have said, some bad things about Kerridge's book but it nevertheless contains a number of crucial insights which, as I hope to show, can throw important light on the development of early medieval landscapes.

The results of many decades of research have thus been considerable and, while much remains contentious, there is general agreement on a number of basic issues. It is apparent that open fields could take a wide variety of forms, could take up widely varying proportions of township area, and could display much variation in the extent to which, and ways in which, they were communally regulated. As a general rule, areas with the most nucleated patterns of settlement had, by the thirteenth century, the most extensive, and most communally organised, open fields. It is likely that areas of subdivided, intermixed arable existed in some places from middle Saxon times, although they increased in area and complexity during the later Saxon period. They probably originated in a variety of ways: through partible inheritance, assarting, and the allocation of land by lords to undertenants according to some equitable scheme. They were perhaps associated, above all, with the proliferation of service-tenancies, as the numbers of dependent peasants increased both through the downgrading of those once holding by free tenure, and through the emancipation and 'hutting' of slaves. Some open fields were presumably laid out on an ordered, regular basis from the start; others were remodelled in regular forms some time after they first came into existence; and some field systems may have been replanned on more than one occasion. Forms of communal organisation, and the imposition of communal forms of cropping, may in some cases have been present from the start, but elsewhere they developed more gradually. Either way, they arose from the needs of small proprietors to co-ordinate their farming activities in order to ensure the efficient use of resources, especially the marginal grazing offered by the fallows and the harvest aftermath – a need which became acute as population rose, and reserves of pasture dwindled, in the course of the tenth, eleventh and twelfth centuries.

The 'Midland system' was the most complex and sophisticated form of open-field agriculture and its adoption in the course of the Saxon period involved major alterations to the existing pattern of settlement, with the abandonment of dispersed farms and hamlets and the emergence of nucleated villages. It developed where it did because the crisis in resources was most acute here; alternatively, or in addition, the hand of lordship was here particularly strong. Manorial lords assisted, or enforced, settlement nucleation and the reorganisation of open fields to protect their own agrarian interests and rents.

As I say, the majority of these contentions would be shared by most, although not all, landscape historians: and, while few are directly supported by archaeo-logical or historical evidence – they are inferences, rather than direct observations – most seem superficially plausible. But a number of problems remain unresolved and in particular, as I shall argue, current models do not in fact satisfactorily account for the overall *distribution* of landscape regions – of 'woodland' and 'champion' countrysides. There is in fact no evidence that areas of nucleated settlement and extensive, highly communal open-field systems were characterised by particularly dense populations or particularly strong lordship. Indeed, as I shall argue, variations in settlement patterns and field systems were primarily the consequence of environmental factors. They were the responses made by farming communities to the challenges posed by soils, climate and topography. By looking more closely and carefully at the environmental context of medieval societies, I shall argue, we can cast a whole new light on the particular issues of village origins and open-field genesis.

Methods and approaches

Before going any further it might be useful to remind readers of some features of the medieval landscape which are sometimes obscured in published accounts by an understandable desire to make comprehensible and manageable a highly complex and varied reality. Firstly, it is important to emphasise, as both Dyer and his colleagues, and Wrathmell and Roberts have recently done, that the contrast between areas of nucleated, and areas of dispersed, settlement has sometimes been too sharply drawn. Not only could nucleated villages be found in many if not most 'woodland' districts – albeit accompanied by isolated farms and hamlets – but dispersed settlements were much more common in the Midlands than has sometimes been assumed.

> The division into 'dispersed' and 'nucleated', while representing a general truth, is inadequate to explain the rich variety of the patterns. Applied too rigidly the antithesis of 'dispersed' versus 'nucleated' could be an obstacle to explaining the origins or evolution of this settlement pattern (Lewis *et al.* 1997 and 2001, 62).

Secondly, it is worth reiterating that while regular open-field systems, comprising extensive areas of intermixed arable grouped into two or three continuous fields or cropping sectors, were largely restricted to the Midlands, open fields *of a kind* had a far wider distribution, and were widespread in 'woodland' districts. Historians, geographers and others have always known this, as the foregoing discussion will have made clear, but it is a point worth re-stating. Open fields are recorded from every English county and in some non-Midland districts they could occupy a very considerable proportion of the land area (Postgate 1973; Roden 1973; Roberts 1973). Indeed, as already intimated, the sharp contrast drawn by early topographers between 'woodland' and 'champion' districts is to some extent a consequence of late medieval and post-medieval developments – of the relative ease with which 'irregular' (as opposed to 'regular') field systems could be removed by informal, piecemeal enclosure. Conversely, although regular open fields were the dominant form of agrarian organisation within the medieval Midlands, islands of less regular field systems – and even areas of enclosed fields – could also be found here, often associated with areas of dispersed settlement. 'Planned' and 'ancient' countryside, 'woodland' and 'champion', were not hermetically sealed, mutually exclusive landscape types.

But even more important than all this, perhaps, is the fact that within that broad belt of champion land two rather different forms of landscape could be found: forms which to some extent merged, as a continuum, but which were nevertheless distinct enough to be considered as essentially different. Within the central core of the Midlands – a region largely composed of heavy clay soils – most parishes had open fields which were highly regular in character and which, by the thirteenth century, often ran to the very margins of the township (Hall 1995, 2). There was very little in the way of 'waste' or common grazing land. On the lighter lands around the margins of this central core, in contrast – on the chalklands of Wessex, in parts of the Chilterns, in western East Anglia, on the South Downs, on the Wolds of Yorkshire and Lincolnshire, and (though to a lesser extent) in the Cotswolds – rather different forms of champion country could be found. Here, in contrast to the situation on the Midland clays, the open fields generally co-existed with extensive tracts of open grazing – downs, sheepwalks, and heaths. Large flocks were grazed here by day and folded by night on the open fields, thus ensuring a continuous flow of nutrients which kept these thin, easily leached soils in heart (Kerridge 1967, 42–51). There were many different versions of such agrarian systems,

22

some of which blurred the notional division, which we have so far managed to adhere to, between 'regular' and 'irregular' field systems. In East Anglia, for example, holdings were often clustered in limited areas of the arable, there were often more than three fields, and areas of periodically cropped 'outfield' land often existed between the permanent 'infields' and the sheepwalks beyond (Postgate 1973, 300–3).

'Champion' landscapes, although they shared a largely nucleated pattern of settlement and extensive areas of unhedged open arable, might thus display a significant degree of variation. But the same was true of 'woodland' districts. In some, substantial nucleations of settlement existed in medieval times within the matrix of dispersion; in others, village were rare or absent. In some districts settlement was largely dispersed around the margins of extensive commons; in others, most commons took the form of small greens, and many farms stood alone within their fields. Some areas of ancient countryside were (and still are) densely wooded; in others, woodland was as scarce as in the champion lands. To better understand the distinction between 'champion' and 'woodland' landscapes, in other words, we also need to understand the nature, and origins, of the different variations on these essential themes, and to appreciate that this diversity includes some blurring between the neat, discrete landscape types implied by the use of this simple, bipartite division.

To a significant extent variations in the human landscape mirrored the patterns of soils, the urgings of topography. The boundaries of human, and of natural, landscape regions often corresponded, and still to a large extent correspond. Where, in north-west Essex, heavy boulder clay plateau gives way to chalk escarpment, the landscape of winding lanes, ancient hedgerows, isolated farms and small hamlets ends abruptly, to be replaced by wide, empty expanses of 'planned countryside', where open fields survived into the nineteenth century. Such correlations should not surprise us, given that we are dealing with landscapes created by farming communities, in intimate relationship with the soil. They would certainly not have surprised an earlier generation of geographers, for whom the complex and intricate relationships between society and environment were meat and drink. But such approaches appear curiously unfashionable in most modern studies of the medieval landscape, which tend to hurry through an obligatory description of geology and soils as if these things were a mildly relevant backdrop to the main objects of enquiry. Some modern landscape historians explicitly reject 'geographical determinism', in a conscious attempt to distance the discipline from the perceived excesses of an earlier generation of historical geographers. As a result, many books and articles on open-field agriculture will often dwell in detail on the role of manorial lords in the reorganisation of the landscape, or on the possible impact on peasant cultivators of an emerging market economy, and yet only discuss in the vaguest terms the actual practice of medieval farming – the types of ploughs employed, or the problems posed by poor drainage, low fertility or soil acidity. Settlement patterns and field systems were certainly moulded by, and to some extent embodied, a vast raft of social and economic realities. But fields are primarily about farming, settlements were largely occupied by farmers, and whatever the importance of other factors the practice of agriculture must have been a very major determinant of their evolution. Farming in a pre-industrial age was influenced in innumerable, subtle and complex ways by environmental factors: and so we should not be surprised to find so close a correspondence between landscapes human, and natural.

Yet here we are immediately faced with a curious paradox: a paradox which has, perhaps more than anything else, made the puzzle of open-field origins so hard to solve. For while it is undeniably true that, at a local level, natural regions and landscape regions tend to be conterminous; yet at the same time, on a wider scale, they appear to display a high degree of autonomy. In northern East Anglia, for example, the dominant form of settlement in medieval times was a loose cluster of farms strung out around the margins of a large common. This occurred, with some variations, in virtually all soil regions; but is comparatively rare or absent, on any soil type, in the areas to the south or west – that is, in the Midlands or the Home Counties. More dramatically, heavy clay soils in Norfolk, Suffolk, Essex or Hertfordshire were invariably associated with some form of dispersed settlement pattern, and with landscapes featuring various mixtures of irregular open fields and ancient enclosures. But on very similar clay soils in the Midlands – separated by only the narrow strip of light land which forms the Chiltern escarpment and its north-eastern continuations – classic champion landscapes of large villages and 'regular' open fields predominated. This essential paradox of landscape – local coincidence of settlement forms and aspects of the environment, but apparent independence of the two on a larger, national scale – has encouraged some historians (from Gray onwards) to see variations in landscapes as, at least in part, quite independent of the natural environment: the manifestation of ethnic or cultural differences, or of unexplained spatial variations in tenurial organisation, or both. Indeed, I have been guilty of such nonsense myself in the past (Williamson 1988). In reality, as I shall argue, the solution to this apparent paradox lies in a more complete understanding of the complexities of the relationship between society and the natural world: of the subtleties of the interaction between social and economic forms on the one hand, and aspects of soils, topography and climate on the other.

Brian Roberts and Stuart Wrathmell have recently suggested that:

> The period of research in which major advances could be made on the basis of broad generalisations from limited cases is over: the past decade or so has seen a rapidly increasing number of local and regional settlement studies which have, inevitably, confused – and to some extent under-mined – initial tenets. The conundrum is that regional studies of regionally variable data inevitably create a regionally based perception of what is supposedly a national picture (Roberts and Wrathmell 1998, 114).

One solution to this problem – and the one adopted here – is to examine not the whole country, nor yet some local area, but something in between: a region wide enough to encompass a broad range of landscape types – both 'woodland' and 'champion' – but small enough to allow a good understanding of the range of settlement forms and field systems, and their relationship with the natural environment. The region studied in this short volume embraces all of East Anglia, a large part of the Midlands, and the northern Home counties: specifically, the counties of Norfolk, Suffolk, Essex, Hertfordshire, Buckinghamshire, Huntingdonshire, Bedfordshire, Cambridgeshire, and the old county of Rutland; most of Northamptonshire; much of Middlesex and Leicestershire; and parts of Oxfordshire (Figure 7). The topography ranges from the rolling uplands of the Chilterns, reaching a height of more than 260 metres in the wooded hills above Wendover; to the level expanses of the silt fens, little more than a metre above sea level. It includes some of the most densely, and some of the most sparsely, settled areas of medieval England; and it embraces a bewildering variety of landscapes.

Soils form an important focus for this book, and in this respect also the study area displays considerable diversity. Around a third of it – towards and west – lies within the Midland Plain, a district dominated by gentle scarps,

FIGURE 7.
The study area,
showing basic relief
and principal rivers.

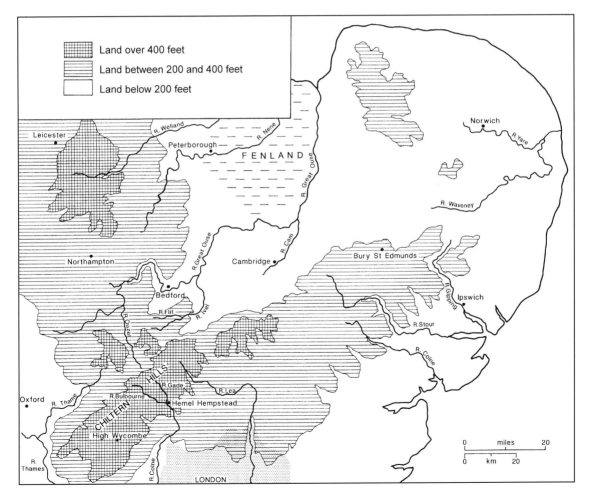

25

wide valleys, and – for the most part – heavy clay soils (Figure 8). These are derived in part from Jurassic and Cretaceous clays, but mainly from glacial boulder clay (Ragg *et al.* 1984; Hains and Horton 1969). The south eastern boundary of this Midland zone is marked by the chalk escarpment of the Chiltern Hills and its more muted north-easterly continuation, the so-called East Anglian Heights. This band of light, calcareous soils corresponds – for much of its length – with the conventional boundary between the 'planned' and 'ancient' countryside: the chalk continues into north-west Norfolk, now as a rather wider if less imposing topographic feature, eventually reaching the sea at Hunstanton (Chatwin 1961).

To the south and east of the escarpment, the chalk is masked by a variety of Tertiary formations but these are themselves mostly buried beneath depths of glacial drift (Thomason 1961; Hodge *et al.* 1984, 12–19). The most important of these latter deposits – in the sense that it covers the most extensive area – is the chalky boulder clay (Thomasson 1969; Hodge *et al.* 1984, 15–16). This extends in a great arc running from north Norfolk, through central Suffolk and the northern half of Essex, into east Hertfordshire. The soils associated

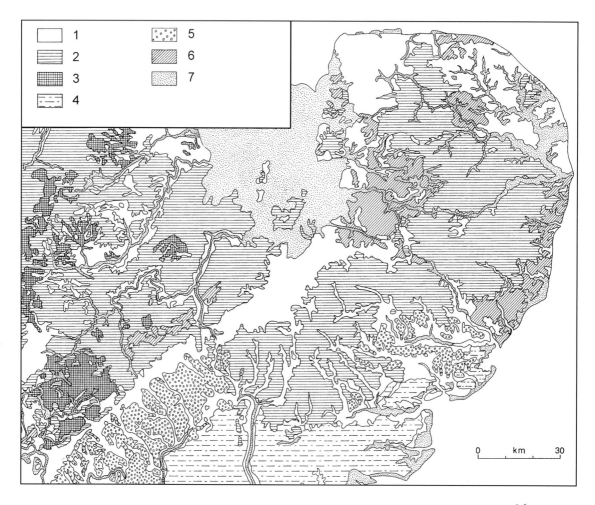

with this deposit are, as we shall see, fertile but generally poorly draining. Other glacial deposits, however, are very different in character. In Breckland, the chalk is masked by flinty and sandy drift of uncertain origin which gives rise to freely draining, acidic, infertile soils. In north-east Norfolk, in contrast – and in a small area of high ground between Colchester and Ipswich – aeolian, sandy drift forms tractable and generally fertile (often very fertile) soils. On the dipslope of the Chiltern Hills *sensu stricto* – in west Hertfordshire and south Buckinghamshire – the chalk is overlain by the so-called plateau drift, of pebbly clay and clay-with-flints, giving rise to comparatively poor, acidic soils.

Only in the extreme south of the region studied does the mantle of drift deposits become patchy, and eventually fade, in south Hertfordshire, south Essex and Middlesex. Here the underlying Tertiary deposits are exposed, laid down unconformably with the chalk but with a similar dip towards the south east (Sherlock 1967). The London Clay, and the sandy and pebbly Bagshot and Claygate Beds, all give rise to soils which are particularly acid, infertile, and uninviting (Gardner 1967, 91–3).

In studying the development of the medieval landscape in this region, I have not embarked on a large-scale programme of primary data collection. Some new evidence is presented here, but this is largely a work of data collation, rather than collection. There is a wealth of information lying available, the fruits of the studies of several generations of historians and archaeologists, amateur and professional. Our problem has not, for the most part, been a paucity of data. It has been our failure to interrogate it in the most effective ways.

FIGURE 8 (*opposite*). The study area, showing simplified soil types: (1) freely-draining, neutral or calcareous loams; (2) soils formed in chalky boulder clay; (3) soils formed in Jurassic or Cretaceous clay; (4) soils formed in London clay and associated deposits; (5) soils formed in plateau drift, clay-with-flints and similar formations; (6), soils formed in acid sands and gravels; (7); soils formed in peat or alluvium.

27

CHAPTER TWO

Field and Forest

Almost all historians and archaeologists agree that the development of 'champion' landscapes was closely connected with important demographic and social changes taking place during the later Saxon period. The most complex and sophisticated forms of open-field agriculture, and settlement patterns of nucleated villages, developed where they did as a result of population pressure, which served not only to subdivide and intermix holdings but, in addition, led to the over-expansion of arable at the expense of pasture and woodland. This in turn meant that it was necessary to use more intensively the grazing offered by the harvest aftermath and the fallows, leading eventually to the regularisation of field systems and the development of nucleated villages. Alternatively, or in addition, the emergence of these distinctive landscapes was connected with the disintegration of large early estates, and the growth of local lordship. Manorial lords, keen to maximise their incomes at a time of expanding markets, took an active hand in the reorganisation of peasant agriculture. It was they who took the lead in the re-modelling of field systems in order to maximise available grazing. They may have intervened to improve the efficiency of peasant agriculture for other reasons, for upon its health the viability of their own home farms – *demesnes* – depended. Nick Higham, for example, has suggested that the nucleation of settlement was carried out in order to pool resources of draft oxen, thus allowing the more efficient use of plough teams and reducing the number of oxen which each cultivator had to maintain (Higham 1990). In short, in a number of ways matters of demography and territorial organisation lie at the heart of the debates about open-field agriculture, and we must first review what evidence there is for the development of both in the period before the Norman Conquest.

Population

It is notoriously difficult to estimate population levels in the period before Domesday. Archaeological approaches, especially field-walking surveys and aerial photography, can provide some evidence for the density of settlements but what this means in terms of *population* is usually open to a range of interpretations. Does a scatter of debris in the ploughsoil represent a single farmstead, or a small hamlet? Even when excavated there are usually grounds for uncertainty over whether a Roman villa, for example, represents the habitation of a nuclear family, or an extended kin group (Smith 1982). Nevertheless, changes in the numbers or distribution of settlements can, with caution, be used to chart overall trends in demography, and there is now a broad consensus among landscape archaeologists over how England's population changed in the period from the late Iron Age up until Domesday.

Population was rising in later prehistoric times, and by the time of the Roman Conquest settlements could be found in some numbers on most of the soils in the region studied here. On the boulder clays of Norfolk, Suffolk, Hertfordshire and Essex, and on the heavy clays of the Midlands, Romano-British settlements occur with an average density of around one per square kilometre (Taylor 1983, 83–4; Brown and Foard 1998, 75; Liddle 1994; Williamson 2000a, 55–9). Only on the poor, leached and intractable London clays and associated Eocene deposits in the extreme south of the region, and in a few limited areas of particularly heavy, upland clays elsewhere, do settlement densities appear to have been much less than this. Here, substantial tracts of woodland may have survived but for the most part the Roman landscape was a tamed, divided and settled one. It is unlikely that many places were, by the third century, more than two kilometres from a farm, hamlet or villa.

Indeed, some archaeologists have argued that, by the third or fourth centuries, population levels across England as a whole were similar to those of early medieval times. Others are more doubtful. Glenn Foard compared the archaeological evidence for Roman settlement in Northamptonshire with the documentary evidence for medieval population density. To judge from the evidence of Domesday and the 1377 Poll Tax, there was an average of around one household for every 0.57 square kilometres in 1086, one for every 0.3 square kilometres in 1377, 'and presumably even more in the 1340s. Can the Roman settlement evidence recognised by field walking, aerial survey and excavation, typically argued as being at a maximum of about one settlement per square kilometre, really match this minimum medieval density?' (Brown and Foard 1998, 75).

Either way, there is little doubt that the immediate post-Roman period saw a significant reduction in population, although its causes remain uncertain. So too does its scale. This is because Romano-British settlements are comparatively easy to recover through field surveys, due to the large amounts of pottery and other debris which they produce. But early Saxon sites are much harder to locate. Early Saxon pottery is in general highly friable, and liable to rapid disintegration once exposed on the surface to the effects of frost and rain. In addition, only small amounts of pottery seem to have been in use and it is possible that during the fifth and sixth centuries some districts were effectively aceramic. Settlements of early Saxon date may be represented on the surface by only three or four small sherds (Foard 1978). On a number of occasions, earth-stripping in advance of construction work has revealed early Saxon settlements which remained undetected during earlier field-walking surveys ((Medlycott and Germany 1994, 17). Conversely, it is also possible that in some cases field surveys may *over*-estimate Saxon settlement densities.

Helena Hamerow has cogently argued that early Saxon settlements were much less long-lived than those of the Roman period. Farms shifted position with some frequency, every few generations, and the number of sites occupied at any one time might thus have been significantly less than the total numbers from this broad period recovered by field surveys (Hammerow 1991). At Witton in north east Norfolk, for example, eight Romano-British settlements were discovered through fieldwalking, but only four areas of early Saxon occupation. Through limited excavation and intensive surface collection, moreover, it was possible to establish that only one of these sites – the largest – was in use throughout the fifth and sixth centuries. Of the others, one was occupied in the fifth century, one in the sixth, and the third could not be dated accurately (Wade 1983, 50–69).

We should note in passing, however, that the concept of early Saxon settlement 'mobility' is often used rather loosely by archaeologists and in many cases took the form of much more localised 'drift', especially where one limited area was particularly favoured for settlement, within less inviting terrain. In such circumstances, what might appear from surface survey as quite a large settlement might, in reality, result from the gradual movement of occupation over time. Thus at West Stow in Suffolk a spread of settlement covering some 1.8 hectares was shown, by careful phasing, to have resulted from the gradual eastward movement of three 'halls', and associated sunken-featured buildings – probably the residences of three family groups. Each 'hall' was rebuilt twice during the period the site was occupied, from the early fifth century to the early eighth, when the area was finally abandoned (West 1985, 151–2). The slow 'drift' of the settlement at Mucking in Essex was in many ways comparable (Hamerow 1993).

In spite of all these difficulties, it is generally agreed that the population declined fairly dramatically in the immediate post-Roman period. The early Saxon settlement pattern was in many ways like that of the Roman period – it consisted of scattered farms and small hamlets, rather than sizeable nucleations – and indeed, occupation often continued on, or close to, Romano-British sites. But settlement was much less widely dispersed across the landscape and in all districts heavy clay soils seem to have been abandoned, with sites now restricted to areas of freely draining chalk, sand or gravel.

During the middle Saxon period settlements become more visible across much of the region studied here: from the early eighth century well-fired, wheel-turned pottery called *Ipswich Ware* is widely found (albeit often in small quantities) on sites in Norfolk and Suffolk, and to some extent in the adjacent counties. But it was only in the late Saxon period – that is, from the later ninth century – that durable pottery came into widespread use across the whole of the area studied, and settlements of all kinds thus become clear once again in the archaeological record. Nevertheless, problems remain for the field archaeologist. Many settlements from this period – not only villages, but numerous hamlets and isolated farms – are still occupied today and their archaeology is thus sealed beneath houses and gardens. Fortunately, by this time the archaeological record is increasingly supplemented by documentary sources, including Domesday Book, and the two approaches together provide a moderately good picture of the late Saxon countryside, its organisation and management.

By the time of Domesday levels of population were probably returning to those of the Roman period across most of the region, and large areas were once again under cultivation, to judge from the distribution of stray sherds in the ploughsoil, derived from manuring, recovered by field surveys. But population densities varied greatly across the country as a whole, and across the region discussed here (Darby 1977, 87–94) (Figures 9 and 10). At one extreme, the claylands of Norfolk, Suffolk and north Essex had the highest

FIGURE 9.
Domesday population in England, showing recorded individuals per square mile (after Darby 1977).

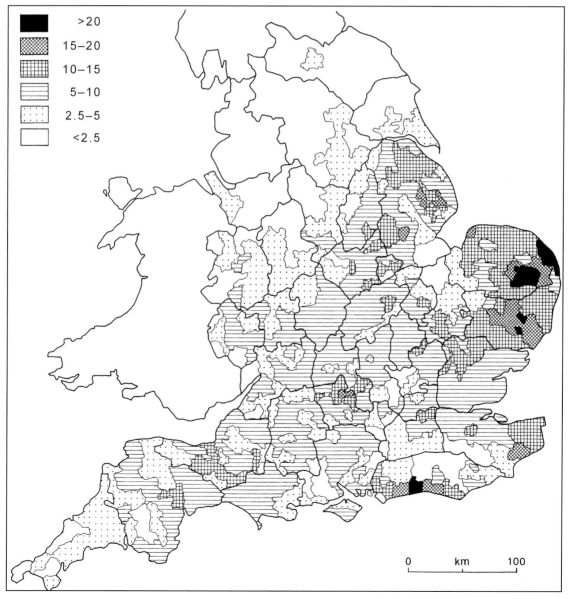

>20
15–20
10–15
5–10
2.5–5
<2.5

0   km   100

31

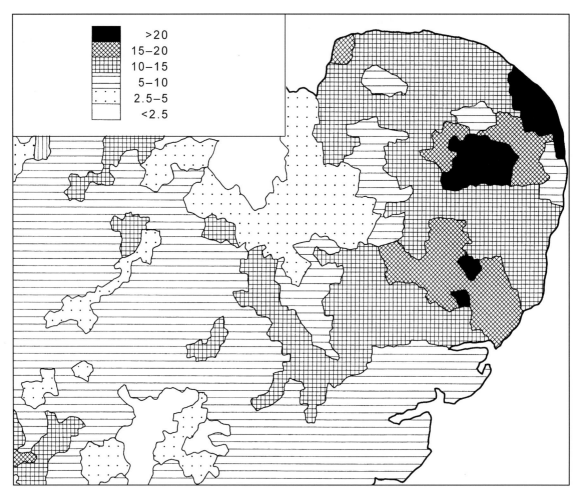

recorded densities in the region: more than 10, and in many districts more than 15, recorded individuals per square mile, probably implying real densities (Domesday records only heads of households) of between 50 and 75 individuals. At the other extreme, the East Anglian Breckland, the Fens, the Chiltern dipslope in south Oxfordshire, south Buckinghamshire and west Hertfordshire, and parts of the London clay district in south Hertfordshire and Middlesex, had densities of less than 5 per square mile. Running roughly from south east to north west was a broad band of territory, extending through central Essex and east Hertfordshire, into north Buckinghamshire, Bedfordshire, and North-amptonshire, which generally boasted densities of between 5 and 10 recorded individuals per square mile, between 25 and 50 individuals. During the following three centuries, there was some change in these relative densities, but Norfolk, Suffolk and north Essex remained the most populous parts of the country (Baker 1973, 196; Pelham 1936, 232).

It might be useful to consider briefly the main reasons for these demographic variations. In early Saxon times population densities were, to judge from the available archaeological evidence, most closely related to the ease with which

FIGURE 10.
Domesday population within the study area, showing recorded individuals per square mile (after Darby 1977).

32

soils could be cultivated, rather than to their fertility. Even areas of light but infertile soils, such as the East Anglian Breckland, appear to have been quite densely settled. By late Saxon times, however, technological developments evidently allowed the successful cultivation of even the heavier clay soils and regional variations in population were now primarily a function of other factors.

Firstly, the wet peat Fenlands of west Norfolk, north-west Suffolk, Cambridgeshire and Huntingdonshire, show up on the map as an area of low population density. This is because, although these wetlands were an important resource to local communities, they were largely exploited from their margins. On the higher silt ground towards the Wash, it is true, permanent settlements were appearing from middle Saxon times but for the most part farms and villages were confined to a few fen islands and overall population densities thus remained low. Secondly, and more importantly, people were generally thin on the ground wherever soils were acid and infertile. Most areas of freely draining sands and gravels were now, in comparative terms, sparsely settled, simply because – compared with most heavier loams or clay soils – they produced only poor or indifferent yields of the principal cereal crops. The reasons for this have long been well known to agronomists (Robinson 1949, 30–5; Hanley 1951, 33–7). Soils formed in such deposits cannot hold nitrogen or other nutrients easily for they are rapidly washed away by rainwater. In addition, the easily exchangeable bases held by soil colloids are removed in solution by rainwater, which is slightly acid due both to the carbon dioxide in the atmosphere, and to the various decay products of humus. Some clay soils within the region studied are likewise naturally acid and infertile, either because the main parent materials are inherently acidic, or because the clay forms a relatively thin layer over a more permeable substrate, usually chalk. The London clays and associated Eocene deposits, with poor acid soils dominated by the Windsor and Essendon Associations; and the clay-with flints of the Chiltern plateau, which gives rise to the acidic Batcombe, Hornbeam, and Oak Associations; both fall into this category, and together show up in the Domesday statistics as an area of sparsely settled territory in the south west of the region studied here (Figure 11). The soils of the London clays were particularly inhospitable, for problems of infertility and acidity were compounded by chronic seasonal waterlogging. The pattern of administrative divisions, and thus the mapping units employed by H. C. Darby (on whose pioneering work this discussion and Figures 9 and 10 are based) tends to obscure an eastwards continuation of this poor tract of land, into south Essex.

Soil acidity limits productivity in a number of other ways. Under acid conditions the roots of cereals, especially barley, become stunted and discoloured; and acidity enhances the solubility (and hence the availability) of certain harmful elements, such as aluminium and manganese. But in addition, nitrogen is converted into nitrites by soil bacteria which are highly susceptible to acidity. In Breckland, and on the Chiltern dipslope, acidity could be ameliorated to some extent by marling or chalking: that is, by sinking pits

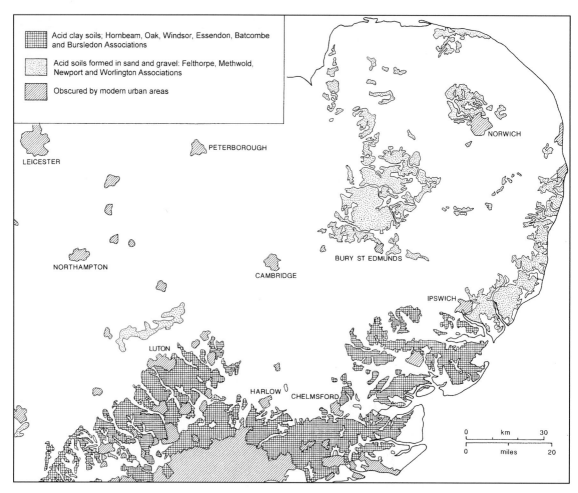

FIGURE II.
The principal areas of
leached and acid soils
within the study area.

down to the underlying chalk or chalk marl, and spreading this on the surface of the fields (Mathew 1993). The use of these methods increased in extent and intensity in post-medieval times but they were certainly practised in the early middle ages, although evidently not on such a scale as to effect regional patterns of fertility to any significant degree (Prince 1964). On the London clays, however, these procedures were never an option, for the underlying chalk was here – except on the fringes of the formation – usually too deeply buried to be reached by surface pits.

Explaining areas of very low early medieval population density is thus relatively straightforward. Areas of particularly *high* density are more problematic, and this issue is perhaps most easily addressed if we adopt for a moment a rather wider perspective, and examine the distribution of population as recorded by Domesday across England as a whole (Figure 9) as well as within the region studied here (Figure 10). It is immediately apparent that there was a general gradient of population from east to west, with the highest recorded densities in Norfolk, Suffolk and to some extent Lincolnshire. This distribution does not correlate in any clear or obvious way with aspects of soils. On the

34

contrary: high population densities are recorded in areas of heavy boulder clay, in north Suffolk and south Norfolk; on the light chalk soils of the Lincolnshire Wolds; as well as on the light but fertile loams of Flegg in north-east Norfolk. The closest correlation is, perhaps, with the distribution of arable land in the early decades of the twentieth century (Figure 12). This was a period in which the completion of enclosure and the development of an integrated national transport system had long encouraged a high degree of regional specialisation in production; but also one in which a long agricultural recession, starting in the 1880s, had ensured that arable farming had retrenched to the areas most suited to cereal cultivation. In the words of L. Dudley Stamp, in the course of the recession 'the cultivation of wheat became more and more restricted to … the drier eastern counties, where a harvest of good grain was assured' (Stamp 1950, 389).

Modern agronomists have studied in some detail the variables affecting crop yields, and modelled them in a number of ways. The CERES model for predicting wheat growth has been employed in a number of contexts, and takes into account soil character, rainfall, temperature and other climatic factors (Ritchie 1984). It has also been used to examine variations in post-medieval wheat yields in Europe, by the historian Liam Brunt. Although temperature and soils have an important bearing on yields, rainfall 'is by far the most important climatic factor determining wheat yields in Western Europe' (Brunt 1997, 7). This is because 'the grain yield is susceptible to rainfall fluctuations *throughout* the growth cycle': when the wheat plant is developing; in early summer when the grains are 'filling'; and in late summer, when the grains are harvested (Brunt 1997, 7). Wheat produces the heaviest yields in areas of modest rainfall, especially in late summer. But not only are heavier yields obtained in drier districts. More importantly, the harvest is less likely to be ruined by high levels of late summer precipitation. In early medieval times it is probable that, in the eastern counties, higher yields and dependable harvests allowed a sustained increase in population, whereas in many central and western areas not only were yields lower, but periodic harvest failures tended to check demographic expansion. Late Saxon population densities, in other words, were in part a function of soil character, but – at least within the area studied here – were primarily a consequence of climate.

The precise reasons for the varying densities of population in late Saxon England may always elude us, but one thing is very clear. In spite of what is still often asserted, there is no correlation between variations in population density, and the ditribution of particular forms of field system or settlement. Both 'champion' landscapes, and areas of dispersed settlement, can be found in districts which Domesday suggests had high, medium and low population densities. Given that many scholars believe that nucleation, and open-field formation, were taking place within a century or so of the Domesday Survey, this lack of correlation is, to say the least, surprising.

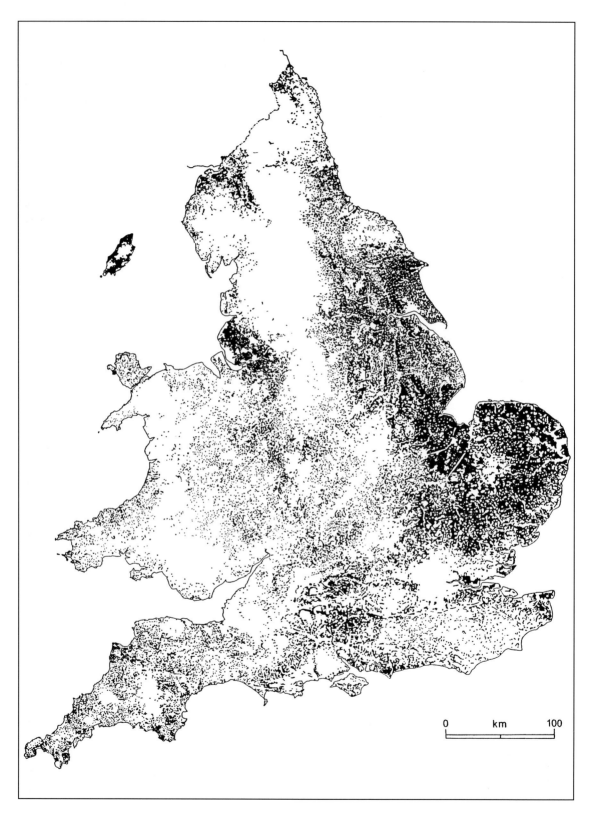

Large terrains and the landscape

The demographic changes of the post-Roman period were accompanied by important developments in economic and territorial organisation. Following the collapse of Roman rule, according to many scholars, political power was highly fragmented. Authority devolved to a plethora of autonomous or semi-autonomous tribal groups, each with territories embracing tens or hundreds rather than thousands of square kilometres (Bassett 1989). Some were still in existence when the Tribal Hidage, probably a tribute list for a Mercian king, was drawn up in the mid seventh century – groups like the *Hicce,* or the *Cilternsætan,* who occupied territory in the west of the region studied here (Davies and Vierk 1974). Most, however – like the *Brahingas* and *Wæclingas* in Hertfordshire, or the *Rodingas* in south-west Essex – had long since disappeared, and are known mainly from place names, or from references in early charters and histories (Williamson 2000a, 62–6; Bassett 1997; Short 1988). For by the time the *Tribal Hidage* was drawn up, larger and more sophisticated polities – tribal kingdoms – had emerged, and most of the area studied lay within Mercia, Essex and East Anglia.

As population began to grow again, and settlement and cultivation to expand, more stratified forms of social organisation gradually developed (Bassett 1989). The rise of large, centralised kingdoms saw the development of systems of territorial organisation necessary to sustain small élites of warriors, bound to the service of their kings. According to many historians, the various kingdoms of England were at this time divided into territorial units much larger than the vills and manors which we meet in Domesday Book, units to which historians sometimes give the name 'multiple estates' (Jones 1971; Jones 1979; Faith 1997). In a world in which markets and market exchange were poorly developed, these of necessity each contained 'the varied resources needed to sustain life' (Sawyer 1979, 7), and often included economically specialised sub-units which, as well as providing sustenance for their inhabitants, also supplied particular goods, or services, to the *caput* or estate centre. Near to the estate centre lay the main areas of arable land, some farmed by bond tenants: the *inland* of the estate. Further away, often on more difficult ground, might be found specialised grazing establishments, or places producing wood and timber. Here, on the outlying *warland,* the dues and duties owed by the inhabitants were generally less onerous (Faith 1997). Although by the time of Domesday most large, ancient estates had fragmented into a mosaic of smaller units, their centres or *caputs* can often be identified, for many retained some administrative importance, as major royal or hundredal manors; while others maintained some claim to jurisdiction over, or services from, groups of privileged peasants – sokemen or *socmanni* – dwelling within what were now alienated portions of the outlying *warland.*

The former existence of large Saxon estates has been demonstrated in many areas, and it is sometimes possible to discern a thread of continuity, from late Roman administrative district or *pagus,* to early tribal territory, to middle

FIGURE 12.
The distribution of arable land in England *c.* 1940, as mapped by the Land Utilisation Survey (after Stamp 1950).

Saxon 'multiple estate'. In those districts within the region studied here in which substantial numbers of pagan Saxon cemeteries from the fifth and sixth centuries are known – essentially, Norfolk and Suffolk, and the Midland counties north of the Chiltern escarpment – their distribution is closely associated with sites of major late Roman importance, such as military installations or major and minor towns. These cemeteries seem to represent the central places of small tribal groups: but these in themselves seem often to have developed into the 'estate centres' of middle Saxon times, for the cemeteries also often lie in close proximity to royal manors or hundredal centres (Williamson 1993, 92–104). In Middlesex, Hertfordshire and Essex large early Saxon cremation cemeteries are a less prominent feature of Dark Age archaeology – possibly because here the indigenous elites were replaced by Germanic immigrants at a relatively late date – but here, too, a measure of territorial and administrative continuity is often apparent. Thus in Hertfordshire the principal tribal groups recorded in early charters or other documents – the *Hicce*, the *Wæclingas*, and the *Brahingas* – evidently occupied territories based on the three largest Roman towns, Baldock, Verulamium, and Braughing (all of which themselves developed from the three main Iron Age *oppida* in the county). The central places of these groups – St Albans, Hitchin, and Braughing – all became, in turn, major royal estates and places of ecclesiastical and administrative importance in later Saxon times. In the same county, similar continuity is apparent at a lower level of the hierarchy, with places like Welwyn or Bishops Stortford developing from major Iron Age and Roman settlements, to central places for minor tribal groups, to Saxon estate centres (Williamson 2000a, 98–130). Their precise economic and social character might change over time, in other words, but these 'large terrains' (to use Andrew Fleming's elegant term) (Fleming 1998a) often displayed marked continuity in boundaries and configuration.

In many districts these enduring territorial units also displayed a recurrent, and perhaps unsurprising, relationship with terrain and topography. From the later Iron Age through to Saxon times the main settlements, and the principal arable areas, tended to be located within the main river valleys, in part because good supplies of running water were available here but also because – in the kind of clayland countryside which occupies most of the area studied – the lightest, most easily cultivated soils tended to be found here. Well-watered areas on spring lines at the foot of escarpments of light soil were also favoured areas for estate centres and their arable cores, for similar reasons. The high interfluves between the principal valleys, in contrast, tended to be occupied by areas of woodland and grazing. Where they comprised – as they often did – level, poorly draining clay plateaux the reasons for this are obvious. But almost irrespective of the character of soils higher ground, away from major valleys, was often occupied by stands of woodland, and wood-pastures, well into the Saxon period. In Norfolk, for example, almost all the major areas of Domesday woodland were concentrated in a 'wooded crescent' running through the middle of the county, from Diss in the south to Catfield in the

FIGURE 13.
The significance of watersheds: (a), the main central watershed running through the county of Norfolk; (b), known Romano-British settlements; (c), the larger areas of Domesday woodland. In Norfolk, areas of relatively sparse Romano-British settlement, and the largest concentrations of Domesday woodland, are related less to soil type than to topography: they correspond with the watershed running in an arc through the centre of the county, between rivers draining east, and those draining north and west (after Williamson 1993).

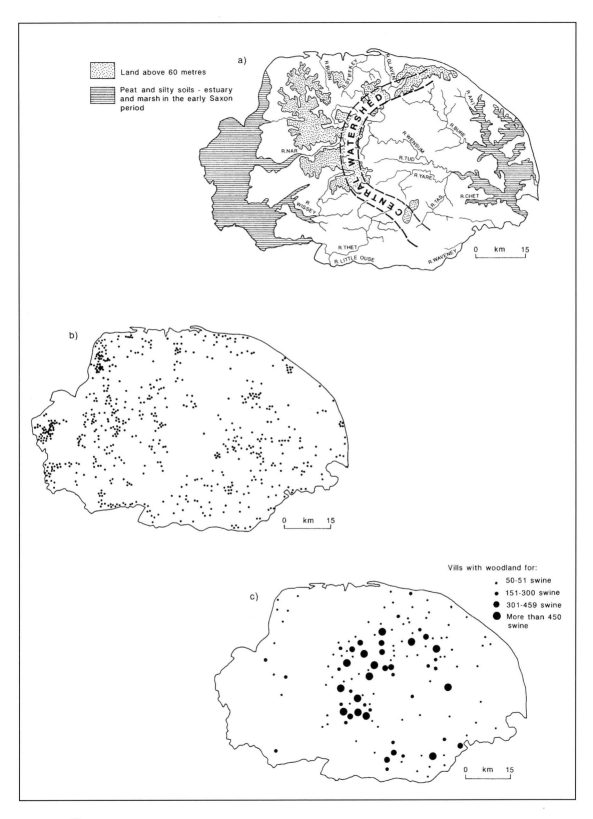

a)

Land above 60 metres

Peat and silty soils - estuary and marsh in the early Saxon period

CENTRAL WATERSHED

R.BURE
R.STIFFKEY
R.GLAVEN
R.ANT
R.WENSUM
R.NAR
R.TUD
R.YARE
R.CHET
R.WISSEY
R.TAS
R.THET
R.LITTLE OUSE
R.WAVENEY

0 km 15

b)

0 km 15

c)

Vills with woodland for:
· 50-51 swine
● 151-300 swine
● 301-459 swine
● More than 450 swine

0 km 15

39

north east. The majority of 'woodland' place names are likewise concentrated here, rather than on the most extensive and continuous spreads of clay soils, which occur in the south of the county (Williamson 1993, 60–2, 113–15) (Figure 13). Most of the other major watersheds within the area studied here were characterised by marked concentrations of early woodland: that between the Nene and the Welland, for example, later occupied by Rockingham Forest; or that which runs more intermittently along the crest of the East Anglian Heights, between rivers draining north, across the Midlands and into the Wash, and those draining south, across Hertfordshire and Essex directly into the North Sea, or indirectly, via the Thames: this still forms a noticeably well-wooded band of territory. These upland, interfluve tracts of woodland and pasture were often described as 'wolds' by the Anglo-Saxons, a terms which survives today in a number of place names (Fox 1989, 81–5).

This essential contrast between the more densely settled valleys, and the less intensively occupied interfluves, underlies much of the early landscape development of southern Britain. And it explains, in part, the long-term stability of many 'large terrains'. When population levels were low, the forested uplands were exploited by scattered farms, some perhaps only seasonally occupied. But even at times of population expansion and colonisation, they remained dependent territory, their inhabitants looking to the neighbouring valleys for their principal social and economic contacts, so that watersheds represented cut-off zones between neighbouring communities. Over long periods of time, social territories thus tended to correspond with drainage basins (Everitt 1977; Phythian Adams 1987; Phythian Adams 1993).

This contrast between upland wooded tracts at the periphery of ancient territories, and lowland arable cores, has in many places left an enduring mark upon the landscape in the form of distinctive road and field patterns of the kind called 'co-axial' by some archaeologists: that is, landscapes arranged around bundles of long, slightly sinuous axes that run for many kilometres in one direction. Fewer boundaries run for any distance at right angles to this dominant 'grain' so that the field pattern resembles, in plan, slightly wavy brickwork. Such arrangements are found in many districts within the region studied here, in the form both of enclosed fields and pre-enclosure furlong patterns, but are especially prominent on the Chiltern dipslope; on the fringes of the London Clays; on the chalky boulder clays in south Norfolk and north Suffolk; and on the light chalk soils of south west Cambridgeshire and north west Norfolk (Hesse 1992; Hesse 2000; Williamson 1987; Williamson 2000a, 144–52; Bryant, Perry and Williamson *forthcoming*). They superficially resemble the extensive planned field systems of Bronze Age date which survive in the form of low tumbled walls on Dartmoor, locally known as the 'reaves' (Fleming 1988), but with the important difference that many, often most of their long axes are formed by roads and tracks. These are invariably orientated at right angles to a major river valley, suggesting that these landscapes originated through the division, and exploitation, of upland grazing grounds and woodpastures (Figures 14 and 15). The tracks presumably existed for the movement of cattle, wood,

FIGURE 14.
Co-axial field patterns on the Chiltern dipslope, mapped from the Ordnance Survey six-inch first edition of the 1880s.

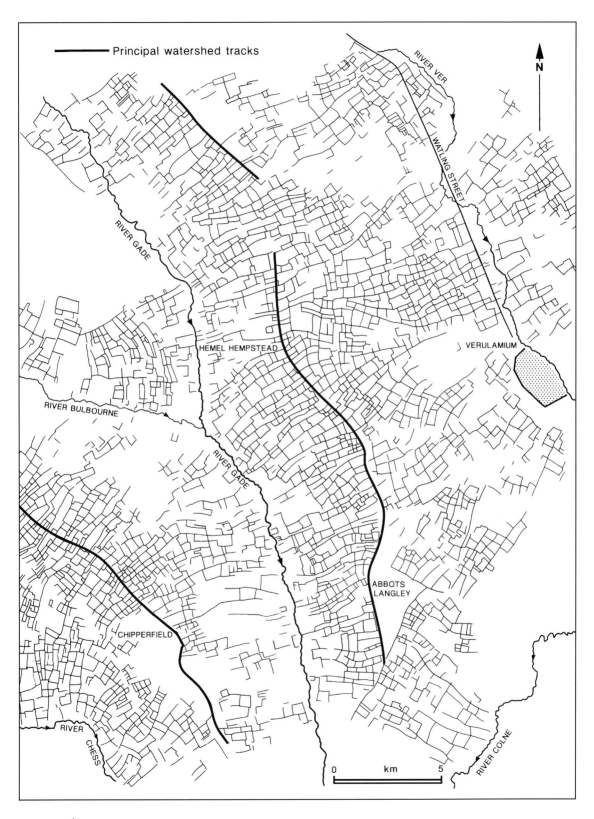

Principal watershed tracks

RIVER VER

WATLING STREET

RIVER GADE

HEMEL HEMPSTEAD

VERULAMIUM

RIVER BULBOURNE

RIVER GADE

ABBOTS
LANGLEY

CHIPPERFIELD

RIVER
CHESS

RIVER COLNE

N

0   km   5

41

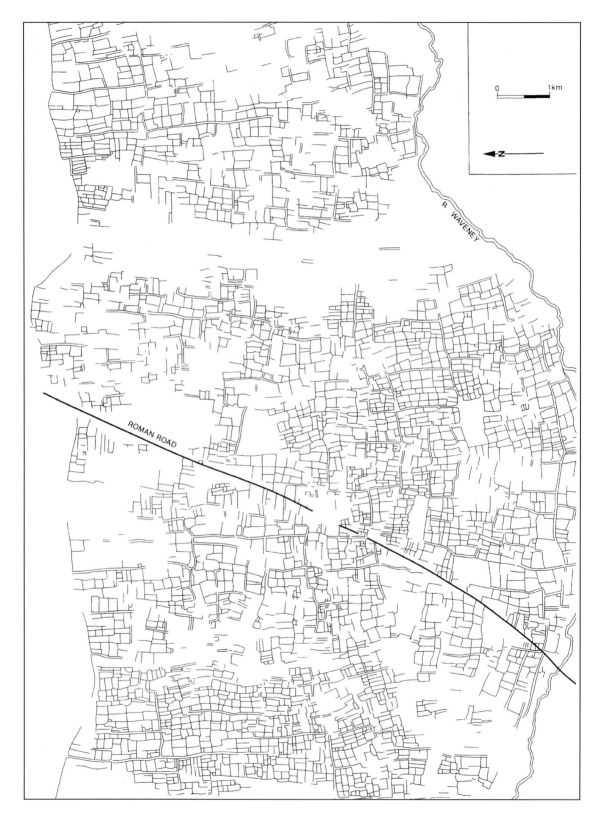

R. WAVENEY

ROMAN ROAD

0   1km

←N

42

timber and swine to or from the core areas of settlement, and the wooded peripheries. A fairly sparse pattern of boundaries separated the woods and pastures allocated to particular sections of communities and this rather loose, ladder-like layout formed the framework within which the more minutely divided brickwork patterns of the medieval countryside eventually evolved.

What I have said so far might suggest that these landscapes were entirely organic in origin, but many display marked regularities which suggest a degree of ancient planning. Regular spacing of trackways is often evident, while in parts of the Chilterns, and in south Norfolk, co-axial 'systems' running up out of adjacent valleys meet at, and are separated by, long lanes or boundaries which follow, uncannily, the lines of the watershed between them (Figure 14). Some of these landscapes may be very old indeed. In the area around Broxbourne and Wormley in south Hertfordshire the main axes of one such 'system' continue, in earthwork form, beneath an extensive area of ancient, semi-natural woodland (Bryant, Perry and Williamson *forthcoming*). In East Anglia, several co-axial landscapes appear to be slighted by Roman military roads, again suggesting a prehistoric origin (Figure 15). Indeed, in some places individual fields appear to predate the imposition of the road, suggesting more detailed partition of the land between major boundaries and tracks, perhaps paddocks associated with upland grazing farms (Williamson 1987 and 1998). Some direct archaeological dating evidence is also now emerging. The extensive co-axial systems which characterise the Chiltern dipslope in Hertfordshire have a number of marked *lacunae*, patches where the original pattern has been erased and new landscapes created. One example coincides with the eighteenth-century landscape park at The Grove, which lies in and above the Gade valley immediately to the north of the town of Watford. Recent excavations within the area of the park, carried out prior to the development of yet another golf course, revealed lost elements of one such system: and these could be firmly dated by pottery finds to the Iron Age (Charles LeQuesne *pers comm*). Landscapes like this remind us that England in 1066 was indeed an 'old country'. In many areas of 'ancient countryside', the earliest strata of the landscape are ancient indeed.

Patterns of transhumance between settled lowlands and upland 'wolds' did not always lead to the creation of regular co-axial landscapes. Sometimes more chaotic, less structured networks of sub-parallel trackways developed, especially where interfluves were wide, upland wolds extensive, and the distance from valley to watershed considerable. Good examples include the bundle of tracks running from the Soar valley for twenty kilometres eastwards onto the drift-covered uplands of 'high' Leicestershire, mapped by Harold Fox (Fox 1989, 88); or those running from the valley of the Great Ouse around Huntingdon and Godmanchester up onto the high watershed with the Nene – an area traditionally known as Bromswold (Rackham 1986, 276). But whether regular or irregular in character, such landscapes testify to the vital importance of outlying wood-pastures to these early economies, a subject to which we shall soon have cause to return.

FIGURE 15.
Co-axial field patterns in south Norfolk (the so-called 'Scole-Dickleburgh field system'). The earliest boundaries in the area form extensive, semi-regular co-axial grids, one of which is apparently slighted by the Roman Pye Road (after Williamson 1999).

Estate fission

The great estates of middle Saxon times were, according to most writers, the patrimony of tribal kings. They were granted out to individuals in the king's retinue for limited periods and did not at first become the permanent possessions of noble families. But in time they became alienated, first to endow the church, subsequently as powerful families gained full rights of ownership over them. Once they had passed into private hands, they tended to disintegrate, through the effects of partible inheritance, or because portions could now be sold, or granted away. At the same time, they tended to disintegrate from below, as lesser men – former administrators, or prospering peasants on the outlying *warland* – received or usurped proprietary rights over portions of the territory (Williamson 1993, 114–26).

Fission of secular territories was accompanied by the disintegration of their ecclesiastical counterparts. Following the conversion of tribal elites in the course of the seventh century relatively few churches existed, each serving an area much more extensive than later parishes. These churches were called *minsters*, were staffed by teams of priests, and their territories or *parochiae* were often conterminous with early estates (Blair 1988). But as population grew, and as estates fragmented, local lords gradually erected churches on their own manors, to serve their families, households and dependants (Morris 1989, 140–67). Most parish churches were originally erected beside the hall of a thegn, and in many villages manor house and church still stand in convenient proximity. Other churches seem to have been built by groups of freemen, perhaps kin groups, especially in parts of East Anglia where, as we shall see, the manorial system evolved in a patchy, uneven fashion in Saxon times (Warner 1986).

Whatever the precise process of estate fission its underlying causes were demographic growth, increasing social complexity, and the emergence of larger and more sophisticated political units. This last process culminated in the creation of a unified English state, although this was actually precipitated by specific political events. The east of England – including the east of the region studied here – was conquered by Viking armies in the later ninth century, something which may, or may not, have been followed by large-scale immigration of Scandinavian peasants (Sawyer 1957; Davis 1955; Stenton 1942). The Viking incursions destroyed the power of Mercia, Essex, East Anglia and the other independent or semi–independent kingdoms, and as England was reconquered from the Danes under the West Saxons during the early tenth century a single unified kingdom was created.

Following the reconquest new forms of territorial and fiscal organisation were introduced throughout the region studied here, often through the adaptation of earlier administrative structures: the old West Saxon system of shires and *hundreds* (Jewell 1972, 42–51; Winchester 1990, 61–4). A hundred was an administrative subdivision of a shire which, at least notionally, comprised 100 *hides* – units of taxation and assessment containing 120 fiscal acres. Each hundred had its own court and its own liability for taxation, which was distributed in turn among its constituent vills on the basis of the notional area of farmland, again measured in hides, which they each contained. All these political and administrative developments were part and parcel of wider and more complex changes. The late Saxon period saw an increasing shift towards a political system based on renders of cash, rather than tribute, something which itself reflected the growing importance of markets, and market exchange (Hodges 1989). The growth of a more market-orientated economy also served as a further encouragement to the fragmentation of large archaic estates, for it rendered less important the complicated forms of *redistributive* exchange with which they had been associated. Great landowners could use cash from rents to buy those commodities which could not be produced on their own lands.

According to most students of the subject, the fragmentation of large estates in the course of the later Saxon period, and the concomitant proliferation of local lords, was associated with an overall decline in the status of the peasantry, especially those more privileged groups living on the outlying *warland*. In effect, the area of *inland* expanded, as new owners increased the burdens on the local population, in order to acquire the labour necessary to service new demesnes (Faith 1997, 153–200). In middle Saxon times a significant proportion of the Saxon peasantry had been of bond or dependent status: those receiving a house and land from a lord, in the laws of Ine of Wessex at least, appear to have been tied to the soil and bound to undertake labour services. But the early law codes and other references strongly imply that the free peasant, the *ceorl* or *geneat*, was the backbone of middle Saxon society. Such individuals owed only sporadic services to estate centres, principally at the main bottlenecks of the farming year – spring ploughing, harvest and hay harvest (Faith 1997, 176–7). By the eleventh century things had changed. Documents like the *Rectitudines Singularum Personarum* or the *Gerefa* seem to assume that the majority of the population were *geburs* or *cottars,* bound to supply heavy and more regular labour services, and pay a range of other dues to estates or manors.

Sokemen – broadly equivalent to the *ceorls* or *geneats* of earlier centuries – remained numerous in some districts. But many disappeared soon after the Norman Conquest. They frequently became villeins and bordars, their holdings incorporated more thoroughly into the organisation of some local manor, and labour services were imposed where none had existed before (Faith 1997, 215–18; Fleming 1991, 125). At Ware in Hertfordshire, for example, Domesday records how two sokemen 'have, since the coming of King William, been annexed to this manor, to which they did not belong in the time of King Edward'. In the wake of the Conquest the status of dependent tenants – the *geburs* or villeins – also declined. Their labour services were increased still further by new lords keen to maximise their revenues. All this, in Faith's words, represented a 'significant reorganisation of rural society in relation to manorial demesnes' (Faith 1997, 216). It was facilitated by the shock of Conquest, but also encouraged by wider developments, especially the increasing pressure on land and resources, which forced tenants to accept tenancies from lords on increasingly servile terms.

One important factor in the post-Conquest decline in peasant fortunes was the continued fission of estates, through the process of *subinfeudation*, that is, the creation of sub-manors within the holdings listed in Domesday. Great landowners in Norman England held their land in return for military service: they needed to supply the king with a given number of armed knights at time of need or, increasingly after 1100, render a money payment in lieu. But the knights to whom the manors comprising a great fief were granted in order to achieve this end often met these demands by creating new manors within their holdings, and thus passing their military obligations down to under-tenants. The creation of sub-manors also bought other benefits, in terms of fines, political and military support, or assistance in estate management. And manors proliferated for other reasons, as for example when a lack of male heirs led, under the terms of feudal law, to the division of a holding between co-heiresses.

Proliferation of manors, the shock of Conquest, the expansion of demesne production at a time of rising prices, all intensified tendencies already well-developed in late Saxon society. There was a general increase in the proportion of peasant farms held for labour rents, and these rents became heavier, and less certain and predictable. The pressures on the peasantry may have abated for a while in certain places during the twelfth century, when some demesnes were leased by their lords (sometimes to the local peasantry) and labour services commuted (Postan 1973; Miller and Hatcher 1978, 204–10), although recent scholarship has called into question the importance of this (Bridbury 1992, 133–53). Either way, in the later twelfth century direct management was usual and, where labour services had been rescinded, they were now widely re-imposed.

Regional variations in late Saxon society

Throughout the period from the ninth to the late twelfth century – when the formation of new manors more or less came to an end, or was at least made illegal – the number of local lords, the number of demesnes or home farms, and their demands on the local population, all steadily increased: and these factors have been seen as critical in the development of the landscape. Yet, as already intimated, the extent and character of these developments displayed a significant degree of regional variation (Figure 16 and 17). By the time of Domesday some areas within the region studied – especially those like south Hertfordshire, or the Chiltern dipslope, where the frontiers of cultivation were still expanding – were still characterised by fairly large estates, many in ecclesiastical hands, which were conterminous with equally extensive vills, and which contained few sokemen. In contrast, the densely settled boulder clays of north Suffolk and south Norfolk, and the fertile loams of east Norfolk had, for the most part, numerous small manors, a plethora of small properties held by *liberi homines* or free men, and a large number of sokemen. In contrast to

FIGURE 16.
Free men and sokemen as a proportion of the recorded Domesday population in England (after Darby 1977).

Field and Forest these two extremes, there was a broad band of countryside embracing most of the Midland counties, as well as north-east Hertfordshire, most of Essex, and parts of south Suffolk, in which medium-sized manors of more 'normal' form predominated and in which freemen and sokemen were relatively thin on the ground (although, again, relatively more numerous towards the east) (Miller and Hatcher 1978, 19–22). This basic pattern was, to a surprising extent, maintained throughout the following two centuries (Hilton 1973, 167–74). In spite of progressive subinfeudation, the far south of the region studied here continued to be characterised by large estates, and (in particular) northern East Anglia remained the land of relative freedom, where demesnes

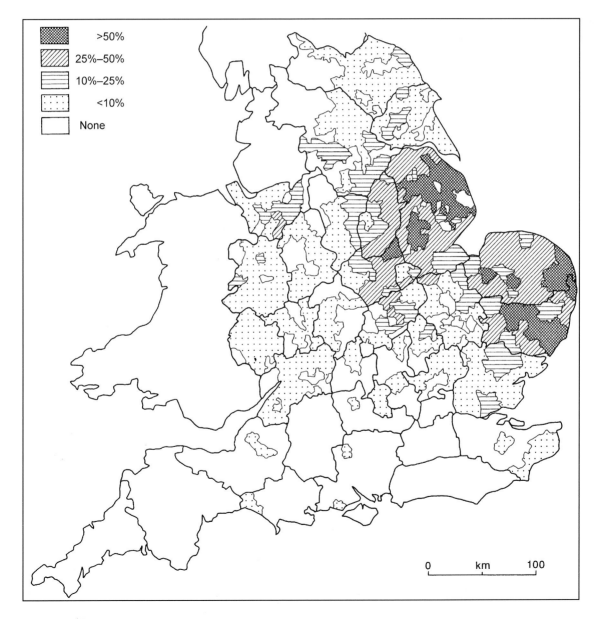

>50%

25%–50%

10%–25%

<10%

None

0   km   100

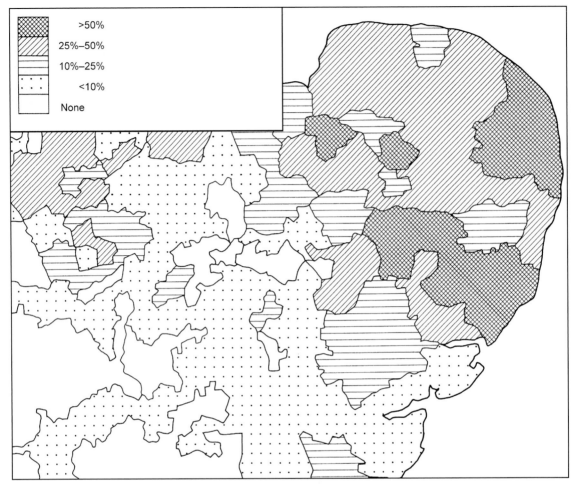

>50%

25%–50%

10%–25%

<10%

None

were small, even villein land often descended by partible inheritance, and peasant land was bought and sold with little limitation (Dodwell 1967). Indeed, the complexities of East Anglian manorial organisation were in some ways increased in the immediate aftermath of the Conquest. Minor free men in pre-Conquest England had usually been 'commended' to a major landowner – that is, had owed him fealty and allegiance. This was a personal relationship, which had little if any effect upon their property rights. The Norman lords who replaced the great Saxon landowners, however, saw things differently. They regarded the commended men as the feudal tenants of their precursors, and thus of themselves. In Abel's words, commendation was transformed into 'an irrevocable tenurial relationship' (Abels 1996, 40). Their land could be annexed completely, and thus numerous small manors, or manors with detached outlying portions, were added to an already confused territorial pattern.

The abundance of free men and sokemen in the east of England at the time of Domesday has often been explained as the consequence of the Viking invasions of the ninth century. In Stenton's words, it was no accident that 'a social organisation to which there is no parallel elsewhere in England occurs

FIGURE 17.
Free men and sokemen as a proportion of the recorded Domesday population in the study area (after Darby 1977).

48

in the one part of the country in which the regular development of native institutions had been interrupted by a foreign settlement' (Stenton 1947, 519). Free men and sokemen represented the lineal descendants of de-mobbed Viking armies, or of Scandinavian peasants who migrated in the wake of conquest. Alternatively, the disruptions brought about by raiding and conquest allowed the inhabitants of the Danelaw to escape the increasing oppression suffered by their fellows in areas which remained under Saxon control (Dodwell 1941; Stenton 1942). Even modern scholars of the calibre of Ros Faith have explained the idiosyncrasies of the east in this way: 'the terms on which Scandinavian landholders took over land seems, in some way not yet understood, to have preserved many aspects of a comparatively free peasantry.' (Faith 1997, 122)

Yet there is very little evidence that early medieval social and tenurial patterns, and Viking settlement, were in fact connected, and there have always been historians who have seen the relative freedom of the east as having more complex causes (e.g. Fisher 1973, 123). There is no real reason to assume that the Danes were, by definition, lovers of 'freedom' in a way that the English were not: Stenton believed that the settlers injected a fresh dose of 'Germanic freedom' into society (Stenton 1947) but few historians would today wholeheartedly accept such a simple notion. Moreover, the scale of Scandinavian settlement, and its distribution, remain contested (Hodges 1989, 153–4; Sawyer 1957; Davis 1955; Williamson 1993, 105–10; Margesson 1996), and there is often in fact a measure of circularity in the arguments of those who believe it was a major factor in the social and tenurial development of eastern England. The distribution of 'free peasants' is thus seen as a consequence of Viking settlement, but at the same time is presented as evidence for the scale and extent of that settlement! While there certainly are dangers in minimising the scale of Scandinavian immigration and influence, as Dawn Hadley has argued (Hadley 1996, 69–96), it is difficult to see the social and tenurial peculiarities of eastern England simply as their consequence, not least because of the very real differences between the northern and southern Danelaw 'not only in law, but also in religion, administration, and the extent of Danish place names' (Davis 1955, 38). In Lincolnshire and adjacent areas place name evidence does seem to suggest intense Viking settlement. But in East Anglia this is not the case and, moreover, the distribution of Danish place names, and that of 'free peasants', is poorly correlated. Sokemen and *liberi homines* were thus dense on the ground across much of Norfolk where, outside the district called Flegg to the north of Yarmouth, Danish place names are rare. To complicate matters further the detailed distribution of free men, and of sokemen, displays much divergence. True, Domesday's use of these terms may have varied from county to county, so that some of the individuals accounted sokemen in Lincolnshire might have been described as free men in Norfolk. But where both terms are employed the people so classified are often found in different kinds of places. Thus in Norfolk sokemen are widely scattered and normally associated with major manors which, in many cases, can be identified with the centres of ancient estates (Williamson 1993, 120). Free men, in contrast, were concentrated on the edges of fens and marshes, and in particular on the heavy plateau clays which occupy the south east of the county. 'Sokeman' is an English rather than a Danish term, and as already noted these individuals are probably best understood as the descendants of semi-free cultivators dwelling within large Middle Saxon estates – ceorls living on the *warland.* Free men, in contrast, were more privileged individuals, paying their own taxes, and might hold anything from a few acres to several hides of land, thus merging without a break into the class of local lords or *thegns* above them. Such people are perhaps most plausibly interpreted as the descendants of individuals dwelling on outlying parts of great estates, involved in the production of sheep and cattle, who had enhanced their status as population rose, the area of arable expanded, and farms grew into villages. They had gained – perhaps usurped – full proprietorial rights over their lands. Domesday sometimes hints that some lived in patrilocal kin groups: at Alby in Norfolk, for example, 'one free man' held a carucate of land in 1066; in 1086 we learn that 'now his four sons hold'.

All this suggests rather different reasons for the spatial distribution of relative freedom, and relative manorial complexity. It will be apparent from Figures 9 and 16 that there was a broad coincidence between areas in which free men and sokemen comprised more than 25 per cent of the population, and areas in which Domesday records population densities of ten or more per square mile. This suggests that both had the same basic cause. Just as favourable climatic conditions – dry summers, and reliable harvests – appear to have encouraged population growth, so also did they encourage the survival and enhancement of peasant freedom as local lords proliferated: they served to reduce 'the extent to which individual lords on individual estates had succeeded in bringing the local peasantry into dependence' (Faith 1997, 122). Perhaps, to judge from numerous ethnographic parallels, frequent harvest failures encouraged bondage, as cultivators were obliged to fall into dependence on social superiors with greater command of resources, and greater facilities for the storage of surpluses. As Stenton suggested long ago, with regard to the *geburas* of late Saxon England: 'A short run of bad luck; a series of poor harvests … might quickly reduce a man to complete dependence upon his lord', forcing him to surrender control of his land 'in return for relief from present necessities' (Stenton 1947, 476). Perhaps, in an expanding market, prospering peasants were simply better able to assert or expand their ancient rights against a rising class of thegns than their fellows living in less agriculturally favoured areas. Indeed, the eastern seaboard had advantages for the agricultural producer in the eleventh century, other than just a favourable agricultural environment. The North Sea basin was a nexus of trade and exchange, an engine for economic growth, and by late Saxon times the largest towns and markets tended to be concentrated around its margins (Hodges 1989). Topography may have been a factor in the high density of 'free peasants'. In the clayland areas in which they were particularly dense on the ground, the well-watered valleys which formed the core areas of both ancient estates and most new manors are separated by wide interfluves. Such men often dwelt

FIGURE 18.
The distribution of 'wooded' and 'open' areas in Saxon England, as mapped by Brian Roberts and Stuart Wrathmell (2000b). The map is based on a combination of place-name evidence and the data provided by Domesday Book: the champion Midlands stands out as a sparsely-wooded district.

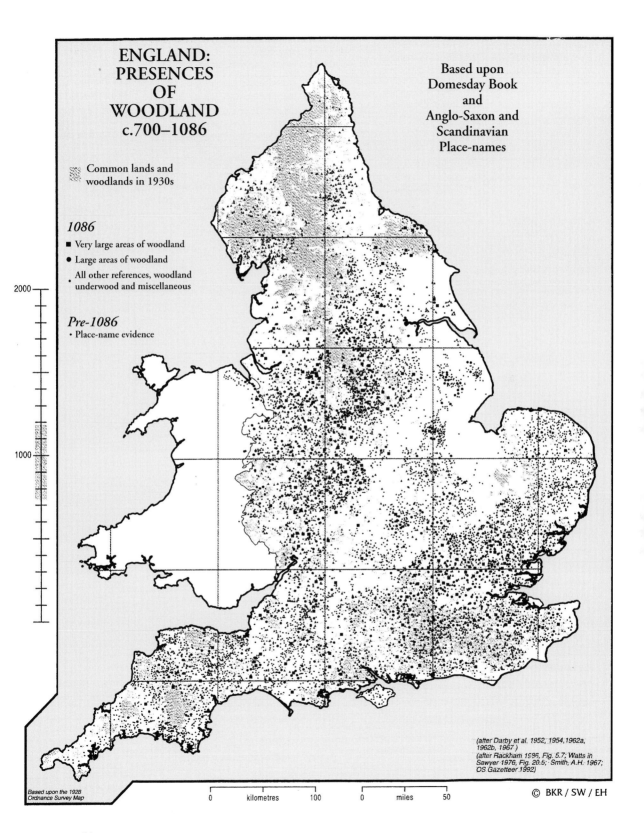

ENGLAND:
PRESENCES
OF
WOODLAND
c.700–1086

Based upon
Domesday Book
and
Anglo-Saxon and
Scandinavian
Place-names

Common lands and
woodlands in 1930s

1086

■ Very large areas of woodland

● Large areas of woodland

· All other references, woodland
  underwood and miscellaneous

Pre-1086

· Place-name evidence

2000

1000

(after Darby et al. 1952, 1954,1962a,
1962b, 1967)
(after Rackham 1986, Fig. 5.7; Watts in
Sawyer 1976, Fig. 20.5; Smith, A.H. 1967;
OS Gazetteer 1992)

Based upon the 1928
Ordnance Survey Map

0   kilometres   100   0   miles   50

© BKR / SW / EH

51

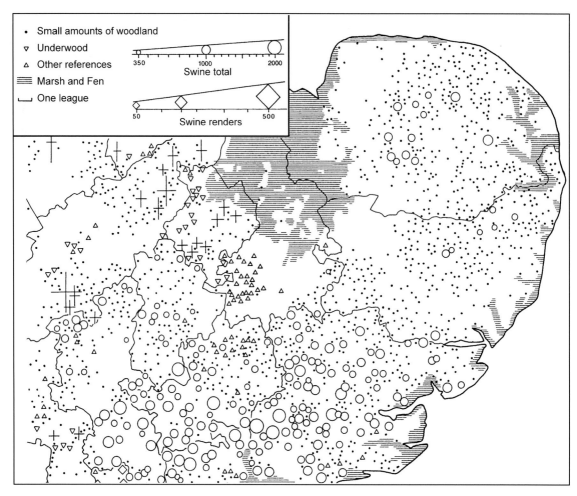

too far from the emerging centres of lordly power to be drawn fully into the organisation of estates, and in particular could not easily be called upon to supply labour services on a regular basis. In addition to all this, it is possible that favourable environmental conditions and high population densities were responsible for the more minute subdivision of lordly estates in these eastern regions, through sale or inheritance. Whatever the precise explanations for spatial variations in tenurial organisation, their overall pattern is not in doubt. Both the proportion of sokemen and free men, and the degree of manorial complexity, were high in the east, and low in the west, of the region studied here: a distribution which, the reader may not be surprised to learn, bears absolutely no relation at all to the broad distinction between 'woodland' regions, and 'champion', with which we are here concerned.

Forest and field

One possible explanation for the lack of correlation between regional settlement patterns and field systems on the one hand, and the population densities and

FIGURE 19.
The distribution of Domesday woodland within the study area (after Darby 1977).

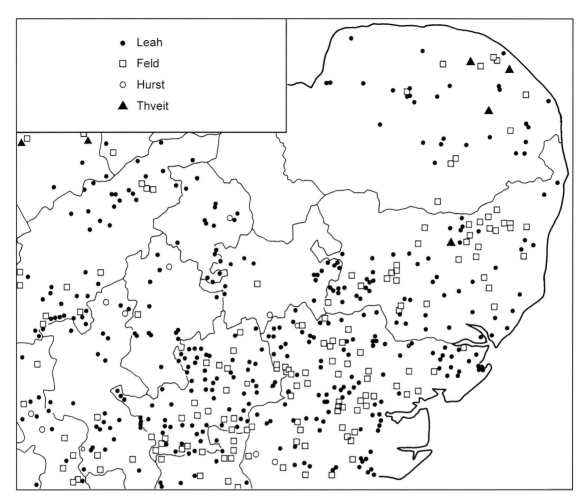

FIGURE 20.
The distribution of
'woodland'
place-names within
the study area.

variations in tenurial and social organisation recorded in Domesday on the other, is that the basic division between 'woodland' and 'champion' areas emerged in an earlier period, and that the geography of population and tenure had changed by the late eleventh century. This is not in itself an unreasonable assertion, given the fact that some have suggested that nucleation of settlement was occurring in many Midland districts as early as the eighth century (Brown and Foard 1998, 76). At this time, perhaps, population densities were highest – and the disintegration of large estates had progressed furthest – in the champion Midlands. Powerful support for such a view comes from place name and documentary evidence for the distribution of woodland in Saxon England.

Oliver Rackham was the first to note the broad correlation between the 'ancient countryside' areas, and districts which were both well-wooded at the time of Domesday, and in which there is a high proportion of place names containing elements relating to woodland or its clearance: *leah*, *feld*, and the like (Rackham 1986, 75–84). More recently, Brian Roberts and Stuart Wrathmell have emphasised the close relationship between 'regions of late surviving Anglo-Saxon woodland and nineteenth-century dispersed settlement on the one hand and, on the other, regions of open land and nucleated settlement' (Roberts and Wrathmell 2000a, 88) (Figures 18, 19 and 20). In some ways this is an old idea. Historians have long associated dispersed settlement with 'forest clearance'. And it is indeed true that many ancient countryside areas were well-wooded in medieval times, and remain so today, so that the farmland often does appear to have been cut from a once continuous tract of forest land, the tattered remnants of which survive as woods, coppices and wide hedgerows. In contrast, in most Midland vills by the thirteenth century even pasture had largely disappeared. In Northamptonshire, as David Hall has shown, most villages had at least 80 per cent and some as much as 90 per cent of their land under the plough (Hall 1995, 3). In Leicestershire, similarly, early extents reveal that 87.9 per cent of demesnes were under arable, 8.7 per cent meadow and only 3.4 per cent pasture (Fox 1984). Woodland was, in many Midland districts, non-existent.

To Roberts, Wrathmell and Rackham the distinction between open and wooded land, later manifested as the great divide between 'champion' and 'woodland' countrysides, had roots which were ancient indeed. It was a pattern largely *inherited* by Saxon farmers, not one *created* by them. Indeed, the regional distinction between well-wooded and sparsely wooded country was 'well marked by the time of the Roman Conquest' (Roberts and Wrathmell 2000, 95). Because the Midland counties were already largely cleared in Roman times, it was here that arable land use was most extensive in Saxon times, leading eventually to the familiar resource crisis described by Thirsk and others, and thus to a thoroughgoing reorganisation of settlement and field systems. In contrast, in the well-wooded tracts to the west, and to the south and east, of the Midland belt settlement remained dispersed, and indeed became more so as colonists cleared further land in the later Saxon and post-Conquest periods.

These are interesting and challenging arguments but before we examine them further we need to be a little clearer about the character of the woodland recorded by place names and other early sources, and about the ways in which it was exploited. This was not, for the most part, managed woodland in the later medieval sense – enclosed, and with a coppiced understorey. Even the woods recorded by Domesday in the late eleventh century were mainly *wood-pastures*: that is, without coppices but with a reasonable quantity of herbage growing beneath the trees and with extensive open glades, occupied by shrubs and rough vegetation (Rackham 1986, 120) (Figure 21).

Such areas were exploited for wood and timber but they were not managed very intensively to this end. Of equal or greater importance was the grazing they provided, and names containing the elements *leah*, *feld* and the like are often interspersed with those such as Chiswick ('the cheese farm') or Hardwick ('the herd farm'). Sheep, cattle and goats were fed not only on the grass and herbage but also on bushes and shrubs, and on the trees themselves, which might be eaten directly or cut and stored for use as 'leafy hay'. The latter was ancient practice, but continued in some districts well into post-medieval times

FIGURE 21.
Staverton Park, near
Wantisden in Suffolk,
is one of the best
surviving examples of
a medieval
wood-pasture in the
study area. The more
extensive 'wastes' of
late Saxon times
would probably have
had fewer pollarded
trees, but the
illustration gives a
good impression of
the mixture of trees
and herbage which
characterised this form
of land use.

(Rackham 1980a, 173–5). Herds of swine were also driven into the woods in the autumn, to fatten on acorns and beech-mast – hence the formula, *silva n porcos* (woodland for *n* swine) which Domesday generally employs within the area studied to record woodland. The use of woods for pannage continued in some districts well into the middle ages but did not imply particularly dense stands of woodland, nor preclude the grazing of other livestock. As late as 1373, on the high Chiltern ridge in west Hertfordshire, the wooded common called 'The Frith' (OE *Frið*, 'the wood') in Berkhamsted was exploited for grazing by a substantial number of people living in communities both north and south of the Chiltern escarpment, except during the pannage season, which ran from the feast of St Michael to that of St Martin (VCH Herts, II, 351, 162).

Such wooded areas were valued for other reasons, of course. They supplied timber and wood for local communities, and for great magnates they provided hunting, an activity which was perhaps of increasing importance in late Saxon times, and which already involved the construction of fences or *hagas* for corralling deer, or funnelling them towards the waiting hunters (Hooke 1998, 97). Woodland was a resource, not simply an obstacle to the plough, land to be cleared and used for something else. It is noteworthy that much Domesday woodland lay far from the manor or vill in which it was recorded. Ancient connections dating back to the time of 'large terrains' had been perpetuated, or new ones had been forged, by late Saxon landowners keen to obtain a share in what was by now often a dwindling resource. It is only because its possession was in dispute that Domesday informs us that an area of woodland lying in Colkirk in Norfolk belonged to Fakenham, a vill lying several kilometres to the north (Williamson 1993, 141). Usually such connections can only be teased out using later evidence, if they survived into the better-documented years after *c.* 1200. The Essex manor of Lawling on the otherwise largely woodless Dengie peninsula is recorded as having woodland for 800 swine, a surprisingly large amount. It is only an extent of 1310 which shows us that this actually lay in the well-wooded country around Danbury and Purleigh some twelve kilometres to the west (Hunter 1999, 78).

But wood-pastures were essentially unstable environments. Unless their exploitation was strictly regulated they tended over time to degenerate to open pasture, for as trees were felled, died or were blown down in gales they were unlikely to be replaced. The growth of new seedlings or suckers was suppressed by the browsing of the herds and flocks. In this context, one of the more interesting aspects of the correlation between the distribution of Domesday woodland, and types of landscape, are the anomalies: those districts which developed 'woodland' landscapes of dispersed settlement but which the survey suggests possessed only limited areas of woodland. The most notable example is the clay plateau of south Norfolk, for the relatively small quantities of woodland recorded across much of this district did not reflect the fact that particularly large areas were under cultivation (Figure 18). On the contrary: numerous extensive tracts of largely treeless common survived here well into post-Conquest and, indeed, into post-medieval times (Figure 32, below, p. 96). Some still carry names associated with woodland and most had presumably once been well-wooded. But, together with other areas of 'waste' in this district, their tree cover had already been largely removed by 1066, as a consequence of high population density and (perhaps) a high density of free tenures, and the difficulties of management which this produced. They survived as relatively open pastures but Domesday passes over them in silence: the survey is notoriously unreliable in its treatment of pasture, except in the south western counties of England (Rackham 1986, 335–6).

The expansion of arable at the expense of wood-pasture was thus not simply the replacement of unproductive by productive land, and nowhere is this more starkly revealed than in the pages of Domesday itself. For by late Saxon times the density of woodland, and of population, were very poorly correlated. True, the sparsely-settled soils of the London clays and the Chiltern dipslope, in the far south of the region, still carried vast areas of woodland at the time of Domesday. But elsewhere there was little obvious relationship between the recorded densities of woodland, and of population. Those areas of light, acid land, such as the East Anglian Breckland, most completely denuded of woodland since prehistoric times, were very sparsely settled. But most striking is the situation on the clay soils of moderate or high fertility which occupy most of the region studied here. The till plateau of north Essex and east Hertfordshire carried much more woodland than the clays of the Midlands, yet at least as many people lived there.

It is easy to assume that the champion lands were the prime arable areas of Saxon and early medieval England, where 'waste' was largely ploughed up to feed a teeming population, whereas 'woodland' districts were, by comparison, backward and under-exploited, so that restricted areas of arable co-existed with extensive woods and pasture. But things were evidently not that simple. Moreover, it is hard to see *why* the Midland clays should have attained arable supremacy in quite the manner, or to quite the extent, suggested. In terms of both soils and climate, as we have seen, the clayland districts to the south and east – the 'woodland' areas of East Anglia, east Hertfordshire, and north Essex – are and presumably always have been much better suited to the cultivation of cereals. If the Midland vales really were ideal places for corn-growing in the prehistoric, Roman and Saxon periods, it would be interesting to know why. Their late medieval and post-medieval history was, to a large extent, one of a gradual but inexorable drift into pasture, as the extensive remains of ridge and furrow which survived here until recently, and the widespread evidence for settlement contraction and desertion, amply testify. Post-medieval landowners and farmers were unanimous in their opinion that most of this land made poor arable, difficult and expensive to plough (below, pp. 153–5).

Above all, we ought to note that most of the 'woodland' districts considered in this study were not *very* densely wooded by the time of Domesday – they were not landscapes of extensive forests, clearings, and pioneers. By the mid eleventh century farmland everywhere predominated massively over woodland, except in the far south of the region, on the Chiltern dipslope and in places on the London Clays. In Suffolk, according to Rackham's calculations, woodland occupied only around 9 per cent of the land area. Even in Essex – once the London clay districts are excluded – the figure was probably not much above 15 per cent. All this suggests other, and more subtle, ways of looking at these particular divisions in the late Saxon landscape. They must reflect the existence of different kinds of agrarian economy – different ways of organising farming. In the champion lands, some factor or factors had allowed and encouraged the wholesale destruction of woods and pastures, while in woodland districts these had been retained to a greater extent – yet with no discernible impact, due allowance being made for variations in climate and soil fertility, upon population densities.

When did this fundamental pattern of regional difference emerge? As we have seen, a number of authorities have argued that it was largely inherited by Saxon farmers, rather than created by them. But the evidence upon which this argument rests requires careful evaluation. The fact that there is a broad coincidence between the distribution of place names relating to woodland or woodland clearance, and areas in which high woodland totals are recorded by Domesday, does indeed suggest some continuity of woodland distribution during middle and later Saxon times. Indeed, a lack of correlation between these two data sets would be very surprising. But whether continuity can be pushed back to the Roman period, or beyond, is more questionable. In many districts the distribution of woodland changed dramatically between the Roman and Saxon periods. In north-west Essex, for example, place names suggest an extensive and perhaps continuous block of woodland occupying the high ground to the west of Saffron Walden – an area identified by Rackham as a late surviving tract of virgin wildwood (Rackham 1976, 57–8). It extends westwards from the Cam valley, through the parishes of Strethall (originally *Strætleah*), Lang*ley*, and Bar*ley*, embracing such hamlets as Craw*ley* End and Elmdon *Lea* in Elmdon. Documentary evidence leaves little doubt that extensive assarting took place in this district in the early medieval period (Monteith 1957; Miller 1957, 97). Yet the results of a systematic fieldwalking survey carried out in this area in the 1980s indicate, clearly enough, that it was intensively settled from late Iron Age times, and by the second century had a density of more than one settlement per square kilometre (Williamson 1986). Moreover, scatters of stray sherds, presumably derived from manuring, indicate extensive arable land use in the Roman period, even on the heaviest soils in the area, and Iron Age and Romano-British settlements exist beneath a number of ancient, semi-natural woods. Clearly, much regeneration of woodland had occurred in the district since Roman times.

This is not to deny that the distribution of Saxon woodland mapped by Roberts and Wrathmell was derived in part from ancient, inherited patterns. Those districts within the study region which had been most denuded of woodland by later Saxon times – the chalk escarpment of the Chilterns, Breckland, or north west Norfolk – had been largely cleared in remote prehistory. And I have already noted the marked continuity in patterns of territorial and economic organisation through the Saxon period, and the close relationship of 'large terrains' and topography. It is noteworthy, for example, how the distribution of known Roman settlements in the county of Norfolk has a marked *lacunae* running in an arc through the middle of the county which corresponds, fairly closely, to the watershed zone already discussed, in which the largest tracts of Domesday woodland are recorded (Figure 13, p. 39). But there is much less reason to believe that the broad *national* patterns proposed by Wrathmell and Roberts – comprising, in particular, a largely woodless belt of countryside occupying the Midland clay vales – can be pushed back into remote prehistory. Such evidence as there is suggests that it emerged *during*, rather than before, the Saxon period.

There is, for example, little in the distribution of known Roman settlements to suggest that the Midlands were deforested to a significantly greater extent than the 'ancient countryside' areas to the south east. On the contrary: certain kinds of Romano-British settlement – notably 'small towns' – are if anything *more* frequent in the latter areas, while in the later Iron Age the large agglomerations of settlement normally referred to as 'oppida' by archaeologists were strongly concentrated here, and rare in the Midlands (Cunliffe 1995, 69–74). It should be emphasised that the overwhelming majority of the names which provide the earliest indications of woodland distribution were coined long after the Roman period, some time between the mid-eighth and the mid-tenth centuries (Gelling 1992, 6). The most common 'woodland' element, *leah* ('a wood, a clearing in a wood') was used 'much more frequently after 730 than it was before that date' (Gelling 1984, 198). It should also be noted that in some parts of the Midlands a comparison of place names, and Domesday, suggests the progressive erosion of woodland in the course of the Saxon period. There is a tight cluster of 'woodland' place names in the west of Cambridgeshire, around Madingley and Eltisley, suggesting a tract of well-wooded country occupying the boulder clay plateau there. But by Domesday only small fragments of woodland remained, recorded by such phrases as 'woodland sufficient for fences'.

Indeed, Harold Fox has argued that most of the principal upland tracts between major valleys in the Midlands within the region studied here were 'wold' areas in early Saxon times – extensive woodland pastures 'supporting a scattering of trees, with larger stands here and there'. Great tracts of ground of this kind were found in 'High' Northamptonshire and 'High' Leicestershire, and in Bromswold, on the watershed between the rivers Nene and Great Ouse. These wooded uplands, to judge from place names, were exploited for grazing from seasonally occupied outstations:

> Foliage within easy reach of browsing animals, the mast of beech and oak and the leaves of fallen trees provided sustenance for livestock; stands could be managed in such a way as to provide browse cut from trees and then spread out for feeding (Fox 1989, 85).

But these upland woods fragmented and disappeared at a relatively early date. By the ninth century, permanent settlements were becoming widely established within them. By the late eleventh century, to judge from Domesday, woodland had become restricted to limited districts, most of which subsequently became royal forests – that is, areas in which the remaining fragments of wooded ground were preserved by law, to provide deer for the king. By the twelfth century most of the former 'wolds' were characterised by landscapes of nucleated villages 'not very different' from those found on lower ground, and the open fields stretched to township boundaries (Fox 1989, 89–95).

Of course, by this time the ancient 'wastes' had also largely disappeared from many 'woodland' districts. Only in areas of low population density, such as the Chilterns, did extensive wood-pasture commons normally survive far into the Middle Ages. But the woods were not simply assarted – turned into farmland. In marked contrast to the situation in the Midlands, many were converted into some other form of non-arable land: managed woods, deer parks, or open commons. The contrast with the boundless arable of the champion lands thus remained stark.

Champion lands are usually, implicitly or explicitly, characterised as 'core' areas of settlement. But they can be viewed in another way: as impoverished zones, deficient in important resources. Not only was woodland generally in short supply. Landscapes of extensive open fields were landscapes without hedges, and without hedgerow trees. Some pollards certainly grew in the boundaries of the tofts within the village, and some doubtless survived in the tattered remnants of waste on the periphery of township territories. But on the whole wood for fences, tools, construction and above all firewood must often have been as scarce in champion regions as it is in some third world countries today. And champion landscapes, on the Midland clays at least, were degraded environments in other ways. Because few resources of woodland or pasture survived, fallow grazing served only to recycle nutrients within the fields – there were no recurrent inputs from outside the 'system'. In Harold Fox's words, Midland fields 'must have functioned at a lower level of productivity than did systems where there were additional flows from a hinterland of rough grazing' (Fox 1984, 145). Moreover, the complex inter-mixture of properties, and the rigid adherence to the fallowing regime, were powerful disincentives to innovation. All in all, the Midland system was a form of agricultural organisation 'appropriate to relatively low levels of popu-lation', and which was 'doomed to remain at a modest level of productivity' (Fox 1984, 146).

Conclusion

The purpose of this chapter was to examine the extent to which the nucleation of settlement and the development of extensive, 'regular' open fields in the early medieval period can be explained as a consequence of population pressure, coupled with the presence of strong lordship. The most striking conclusion is that by late Saxon times neither population densities, nor aspects of tenurial organisation, were correlated in any obvious way with the variations in the medieval landscape with which we are concerned. Nucleated settlement pat-terns could be found in areas of high and low population density, weak and strong lordship. For an earlier period, regional differences in tenure and population are much harder to reconstruct but some historians have posited a broad correlation between areas most extensively deforested by the end of the Roman period and those in which champion landscapes developed during the Saxon period. I have argued that important regional differences in the extent of woodland certainly existed by the time of Domesday, but that they probably emerged during the Saxon period, rather than before. Saxon farmers in 'champion' districts evidently did remove more woodland, and pasture, than their counterparts in 'woodland' areas. Moreover, this distinction hard-ened still further in post-Conquest times, for while Midland farmers often ploughed up almost all their grazing land, in 'woodland' areas much surviving 'waste' was converted into commons, managed woods and deer parks. Yet why this difference should have emerged is not immediately apparent. The

Field and Forest   Midland clay vales are not characterised by soils or climate particularly suited to arable cultivation, as their post-medieval land use history so clearly testifies. And these different ways of managing the landscape were not, it may be as well to emphasise yet again, reflected in the distribution of population, either at the time of Domesday or, indeed, thereafter. By the thirteenth century farmers in the Midlands had, on average, extended their arable acreage at the expense of woodland and grazing to a much greater extent than their fellows living in districts to the south and east. But this, evidently, did not allow them to grow more food.

CHAPTER THREE

Champion

In this chapter I will discuss the formation of nucleated settlements, and their associated open fields, within that broad region described by Rackham as 'planned' or 'predominantly planned' countryside – essentially, the Midlands and the adjacent areas of light soils lying to the south and east, along the Chiltern escarpment and in northern and western East Anglia. Many historians have implied that the nucleation of settlement, and the development of open fields, occurred for the same general reasons, and at roughly the same time, across the whole of this extensive area but, as we shall see, this is probably untrue. It is also often assumed that nucleated villages and open fields of 'regular' form were almost ubiquitous here but, once again, this was far from the case. In most districts some hamlets and isolated farmsteads could be found, as well as villages; but in parts of north Bedfordshire especially their numbers approached those of classic 'woodland' districts. In many 'planned countryside' areas, moreover, villages were only poorly nucleated and their field systems were complex and irregular, varying greatly from the textbook Midland 'norm'. In other words, even a cursory inspection soon reveals that the 'planned countryside' is not one kind of landscape, but many. In a volume as short as this some simplification is unavoidable, and in the pages that follow I will divide this extensive region into three main districts.

The Midland clays

I will begin with the clayland 'core' of the Midlands – essentially, the counties of Northamptonshire, Leicestershire, Rutland, and Buckinghamshire north of the Chilterns – because it is here that archaeologists and historians concerned with open-field origins have focused most of their attention (Figure 22). In part this is because it was in this area that champion landscapes reached their most developed and characteristic form. But it is also because, until post-War agricultural intensification, the medieval landscape was here preserved in a more obviously "archaeological" form than anywhere else: as earthworks of villages deserted in the late middle ages and after; and as ridge and furrow, the plough ridges of open fields fossilised under pasture. And it was in Northamptonshire that the Royal Commission on Historical Monuments produced what are arguably their best surveys in the 1960s and 70s, and where a number of prominent archaeologists undertook important research into the

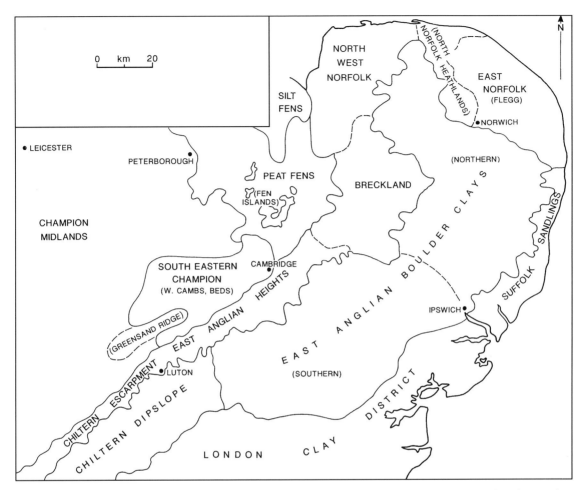

development of the early medieval landscape – Glenn Foard, Christopher Taylor, and David Hall. It is not surprising, then, that studies of other areas of medieval England have often been examined against the background of this Midland 'norm'.

This is a region of varied and undulating terrain, and with a complex underlying geology, structured by a series of inclined planes, dipping towards the south east, which are overlain by drift deposits. Areas of high ground are interspersed with wide valleys, cut by a series of substantial rivers – the Great Ouse, Nene, Welland and their principal tributaries. Although their parent materials are thus very varied, the soils in the region can be divided into four main groups. Firstly, on the floors of the principal valleys particularly wide areas of alluvial soils can be found, more extensive than in any of the other regions discussed in this book – principally those of the Fladbury 1 and Thames Associations.[1]

1. Throughout this book I adopt the system of soil classification, and the terms, employed by the Soil Survey of England and Wales. Soils are grouped into *Associations,* each of which contains a number of co-varying soil types or *Series,* defined in terms of mineralogical content, physical structure, drainage potential etc. The Association takes its name from the dominant series within it.

FIGURE 23.

The open field system of Brixworth in Northamptonshire in 1422, as reconstructed by David Hall. The demesne lay in a single block, close to the village (stippled); one of the yardlands is shown, scattered fairly evenly through the three great fields of the vill.

Secondly, on the sides of the major valleys, a mixed range of soils occurs, derived from chalky boulder clay, Jurassic and Cretaceous clays, and Jurassic limestone (Ragg *et al.* 1984). Many of these, such as the Moreton Association, are comparatively free-draining, but others – those of the Flint and Ashley Associations – are only moderately well drained, and subject to a degree of seasonal waterlogging. On the extensive areas of higher ground between

the main valleys the soils are for the most part fairly intractable, with large areas occupied by the Ragdale and Denchworth Associations. While areas of freely draining soils can be found, on the whole this is a region of heavy clay soils.

By the thirteenth century this was classic champion countryside. Farmsteads were clustered in villages, or large compact hamlets, and the standard villein holding comprised a virgate of 12 or 16 acres divided into a large number of small, unhedged strips (*selions* or *lands*), most covering between a quarter and a third of an acre, which were evenly scattered across the territory of the township (Hall 1989, 194–5). Because the soils were so heavy it was usual for each land to be ploughed in ridges, in order to facilitate drainage, thus producing the characteristic earthworks called 'ridge and furrow'. Strips were grouped into bundles called *furlongs*, which formed the basic unit for cropping; and these in turn were grouped into large blocks called *fields*, usually two or three in number, which formed the basic unit for fallowing: i.e., each year one field lay completely unsown (Hall 1982 and 1995). The layout of the furlongs was usually quite unrelated to that of the earlier landscape: 'the pattern of medieval fields generally bears no relationship to the underlying Iron Age and Roman field systems revealed as crop marks by aerial archaeology' (Brown and Foard 1998, 73) (Figure 24).

The existence of a continuous fallowing sector and the wide and even scattering of strips were connected, for if strips had been clustered in restricted areas of a township then in some years all or most of a man's land might lie fallow and uncropped. The other fields would be sown with 'winter corn' – autumn-sown crops like wheat or rye; and 'spring corn', such as oats, barley, peas or beans. Within any one furlong the same crop would normally be grown in any one year.

The ploughlands were extensive. Although almost all villages possessed some meadow land – often in very considerable quantities – there was often little other grass (Hall 1995, 2; Fox 1984, 121). Livestock were, however, grazed on the fallow field and (after harvest) on the land destined for spring corn. Their dung returned nutrients to the soil, which were constantly depleted by cropping, although the importance of this has perhaps been over-played by some authorities. Because of the heavy and intractable nature of most Midland soils, and their tendency to compact and 'puddle' under pressure, sheep flocks could not be close-folded as they were in light land areas, and stocking densities were generally low (Kerridge 1992, 77–8; Fox 1984, 131–3). The manure from stalled oxen and dairy cattle, fed over winter on hay from meadows, was probably of more importance in restoring fertility to the fields, especially as the straw with which it was mixed would help give 'body' to the soil, improving its structure, aeration and drainage (Fox 1984, 131). A more important function of the fallow was probably that it provided a measure of weed control, particularly necessary on these damp and fairly fertile soils, which encouraged rank weed growth. Repeated ploughing at the end of the year destroyed the weeds and their remains provided further nutrients for the soil, as a form of 'green manure'.

Most Midland parishes contained a single village, albeit one often divided between more than one manor. But more complex arrangements could be found, especially in north Buckinghamshire but also sporadically in Leicester-shire and Northamptonshire. Sometimes there were two settlements in a parish, occasionally three, although both or all were usually significant, compact nucleations, farming their own field systems, rather than the kind of small hamlets or isolated farms characteristic of 'woodland' countryside (RCHME 1981, xxxviii). In most cases the demesne land was scattered throughout the territory of the vill, intermingled with the land of the tenants, but in some cases it formed a compact block, often close to the village.

As we saw in chapter 1, much has been written about the origins of Midland villages but one fact stands out above all others as the result of many decades of research. Although some may have come into existence in late Saxon or even post-Conquest times, the majority began life in the middle Saxon period – that is, in the eighth and ninth centuries. The most detailed evidence comes from Northamptonshire, thanks to the field-walking surveys carried out by David Hall, Glenn Foard and others. A proportion of the scattered settlements of early Saxon times – farms and small hamlets – was abandoned and their inhabitants moved, or were moved, to a smaller number of surviving centres lying on, or close to, the sites of medieval and modern villages. Sometimes there was a single middle Saxon settlement. Sometimes there was more than one but in close proximity, which later fused to produce the multi-centred 'polyfocal' plans characteristic of villages like Cottesbrook, Kelmarsh, or Fawsley (RCHME 1981, 54, 111–13). The development of the new settlement pattern was largely completed before the introduction of late Saxon ceramic types, Saxo-Norman pottery, some time around 850. Many of the surviving settlements were probably already more important places than those which became deserted, to judge from the quantities of pottery recovered by excavation from early/middle Saxon contexts at surviving villages like Higham Ferrers and Raunds (Brown and Foard 1998, 76). Conversely, field names attached to the sites of the deserted settlements, which often feature the term *cote*, imply their relatively lowly, dependent status.

Archaeological fieldwork in the neighbouring counties – north Buckinghamshire and Leicestershire – suggests a similar pattern. The small, outlying sites discovered by fieldwalking, characterised by early/middle Saxon pottery, seldom produce Saxo-Norman wares as well: conversely, excavation within, or fieldwalking beside, modern villages frequently does produce such material. In Leicestershire, 90 per cent of finds of Saxo-Norman pottery were from within, or immediately beside, the area of later medieval villages; in Buckinghamshire the figure is around 80 per cent (Lewis *et al.* 1997 and 2001, 81). Evidently, across this extensive region settlement nucleation had been largely completed before the middle of the ninth century. Nucleation was a middle Saxon, rather than a late Saxon, phenomenon.

Yet at the same time we need to be a little cautious in using this term – in accepting that the change from early to middle Saxon settlement in these Midland counties *always* or *only* involved the replacement of a dispersed pattern of small farms and hamlets by one comprising nucleated villages. Few middle Saxon sites in the region have been excavated, because they lie under modern villages. While those that have been (such as Raunds in Northamptonshire or Pennyland in Buckinghamshire) do indeed represent sizeable 'villages' it is possible that others were, initially at least, small hamlets or even single farms – especially those in high 'wold' areas. This might explain why a number of excavations carried out on deserted medieval village sites in this region have failed to produce evidence of middle or even late Saxon occupation – the latter may have covered a limited area, beyond the bounds of the excavated site. As already noted, early Saxon settlements were often relatively short-lived and mobile, and while the change in settlement patterns occurring in the eighth and ninth centuries often involved the emergence of sizeable nucleations it also represented, in Helena Hamerow's words, a 'fundamental change from essentially mobile to essentially stable communities' (Hamerow 1991, 16–17).

In some cases, this probably involved the fixing at single points in the landscape of single farms, or small hamlets, which only later expanded into true 'villages'.

In some cases, it is true, settlements continued to exhibit continued short-range 'drift' even in Middle Saxon times: Yarnton, on the Thames gravels above Oxford, just outside the study area, is a case in point (Hey 2001). But for the most part, both stabilisation and nucleation occurred in the eighth and ninth centuries, rather than later. It is important to repeat and emphasise this, because many authorities have assumed that these were rather later phenomena (Hamerow 1991; Lewis *et al.* 1997). Explanations for village origins are thus usually framed in terms of the relatively settled and familiar world of Edward the Confessor, William I, and their successors: a world of high population densities, a nation state, an expanding market economy, and local territorial lordship. Yet the first stages of nucleation, at the very least, took place in a very different context: one of rather lower population densities, tribal kings, warrior entourages and a redistributive, rather than a market, economy. The first villages existed within large estates, rather than splintered local lordships. Indeed, Glenn Foard has recently suggested that settlement nucleation was in fact linked, not with the *fragmentation* of large estates, but rather with their emergence and refinement. It was intended to improve in some way the efficiency of agriculture and was associated with a decline in the status of a proportion of the peasantry. 'The forcing of complex free tenancies into the feudal mode known to have taken place after the Norman Conquest can thus be seen as the last stage of a long process of manorialisation' (Brown and Foard 1998, 91).

Much controversy surrounds the character of the fields associated with these middle Saxon settlements. Some historians and archaeologists believe that open fields were, indeed, first laid out in middle Saxon times (Hall 1981, 36–7); and that some originally took the form of very long furlongs, up to a mile in length in extreme cases, which were only later subdivided and realigned to create the patchwork more familiar from post-medieval maps. No unaltered examples of such 'long furlongs' survived the middle ages in the Midland counties, although they are known from outside the area, most notably from Holderness in Yorkshire (Harvey 1981). Some archaeologists and historians, however, take a rather different view and believe that open fields were created some time *after* the nucleation of settlement, in the ninth or tenth centuries, and doubt whether they were originally laid out in the form of 'long furlongs' (Brown and Foard 1998, 82–90).

Central to this particular debate are the tenurial structures which seem to underlie the layout of the open fields. In many villages the virgates or 'yardlands' (or, in Leicestershire, the bovates or 'oxgangs') were laid out with great regularity, although this pattern had often been partially obscured, by the time the earliest terriers or field books were produced, through the operation of the land market. Each holding comprised a single strip of land in every furlong of the vill or, where furlongs were particularly large, two or three well-spaced strips. In each furlong the lands of the tenants would follow a fixed sequence, so that the same neighbours always lay adjacent (Hall 1989, 195). It has been argued, in Northamptonshire at least, that the number of yardlands within each vill was originally related to that place's taxation assessment; and that this, and the physical layout of holdings within the fields, was fixed when nucleation first occurred in the eighth or ninth centuries (Hall 1989, 196). But there are a number of problems with such a view.

Even if the structured layouts of holdings which we meet in medieval documents are indeed of pre-Conquest origin, it is unlikely that most were created as early as the middle Saxon period. The fiscal assessments with which they have most convincingly been linked were only imposed across much of this district following its re-conquest from the Danes in the tenth century. But there are grounds for doubting the validity of this connection. Early forms of taxation, as well as the late Saxon land tax called the *geld*, were based on units called hides or carucates – areas, notionally, of 120 acres – which were subdivided into four units also called virgates or, in some north eastern districts, eight units called bovates. The fact that these same terms were used for the customary holdings in the open fields has suggested to some that tenurial and fiscal structures were originally related, and of comparable antiquity. But even before the old land-based tax fell into disuse in the late twelfth century 'manorial' virgates and 'fiscal' virgates were evidently of different size, the former usually comprising 12 or 16 rather than 30 customary acres (Harvey 1984, 21). This in itself implies that the virgates we meet in the open fields (and the ways in which these were laid out on the ground) are rather later in date, relating not to taxation assessments but instead to the systems of exaction imposed upon peasant communities as demesnes proliferated during late Saxon or even post-Conquest times. True, a number of authorities have argued cogently that, in spite of the differing size of the units in question, the tenurial structures recorded in thirteenth century or later documents were, nevertheless, quite closely related to Saxon taxation assessments. Unfortunately, they disagree about the precise nature of the linkage. Some see a direct relationship between the number of hides at which a vill was assessed at the time of Domesday and the number of yardlands, most frequently at a ratio of ten or twelve yardlands to the hide: thus at Great Billing there were 48 yardlands in the open fields, and Domesday records an assessment of four hides in 1086 (Hall 1989, 195–6). Others, however, have discerned different relationships, suggesting that the yardlands recorded in medieval documents are, in fact, related to the number of *ploughlands* recorded by Domesday, at a ratio of 8:1 (Brown and Foard 1998).

We should also note, perhaps, that the structured and regular patterns of holdings often extended throughout the fields of a township, all the way to the township boundaries. Yet it is hard to believe that the area under cultivation did not expand significantly during the tenth, eleventh or even twelfth centuries, especially in the high 'wold' areas. True, it is sometimes possible to discern 'subtle differences' in the layout of holdings in the more peripheral furlongs of a vill, suggesting that arable had been added through assarting after the regular pattern had been laid out (Hall 1989, 196). And it is possible that once established, a regular sequence of strips would simply be replicated as new furlongs were formed. Nevertheless, the idea that the tenurial structure and layout of townships recorded in medieval and post-medieval documents normally perpetuate, to a significant extent, arrangements made when villages were first established some time before *c.* 850 must be treated with caution (Lewis *et al.* 1997, 148–9).

All in all, it is probable that open fields featuring regular patterns of holdings were associated with some middle Saxon settlements – perhaps those occupied by bond cultivators on the *inland* of great estates. Even these, by the time we see them clearly in later medieval documents, had undergone one, perhaps several, phases of re-organisation, including in particular the subdivision and realignment of 'long furlongs'. In most vills, however, regular tenurial structures were almost certainly a late Saxon or even, in some cases, post-Conquest imposition, associated with the proliferation of demesnes in the course of the tenth and eleventh centuries, and the steady integration of the peasant population, and their labour services, into emergent manorial economies.

There were certainly other changes in the Midland landscape during the later Saxon period, and through the twelfth and thirteenth centuries, as population rose and manors subdivided. Some neighbouring middle Saxon foci, as already noted, fused to form 'polyfocal' villages. Many existing village were re-planned in more regular form, as at Raunds in Northamptonshire, where excavations have revealed how late Saxon tofts were laid out in a measured pattern (Youngs *et al.* 1988). Villages sometimes expanded over their own fields, as at Canons Ashby or Walgrave in Northamptonshire. Many gained planned extensions, such as Stoke Albany in the same county (Taylor 1983, 159). Occasionally new settlement foci might be established a little distance away from the margins of existing villages, subsequently becoming linked to them through 'infilling': another cause of 'polyfocal', multi-centred village plans. Sometimes settlements even moved away from their old sites, often to be beside major roads which, as trade increased in the post-Conquest period, became more attractive locations – as at Harringworth in Northamptonshire. It is also clear that entirely new nucleated settlements appeared in the late Saxon or even post-Conquest period, some perhaps indicated by the name 'Newton'. A number of the 'subsidiary hamlets' in Midland parishes, like Cotton End in Long Buckby, or Milnthorpe between Weedom Lois and Weston, appear to have been established on top of existing open-field arable, their property boundaries replicating the sinuous pattern of the surrounding open field strips (Taylor 1995, 30). A few, such as Thorpe Underwood in Harrington parish in Northamptonshire, do not appear in Domesday Book and may have been created as the final areas of woodland were cleared on the margins of townships as late as the twelfth century. At Newton near Geddington in Northampton-shire, certainly, an entirely new settlement appears to have come into existence in the eleventh century following a phase of woodland clearance on the edge of Geddington township (Brown and Foard 1998, 81).

The important point to emphasise, however, is that throughout all these many and varied changes settlement patterns in this core area of the Midlands remained predominantly nucleated. Neither the growth of population nor the proliferation of sub-manors led to the wide dispersal of settlement across the surrounding landscape, as they generally did in 'woodland' districts. The settlement pattern remained dominated by compact villages, or large non-parochial hamlets.

Of course, even within this heartland of the Midland system pockets of more dispersed settlement could be found: on the Bedfordshire Greensands, for example, where infertile, acid soils ensured the survival of extensive tracts of heath and woodland well into post-medieval times; or in the various royal forests which formed islands of well-wooded country within the open, champion landscape. A string of forests ran through the centre of Northamptonshire and into Buckinghamshire – Rockingham, Salcey, Whittlewood and Bernwood; while to the east, in Rutland, lay the forest of Leighwood. These generally corresponded with high interfluves occupied by particularly poorly draining boulder clay, Lias clay or Oxford Clay soils, although Rockingham lay partly on a deposit of infertile sand. They were all forests in the legal sense – areas subject to forest law, a bundle of legislation designed to conserve deer and their habitats for the king's hunt (Steane 1974, 193–4) and which, *inter alia*, tended to limit the expansion of cultivation at the expense of wood-pasture and 'waste'. Nevertheless, in all these areas cultivation did expand, even in post-Conquest times, the fines on assarting levied by the forest authorities gradually transmuting into regular rents.

Most forest areas were characterised by fairly dispersed patterns of settlement, featuring poorly nucleated hamlets and large common-edge agglomerations. But not all: and those who believe in some relatively direct and simple relationship between the extent of woodland and waste on the one hand, and the intensity of settlement dispersion on the other, could do worse than spend a day looking at maps of Rockingham Forest. Places like Weldon, Stanion, Deene or Deene Thorpe have no outlying settlements other than the lodges associated with deer parks, a common feature of the district. Numerous areas of common waste existed but none attracted peripheral settlement in the way that they would have done, for example, in Norfolk. Thus in the south eastern part of Weldon parish the former area of a large open common called Weldon Plain is flanked on its north western and eastern sides by enclosures. But these were not the sites of long-abandoned, common-edge farms. 'All ... have ridge-and-furrow within them, with headlands inside the field boundaries. This presumably represents early enclosures on the edge of the waste' (RCHME 1979, 166).

Perhaps because cultivation continued to expand in these forest districts well into post-Conquest times their field systems were usually fairly irregular, compared to those in villages lying outside the forest. But here again there were exceptions. One of the earliest maps in England, surveyed in *c.* 1440, thus shows Boarstall in Bernwood Forest, surrounded by its three open fields – Frith Field, Cowhouse Field, and Arnegrove Field (Reed 1979, 127). Even in 'forest' areas, in other words, the strong Midland tendency towards nucleation of settlement, and regularity of field systems, could sometimes be found.

West Cambridgeshire, south Huntingdonshire and east Bedfordshire

Towards the south-eastern edge of the conventional 'champion' or 'planned countryside' belt – in an area embracing west Cambridgeshire, southern Huntingdonshire, and much of northern and eastern Bedfordshire – lies a region which differs in a number of significant respects from that just discussed. To the east, it is bounded by the edge of the peat fens but to north and west its boundaries are not clearly defined, while to the south west it merges with the Greensand Ridge, the district of infertile soils, scattered settlement and low population densities already mentioned (Figure 22, p. 63). But the region under discussion here was by no means thinly populated in late Saxon times, for Domesday suggests that it had population densities more or less identical to those of the districts lying immediately to the west which I have just discussed. Nor is it an area of particularly poor soils, for most of it comprises low, boulder clay-covered plateaux occupied by the calcareous soils of the Hanslope and Evesham Associations (Hodge *et al.* 1984). Nevertheless, although usually classified as a 'champion' district, a number of features aligns this area more with the 'woodland' regions of East Anglia and the south east.

In many places nucleated settlements farming regular two- or three-field systems existed by the thirteenth century. But elsewhere there were many deviations from the familiar Midland norm. In west Cambridgeshire, for example, some vills farmed four fields (Barton) or five (Eversden) (Postgate 1964, Appendix II, ii, v). In some north Bedfordshire vills there were large areas of land held in severalty and evidently enclosed directly from the waste, and open field systems were often multiple and complex. In Thurleigh, for example, there were eleven distinct open fields when the parish was enclosed in 1805: Cooks Field, Cow Hill Field, Little Field, Park Field, South Field, Church Field, Mill Field, Just Field, Hopkins Field, Langley Field and Riddens Field (Brown and Taylor 1989, 62) (Figure 25). There was much blurring of the boundaries between 'enclosed' and 'open' arable, so that in many vills enclosed land was subject to rights of common grazing: an agreement for the Grange Field at Putnoe in Bedfordshire, drawn up in 1240, thus arranged for it to be open at particular places 'so that when the crops have been carried those who want may common there' (Roden 1973, 353).

Even where two- or three-field systems of 'normal' Midland form existed these were sometimes the result of relatively late remodelling of more 'irregular' arrangements, made well into the post-Conquest period. Hardwick in Cambridgeshire had three named fields in the seventeenth century but six in 1272; Little Gransden in the same county had three fields in 1615 but no fewer than ten in 1272 (Postagte 1964, Appendix II, vi). Harold Fox has discussed the

FIGURE 25.
The parish of Thurleigh in Bedfordshire before enclosure in 1805 (after Brown and Taylor 1989). Although well within the 'champion' Midlands, Thurleigh and the surrounding parishes display the kind of dispersed settlement patterns and complex, irregular field systems characteristic of 'woodland' regions.

72

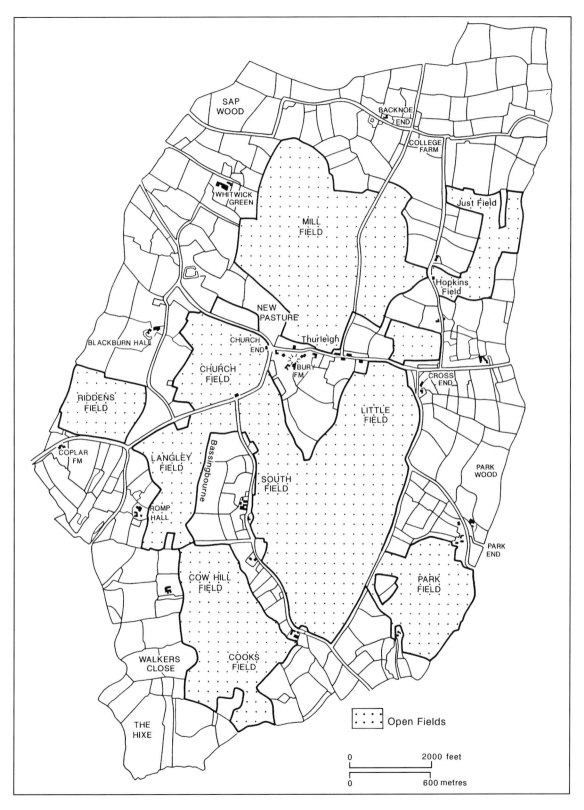

SAP
WOOD

BACKNOE
END

COLLEGE
FARM

WHITWICK
GREEN

Just Field

MILL
FIELD

Hopkins
Field

NEW
PASTURE

BLACKBURN HALL

CHURCH
END

Thurleigh

CHURCH
FIELD

BURY
FM

RIDDENS
FIELD

LITTLE
FIELD

CROSS
END

COPLAR
FM

LANGLEY
FIELD

PARK
WOOD

Bassingbourne

SOUTH
FIELD

ROMP
HALL

PARK
END

COW HILL
FIELD

PARK
FIELD

WALKERS
CLOSE

COOKS
FIELD

THE
HIXE

:::::: Open Fields

0   2000 feet

0   600 metres

cases of Segenhoe in Bedfordshire and Dry Drayton in west Cambridgeshire, where the reorganisation of field systems along more 'regular' lines is apparently described in twelfth-century documents (Fox 1981, 95–8). At Segenhoe an agreement was drawn up in the 1160s in order to bring some order to a pattern of holdings which had become confused through an earlier manorial division, by unjust seizures of land during the 'Anarchy' of Stephen's reign, and perhaps by the expansion of cultivation. At the court of each of the two manorial lords, and under the supervision of six old men, 'knights, free men and others … surrendered their lands under the supervision of the old men and by the measure of the perch, to be divided as if they were newly won land, assigning to each a reasonable share' (Fox 1981, 96). The document does not, unfortunately, make clear the nature of the new landscape being created, but a regular two-field system appears to have been in operation here by the early thirteenth century (Fox 1981, 97). In the case of Dry Drayton an agreement from the 1150s – preserved in the cartulary of Wrest Park – shows the five lords of the vill agreeing to a 'new partition' of the land of the vill, 'both field land and meadow'; a reorganisation which was necessary because the land, or parts of it, had been 'for long uncultivated' on account of being 'dispersed in certain minute parts'. Other documents in the cartulary record the agreement's confirmation by Henry II, and a subsequent adjustment to the original *commutacio* (Fox 1981, 95). Again, the document does not specify the precise nature of the reorganisation, but by the thirteenth century the parish appears to have had a regular three-field system.

Not only do regular field systems appear to have been established relatively late in many of these townships. In contrast to the situation in Northamptonshire, Leicestershire and north Buckinghamshire, they sometimes developed in such a way that they preserved fragments of earlier landscapes. At Tadlow in west Cambridgeshire, for example, the basic plan of the village, as well as the boundaries of the open-field furlongs, perpetuated the framework of a semi-regular grid so ancient that the county boundary between Cambridgeshire and Bedfordshire respects it, carefully picking its way around the margins of lost fields (Rackham 1986, 177). Sue Oosthuizen has noted how at Caxton in Cambridgeshire the Roman road, Ermine Street, appears to cut through the medieval furlong pattern, and in many of the surrounding parishes roads and furlongs display co-axial forms, running in typical fashion from rivers to watersheds (Oosthuizen 1997). The implication, as Oosthuizen noted, is that here the open fields were not created through the systematic replanning of the landscape, but instead 'earlier fields were straightforwardly incorporated into the open field layout' (Oosthuizen 1997, 150).

But perhaps the most striking feature of the medieval landscape of this region is that the settlement pattern often included isolated hamlets and farms as well as nucleated villages, and that the villages themselves were often sprawling and poorly nucleated: places like Caldecote in Cambridgeshire, where 'from relatively early times, if not from the beginning, the houses … seem to have been spaced a considerable distance apart' along the north–south road running down the centre of the parish (RCHME 1968, 32). Brown and Taylor observed in 1989 how 'The pattern of settlement in central and north-east Bedfordshire is a classic mixture of dispersed and nucleated settlement. On the whole, the villages are generally small, and are surrounded by numerous small hamlets and single farmsteads' (Brown and Taylor 1989, 61). Much earlier, in his discussion of the Cambridgeshire landscape, Taylor had emphasised the importance of many 'daughter hamlets' around the villages of west Cambridgeshire (Taylor 1973, 77–85); while in their 1998 discussion of dispersed settlement in England, Wrathmell and Roberts similarly noted how southern Huntingdonshire, together with much of the adjacent areas of Bedfordshire and Cambridgeshire, formed a 'sub-province in which a mixture of "Central" and "south eastern" – "champion" and "woodland" – characteristics appear' (Roberts and Wrathmell 1998, 102).

The dispersed settlements took, and take, a variety of forms. There are many moated sites, often located in remote corners of parishes, on clay uplands; a large number of hamlets bearing the suffix 'end', generally strung out along one or two sides of a road or lane; and a smaller (though still significant) number of 'greens', groups of farms ranged around (or formerly ranged around) an area of common grazing. The origins and character of these outlying settlements is often obscure, not least because their form as depicted on the earliest surviving maps had often undergone radical change since the high middle ages, largely as a consequence of settlement contraction in the course of the fourteenth and fifteenth centuries. But it is possible to pick out subtle variations in the character of dispersal, which to some extent mirror variations in the character of the topography.

In west Cambridgeshire the upland clays form extensive, gently undulating blocks cut by the valleys of rivers and major streams. Most of the principal villages are located in the valleys but in addition to these many parishes contain isolated farms located towards the parish boundaries on higher, heavier ground. Some are moated and, while they do not all have medieval origins, the majority evidently do. Some appear to represent sub-manors, others freehold farms. Many are associated with tracts of former common grazing but, by post-medieval times at least, they did not lie on a well-defined and continuous common edge, as was normally the case in Norfolk or Suffolk (below, pp. 94–6). Instead, the commons themselves generally had complex, indented outlines, and the farms were set back from them, separated by an area of enclosed fields, often containing traces of ridge and furrow.

A good example of this kind of landscape can be seen on the tract of high ground bounded to the south by the Bourn Brook, and to the north by the lower land on the edge of the peat fen (Figure 26) (Taylor 1973, 77–87). The line of the watershed running between these lowlands is followed, fairly closely, by the Ridge Way – a track of probable prehistoric origin which forms, for almost all its length, the boundary between parishes based on either side. In medieval times a line of common grazing also ran along the watershed. The majority of villages – themselves straggling and poorly nucleated – are located

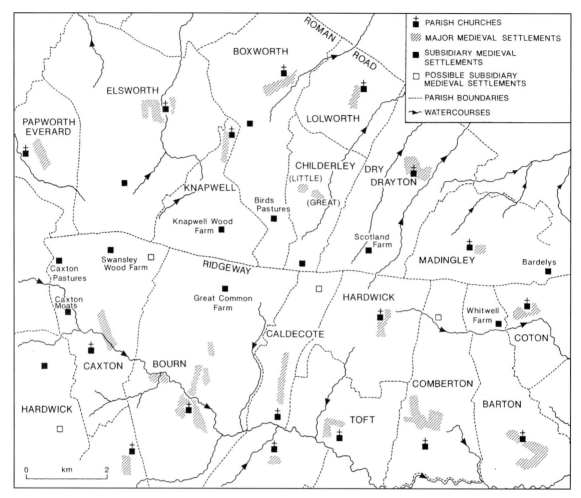

on lower ground: the isolated farms are on the high ground, towards the line of the Ridge Way.

The parish of Caxton lies to the south of the Ridge Way and in its remote, upland portion there are two isolated sites with medieval origins: the moated Swansley Wood Farm and Caxton Pastures. The former marks the site of the manor of Swansley, first recorded in the late eleventh century (RCHME 1968, 41); while Caxton Pastures represents the manor house of Buckholt, which was separated from the main manor of the vill in 1166 (Taylor 1995, 31). Both have names indicating the presence of woodland or wood-pasture, but while both are associated with anciently enclosed fields lying between the upland common of Caxton and the open-fields of the vill, they do not simply represent assarts carved out of woodland. The enclosed fields not only contain ridge and furrow but also have the sinuous boundaries characteristic of piecemeal enclosure. In other words, open arable had reached these far corners of the parish before these manorial sites were established here, close to the common edge.

Moving to the east, but still in Caxton parish, another isolated site –

FIGURE 26.
The pattern of settlement to the north of the river Bourn in west Cambridgeshire (after RCHME 1968 and Taylor 1973).

Common Farm – may have medieval origins; and across the parish boundary to the east, in Bourn, Great Common Farm is evidently of medieval date as it contains the remains of a timber-framed open hall (RCHME 1968, 25). Both are again set in fields enclosed piecemeal, lying a little way back from the common edge. In Caldecote, the next parish, Highfield Farm occupies a similar position. But still further to the east complications emerge. Caldecote is bordered to the east by not one but by two parishes, Hardwick to the north and Toft to the south. These, to judge from the configuration of the parish boundary, were originally one, although they are accounted distinct vills in Domesday (Taylor 1973, 80). The interesting point here is that Hardwick village, always a small settlement, occupies the same topographic position as the isolated sites, moated or otherwise, already discussed. It would form the next in the line, and it is tempting to see it as essentially similar in character, with the important difference that it managed to achieve a separate ecclesiastical and administrative identity. The name, 'cattle ranch', indicates its origins as an upland grazing farm but it must have come into existence at an early date, for is referred to in a charter of 991 (Taylor 1973, 80). It is noteworthy that, unlike the villages lying in the valley of the Bourn Brook, Hardwick was, before enclosure in 1836, clustered around a large green. This covered ten acres but had probably once been more extensive (RCHME 1968, 127: infilled greens are a feature of a number of other villages in this general area, such as Knapwell – Oosthuizen 1993, 100). The pattern of isolated subsidiary sites resumes in the next parish, Comberton, with the undated but pre-enclosure Common Farm; and in Barton, where the isolated Whitwell Farm was actually a separate vill in Domesday, and survived as a small hamlet within Barton parish until the end of the thirteenth century (Taylor 1973, 82).

The same pattern can be picked up to the north of the watershed. Here too we find a string of isolated farms lying this time at the *southern* extremities of parishes based on lower ground. Here too such subsidiary settlements appear to be of tenth, eleventh or twelfth-century date, set close to common edges but within their own fields, most of which appear to be enclosures made piecemeal from the open fields rather than assarts carved from the virgin waste. These include, moving now from east to west, the manorial site of *Bardelys* in Madingley; Scotland Farm in Dry Drayton (the open fields of which were, as we have noted, subjected to some kind of reorganisation in the mid twelfth century); an unnamed moated site in the south of Childerley parish; Birds Pastures Farm in Boxworth; and Knapwell Wood Farm in Knapwell, first recorded in 1311 but 'probably much older than that' (Taylor 1973, 83).

Elsewhere in west Cambridgeshire, and across the county boundary into southern Huntingdonshire, the same basic patterns can be seen. Although the settlement pattern is clearly dominated by villages, these are frequently loosely nucleated and subsidiary settlements, usually located on higher and heavier ground towards the parish boundaries, are common. Most appear to have originated in late Saxon or early post-Conquest times and while some were apparently established in areas of woodland and waste most – such as Pincote in Tadlow, first mentioned in 1176 but probably identifiable with a Domesday holding – overlie ridge and furrow, or have boundaries suggesting the early piecemeal enclosure of open fields (RCHME 1968, 206; Taylor 1995, 31).

In parts of Bedfordshire, usually on more extensive tracts of plateau clay, an even greater degree of dispersal is evident. The parish of Thurleigh, whose complex field system has already been mentioned, contained a plethora of small settlements in medieval times, both isolated farms and hamlets (Brown and Taylor 1989, 63–9) (Figure 25). Some appear to have been established in areas of woodland or wood-pasture but others – like Scald End – were at least in part laid out across existing open arable. Some were strung out along roadsides but many were grouped beside areas of common, or around small greens, such as Flightwood Green or Whitwick Green. Many places which appear as single farms on the earliest surviving maps turn out, when surveyed and fieldwalked, to have been substantial hamlets in the Middle Ages. In Odell parish, as Brown and Taylor have demonstrated, Hobbs Green – now a single farm – was once a long row of farms and cottages, probably fronting on an area of common pasture. It extended for nearly a kilometre to the north of Odell village and was largely created at the expense of existing open arable (Brown and Taylor 1989, 69–71).

What is particularly intriguing is that some of these dispersed settlements appear to exhibit signs of regular planning, and Brown and Taylor have drawn attention to the Bedfordshire parish of Liddlington where several of the 'Ends' associated with a ring of old enclosures around the periphery of the parish appear to have been laid out as rows of measured, equal-sized tofts. They argued that the expansion of cultivation at the expense of wood-pasture in the course of the twelfth century led to the planned establishment of 'rows of farms close to the edges of quite large areas of common pasture or woodland' (Brown and Taylor 1989, 77).

At places like Liddlington it is sometimes hard to distinguish between settlement *dispersion*, and settlement *movement*. A small cluster of dwellings beside a parish church, surrounded by outlying hamlets, might represent a nucleated village which has failed to grow (expansion taking place on other sites) as easily as one from which farms and cottages have actually migrated – or something in between. Although settlement movement in the course of the eleventh, twelfth and thirteenth centuries was certainly a feature of the 'core' champion areas to the west, it seems to have been more common in the district under consideration here. In west Cambridgeshire many parish churches lie in marginal or isolated positions. Examples include Comberton (RCHME 1968, 40); Graveley (RCHME 1968, 119); Great Eversden (RCHME 1968,160); and Toft (RCHME 1968,208). Of particular note are the villages clustered along the Great North Road, the Roman Ermine Street. Arrington, Caxton, Kneesworth, and Papworth Everard all have isolated or near-isolated churches lying 200–600 metres away, almost certainly the consequence of the migration of the main area of settlement to the road in the twelfth and thirteenth centuries (Taylor 1973, 227; RCHME 1968, 34–5, 196–8).

The differences between the medieval landscape of this district, and that of the region lying to the west, were ones of degree, not kind. Some vills with outlying, isolated settlements, and with multiple, irregular field systems, could be found deep in Northamptonshire, north Buckinghamshire or Leicestershire; and in this region too it is probable that regular forms of open field were sometimes the consequence of comparatively late, post-Conquest re-modelling. But there is little doubt that the *extent* of settlement dispersion, settlement mobility, field system irregularity, and late re-organisation of fields, is much greater in west Cambridgeshire, south Huntingdonshire and Bedfordshire than in areas further to the west, in the 'core' of the champion Midlands.

The 'sheep-corn' lands

A third variety of 'champion' landscape could be found to the south and east of the Midland clays, and on very different terrain – on well-drained soils formed in chalk and acid sands. These had been open, largely treeless landscapes since prehistoric times, and by the time of Domesday carried little if any woodland. The Chiltern escarpment and its north-easterly continuation, the East Anglian Heights, were areas of mainly calcareous soils. Breckland, in contrast, was an area of acid sands, large tracts of which remained as heathland well into post-medieval times. Northern and north-western Norfolk were different again. These were districts of mixed soil, with calcareous associations in the valleys and on the lower ground towards the coast, and more acid soils, formed in sandy drift, on the 'uplands' (Figure 22, p. 63). Today, all are quintessential 'planned countrysides' of large villages, outlying post-enclosure farms, and big fields defined by flimsy hawthorn hedges or (in parts of Breckland) by rows of Scots pine trees.

As noted in chapter 1, there were a number of important differences between the medieval landscapes of these districts and those of the champion Midlands. Open fields were seldom ploughed in ridges here and whereas in the Midlands the area of grazing was, by the twelfth and thirteenth centuries, usually very limited, here it was often extensive. Until well into the post-medieval period all these light-land districts operated some form of 'sheep-corn husbandry'. Nutrients were constantly leached from the light, porous soils, and had to be regularly replenished. Large flocks of sheep were therefore systematically grazed on the downs and heaths by day – usually, although not invariably, located on the higher grounds – and folded by night on the arable land, when it lay fallow, after the harvest, or when the crop was still young. The downs and heaths were nutrient reservoirs, without which the poor, thin soils could not be kept in heart; the sheep were primarily valued as 'mobile muck-spreaders' (Kerridge 1967, 42–5).

Across these regions field systems displayed much variation but often deviated markedly from the familiar two- or three-field Midland norm. In the more agriculturally marginal areas – especially Breckland, but also elsewhere in western Norfolk – the distinction between arable and pasture was sometimes blurred by the existence of temporarily cultivated outfields, often called 'brecks' (Postgate 1973, 300–3). Their use was developed, and elaborated, in the fifteenth, sixteenth and seventeenth centuries, but seems nevertheless to have been widespread in the early middle ages. More importantly, in western East Anglia especially most parishes contained more than two or three 'fields'. Marham in Norfolk, for example, had five in the sixteenth century, Tostock in Suffolk nine, Brandon in Suffolk twelve (Postgate 1973, 292). Further towards the south west, along the chalk escarpment running through south Cambridgeshire, north Hertfordshire, Bedfordshire and Buckinghamshire, field systems tended to be more 'regular' in character but even here there were many exceptions. In south Cambridgeshire Pampisford, for example, had four fields, Babraham and Sawston six, Brinkley, Dullingham and Linton seven, and Chippenham no fewer than nine (Postgate 1964, Appendix, i–iv, vii, ix). In such essentially 'irregular' systems, rotations were communally controlled but the fallowing sector was usually discontinuous, comprising groups of disconnected furlongs rather than forming a single block embracing a half or a third of the vill, as was usually the case in the Midlands. Even where more 'normal' arrangements existed this was sometimes at least a consequence of comparatively late remodelling. Fen Ditton in Cambridgeshire, for example, had three fields in 1357, but no fewer than eleven are recorded in 1251 (Postgate 1964, Appendix II, v). Moreover, in all light land areas, even where the number of fields appearing in early documents equalled the 'normal' medieval total, this does not necessarily mean that a compact and continuous fallowing sector – a 'field' in the Midland sense – existed. In many cases 'fields' were topographic terms only, used by documents to locate particular pieces of arable land (Bailey 1989, 41), and the furlong was the real unit of fallowing. All this reflected the fact that farms were often clustered in particular parts of the fields, instead of being scattered evenly throughout them. In eastern areas – in Breckland and west Norfolk – this tendency was particularly marked and was reflected to some extent in the character of customary holdings, for here the *tenementum* – the East Anglian equivalent to the *virgate* or yardland, commonly composed of either 12 or 24 notional acres – was 'relatively ... compact by comparison to its Midland counterpart' (Postgate 1973, 311). In these same districts, moreover, there was usually little regularity in the layout of holdings, as these are recorded in thirteenth-century or later documents, of the kind evident in many Midland vills: perhaps in part because of the early workings of an active land market. A holding of eleven acres in the fields of North Creake, described in a charter of the 1220s, was thus bounded by the strips of different tenants in every furlong but one (Bedingfeld 1966, 9–10). Strips often varied greatly in size, even within the same furlong.

In many eastern light soil parishes field systems were organised around the institution of the *fold course*. Under this particular version of sheep-corn husbandry the manure was a manorial monopoly. The tenants might benefit from the dung dropped by the sheep as they roamed over the fallows by day, or immediately after the harvest. But the intensive night-folding or 'tathing' was the prerogative of the manorial lord (Allison 1957). The sheep were organised into flocks dominated by the stock of the lord and under the care of a manorial shepherd. But because there were usually several manors in a vill, each had its defined 'fold course' which included both upland heath and arable land, each of which was, by custom, allowed to carry a certain number of sheep. Often there were only two or three courses but sometimes many more: Elveden in Suffolk had eleven, Weeting in Norfolk twelve (Postgate 1973, 315).

In these light land districts, even more than in west Cambridgeshire or Bedfordshire, medieval fields often appear to have developed within existing frameworks of roads and boundaries, sometimes of extreme antiquity. As long ago as 1978 Christopher Taylor and Peter Fowler noted places in south Cambridgeshire where medieval furlong boundaries overlay ditches containing unabraded Romano-British pottery (Fowler and Taylor 1978). In north and west Norfolk, and across much of south Cambridgeshire, open-field furlongs appear to have developed within co-axial landscapes which extend across several adjoining parishes, the long axes running – in characteristic fashion – at right angles to the contours, and with the majority of constituent strips running at right angles to these. As in other contexts these co-axial frameworks appear to have been inherited from an earlier 'large terrain' economy, involving short-range transhumance. In south-east Cambridgeshire, for example, Harrison has recently argued that the layout of the open fields of Westley Waterless, Weston Colville, Brinkley, Burrough Green, Carlton, and West Wratting was structured by a network of sub-parallel trackways and boundaries, running from the edge of the peat fens, across the chalk escarpment, up onto the edge of the boulder clay plateau. The antiquity of these tracks is uncertain, but they evidently predate parish as well as field boundaries: Harrison tentatively suggested a prehistoric origin (Harrison 2002). Similar patterns have been discussed by Mary Hesse on the light chalk soils of south west Cambridgeshire (Hesse 2000).

Some indication of the way open fields might develop within such earlier frameworks is provided by the results of a recent excavation at Burnham Market in north Norfolk. No early maps survive for this parish, but they do for a number of neighbouring parishes, where co-axial furlong patterns are ubiquitous, such as those studied by Mary Hesse, further to the south along the Burn valley, which extend across North and South Creake and into parts of the neighbouring parishes (Hesse 1992). An area of just over four hectares to the south of Burnham Market village was stripped prior to development, revealing a complex palimpsest of ditches (Norfolk Archaeological Unit: information from Sarah Percival). The earliest, and most substantial, defined a pattern of large co-axial enclosures: pottery finds suggested a Romano-British or, just possibly, a middle Saxon date. These enclosures were succeeded by a pattern of narrow strips, defined by slight ditches, their width comparable to local open-field strips. These were aligned with the co-axial enclosures and were, apparently, slotted into them. In a third phase, the strips were turned through ninety degrees, thus creating a pattern identical to that displayed by the co-axial furlong patterns in the area. Hesse argued for a similar pattern of development for the Creake fields, on topographic grounds (Hesse 1992, 322–3).

The essential irregularity, in terms of cropping and holding layout, displayed by most field systems in these light soil districts is mirrored in the often poorly nucleated character of their settlement patterns. Villages were generally less compact, much more 'polyfocal' in plan, than those found in Northampton-shire or Leicestershire. The chalk escarpment of the East Anglian Heights, for example, was farmed in part from settlements located along its southern margin, at the edge of the boulder clay plateau which extended southwards, deep into Hertfordshire and Essex. Some were small hamlets – many bearing names featuring Old English elements – but most were loosely nucleated, polyfocal villages, often with a number of separately named 'ends'. Some of the latter feature as separate Domesday vills, or can be plausibly identified with particular Domesday holdings. Water was unobtainable on the escarpment itself so settlements farming the land here had, per force, to cluster on the edge of the clay, where a perched water table could be exploited by ponds or shallow wells. A few Iron Age and Roman farms had existed on the chalk scarp but most had likewise clustered in this junction zone, often forming quite dense agglomerations, and in some cases at least there may have been continuity of settlement from Roman through to early medieval times. Villages like Strethall or Chrishall in north Essex appear to have developed through the fusion of separate late-Saxon settlement foci, some of which had originated during the Saxon period, some possibly with earlier origins (Williamson 1984, 142–8, 217–18, 276–80; Williamson 1986) (Figure 27). Westwards, along the Chiltern escarpment in Bedfordshire and Buckinghamshire, very similar arrangements could be found.

The naming of open fields often reflected the distinct character of the various foci of these somewhat amorphous settlements: individual fields were often associated by name with the particular hamlet, or named section of a polyfocal village, from which they were farmed. A survey of Saffron Walden, drawn up in 1400, thus describes how Bolisgrove lay next to Bolisgrove Field, Westley to Westley Field (Cromarty 1966, maps 3–6). This pattern, of small hamlets and associated open fields, was also a feature of the 'ancient countryside' landscape of the boulder clay plateau of Hertfordshire and Essex, which stretched away to the south and east of the chalk belt, and in some ways the clay/chalk interface can be regarded as a kind of 'junction zone' between 'woodland' and 'champion' regions. But loosely nucleated, polyfocal plans were also a feature of many villages at the *foot* of the chalk escarpment, firmly on the 'champion' side of the notional dividing line. Extreme examples of this tendency, like Steeple Morden in south-west Cambridgeshire, exhibited a degree of dispersion more usually associated with 'ancient countryside' areas with, in this case, a main settlement beside the parish church but subsidiary foci at North Brook End (originally called Glitton); Brook End; Gatwell End; and Morden Green (Barker *et al.* 2000).

FIGURE 27 (*opposite*). Crawley End, Chrishall, in north west Essex. The light chalk soils of the 'East Anglian Heights' were farmed in part from settlements located along their southern margin, at the edge of the boulder clay plateau. Some were small hamlets – many bearing names featuring Old English elements – but most were loosely-nucleated, polyfocal villages, often with a number of separately-named 'ends'. The boulder clays provided a perched water table: most of the settlements are still liberally provided with ponds. Crawley End was a separate vill at the time of Domesday.

Even where more strongly nucleated villages existed in this district by late medieval times they often developed in ways rather different from those on the Midland clays. Sue Oosthuizen and Christopher Taylor have shown how, as late as the eleventh century, south Cambridgeshire villages like Bassingbourne or Litlington comprised loose 'polyfocal' scatters of separate settlement foci around enormous greens or commons, one of which was usually a manorial complex with a church. Most of these commons occupied areas of damp, low-lying 'hummocky ground'; that is, places where permafrost conditions at springlines in glacial times had created features analogous to pingoes which, in warmer conditions, contributed to the marshy conditions created by the continued existence of the springs (Oosthuizen 1994; Oosthuizen 1997; Taylor and Oosthuizen 2000). The majority of these areas occur at around 30–35 metres OD in a rough line running east-west through south Cambridgeshire, at the junction of the Upper and Middle Chalk, especially in marked embayments like that occupied by the village of Thriplow. Similar late-Saxon scatters of farms could be found around areas of low-lying peaty ground in major river valleys, as, for example, at Great Shelford beside the river Cam (Taylor 1973, 74), where the village developed from two separate hamlets, over a kilometre apart, separated by a broad, roughly triangular area of common pasture (Taylor 1973, 74). At nearby Sawston late Saxon occupation took the form of a number of discrete hamlets: two overlooking the floodplain of the Cam, at Sawston itself and at Durnford Farm (recorded in a charter of 954) some two kilometres to the north; and a third on the edge of the marshy area called Deal Grove, near the river Granta (Taylor 1973, 60). The late Saxon settlement pattern of south Cambridgeshire was not a highly dispersed one – the farms and hamlets were 'confined to the edges of the main valleys or occasionally along minor tributary streams' (Taylor 1973, 61) – but it was considerably more scattered than that found, for example, in Northamptonshire. Sprawling villages emerged as neighbouring foci expanded and fused in the course of the medieval period, but some isolated farms and subsidiary hamlets survived in many parishes. Often the emergence of nucleations was associated with the progressive encroachment upon and infilling of large commons, sometimes in a series of planned blocks. Oosthuizen has suggested that the Norman Conquest accelerated this process, in some places at least. Before the Conquest south-west Cambridgeshire had been characterised by a high density of soke holdings, most of which had been absorbed into manors by the time of Domesday. Demesnes were extended into the commons and new villein and bordar farms established there. The end result was the fragmentation of the once extensive common pastures into narrow and often discontinuous ribbons, or in some cases their complete disappearance. Only at Barrington does a significant green still survive, although even this has been much encroached upon since Saxon times (Figure 28).

The damp commons, it should be noted, were replaced not only by buildings, but also by their associated enclosures of meadow and pasture (Taylor and Oosthuizen 2000, 41). Infilling was doubtless encouraged by the simple fact that, in areas dominated by moderately fertile but exceedingly dry soils, an increasing population could only be conveniently housed by building on these damp areas, where water could be easily obtained from ponds and wells. Such villages evidently developed in ways very different from those in the clayland core of the Midlands: so much so, indeed, that Oosthuizen has recently noted how 'The unexpected discovery of huge greens or commons along the spring line has challenged earlier understandings of the interface between 'ancient' and 'champagne' landscapes', significantly blurring the distinction between the two (Oosthuizen and Hesse 2000, 1).

Moving eastwards, into East Anglia proper, we encounter further variations on these same essential themes. Late Saxon settlements were loosely clustered beside springs, watercourses, or areas of damp clay, leaving extensive areas of dry, waterless ground between them quite devoid of habitation. These clusters gradually developed – often at a relatively late date – into 'villages' displaying very variable degrees of nucleation. In north-west Norfolk, for example, the long, gentle chalk escarpment is capped by sandy drift, with only sporadic patches of impervious clay, carrying a perched water table. These, in a way analogous to the areas of 'hummocky ground' in south Cambridgeshire, became the foci for agglomerations of settlement strung around their margins. Often

FIGURE 28.
The green at
Barrington,
Cambridgeshire.

the damp clay 'core' was progressively infilled, as in south Cambridgeshire, to produce a series of small, disconnected greens, as appears to have happened at Docking. But elsewhere, as at Great Massingham, infilling was limited and the farms and cottages, and the parish church, are still today strung around the edges of a large, rambling green. Elsewhere farms clustered on lower ground, beside scattered areas of damp soil watered by springs or watercourses. In many places, sixteenth- and seventeenth-century maps show 'villages' considerably less nucleated than those which exist today. To judge from an undated seventeenth-century map Ringstead, for example, was – well into post-medieval times – no more than a scatter of disconnected farms across a kilometre or more of ground between the two parish churches of St Peter (now ruined) and St Andrew (NRO Le Strange OC1 M5). Here, as elsewhere in Norfolk, the existence of more than one church in a village emphasises the extent to which the development of early medieval settlement deviated from the Midland 'norm'.

Work on the village of Sedgeford, carried out by the historian Janet

Hammond, the archaeologist Neil Faulkener, and the Sedgeford Historical and Archaeological Research Project, has thrown important new light on the development of villages like these (Cox, Fox and Thomas 1997; Davies 2000). Today Sedgeford is a long settlement, mainly strung along an east-west road which runs parallel to, and immediately to the north of, the floodplain of the Heacham River (Figure 29). Ignoring farms established following enclosure in the late eighteenth century, there are three other settlements in the parish. East Hall in the far east, and Eaton in the west, are both now single farms; Southgate, in the south east and close to the boundary with the neighbouring parish of Fring, comprises a farm and several cottages. The present pattern of settlement is, however, largely a consequence of post-medieval developments, for a map of c. 1630 (NRO le Strange OB5) shows that at this stage the village itself comprised two quite separate hamlets, West Hall (containing the parish church) and Cole Green, or Eastgate, separated by c. 400 metres. It was only in the course of the last two centuries that these have become amalgamated, through the progressive infilling of the space between them. Moreover, Eaton and East Hall were at that time sizeable hamlets, with eight and ten houses respectively, while Southgate was also a more substantial place than it is today. Rather than being a nucleated village with a few outlying farms, in other words, well into post-medieval times Sedgeford consisted of five quite distinct hamlets.

FIGURE 29.
Sedgeford in west Norfolk, as depicted on the first edition six-inch Ordnance Survey map. The site of the middle/late Saxon settlement is shown. 'Villages' in western East Anglia are often little more than loose collections of discrete hamlets.

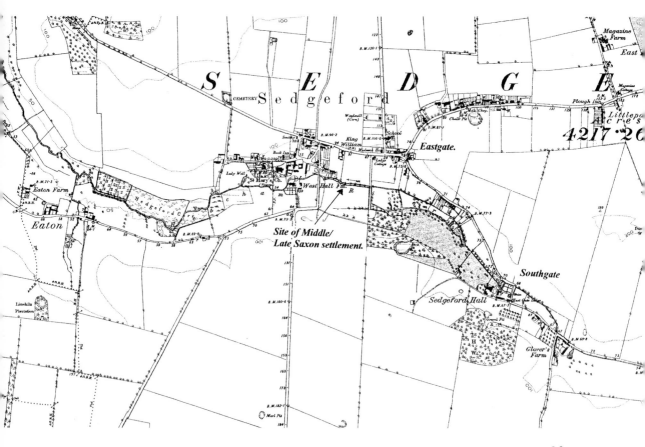

Eaton had, at the time the *c.* 1630 map was made, its own distinct open-field system: it had long been divided between a plethora of small manors, mostly located some distance away from the parish. As Janet Hammond has suggested, the place can be plausibly identified with an estate held by eight freemen at the time of Domesday: the later state of manorial confusion arose, as so often in Norfolk, from the post-Conquest assertion of proprietary rights by lords to whose predecessors the free men had only been 'commended', that is, owed fealty and allegiance (Hammond 1984). East Hall was also a distinct holding at the time of Domesday. Indeed, it was accounted a separate vill, called *Gnatingdon.* West Hall has produced archaeological evidence for late Saxon occupation. The origins of Eastgate and Southgate remain obscure, but it is possible that these too existed by the time of the Conquest.

Gnatingdon lay some way to the north of the Heacham River, deriving its water from springs in the chalk. West Hall and Eastgate also lay to the north of the river, but much closer to it, overlooking the damp ground of its flood plain. Eaton and Southgate lay to the south of the river, but were separated by a rather greater distance – around two kilometres. About half way between them, stray finds made over a number of years led to the excavation, currently in progress, of a middle and late Saxon settlement which overlies in part a middle Saxon cemetery. Evidently, in early medieval times – and apparently in the late Saxon period – Sedgeford comprised a scatter of farms or hamlets, most of which were strung around the marshy flood plain of the river. In other words, we have again a loose cluster of settlement around damp, low-lying ground, similar to those we have already seen around the areas of 'hummocky ground' in south Cambridgeshire. At Sedgeford, however, subsequent develop-ments followed a different course. The low ground was not here gradually encroached upon by farms: this would have been virtually impossible, given the waterlogged nature of the site. Instead, probably in the course of the twelfth century, it became more intensively managed. Dams were erected, and channels dug, to facilitate reed growing in some areas – and to create improved meadow land in others (Hammond 1992; Cox, Fox and Thomas 1997; Davies 2000).

Other medieval villages on the light lands of west Norfolk evidently developed in a similar way, through the gradual amalgamation of late Saxon settlements scattered around the margins of damp ground. Barton Bendish, researched by Andrew Rogerson, is a case in point. Here, both Romano-British and early Saxon settlements had been quite widely dispersed across the parish (Figure 42, p. 126) (Rogerson 1997, 6–19). But by the eighth century there was only a single settlement, continuing the site of one of the early Saxon foci, located beside an area of low-lying peat ground in the north of the parish (Rogerson 1997, 20–1). In later Saxon times this expanded to form a line of discrete farmsteads, more than a kilometre in length, strung out along the edge of the damp ground. These subsequently fused to form the present 'street village' (Rogerson 1997, 21–9).

Barton Bendish was served by no fewer than three parish churches: two are recorded in Domesday, a third was almost certainly present, but omitted. Although it eventually became a large, nucleated village, multiple religious foci again emphasise the difference between such Norfolk villages and the classic nucleated settlements of the Midlands. As Rogerson asked rhetorically: 'How far was this street village really united ... In what ways did three-churched Barton Bendish differ from three distinct but adjacent vills with closely spaced parish churches?' (Rogerson 1997, 25). One wonders at the social background to this ecclesiastical over-provision. The middle Saxon cemetery at Sedgeford hints that multiple religious foci might predate the erection of the churches themselves. Perhaps they represent the burial places of distinct kin groups, in this relatively free region of late Saxon England.

Not all medieval villages on the light lands of northern and western East Anglia developed through the fusion of several late Saxon settlements. Where pockets of damp ground were limited in area many probably began life as single farms, some never rising much above this status and remaining as hamlets or tiny parishes before shrinking back to their original state as population declined in the late middle ages. Most of the 'Deserted Medieval Villages' in this part of the world fall into this category – Waterden or Egmere in north Norfolk, for example. Moreover, where late Saxon population densities were low, soils particularly poor, but areas of damp ground on valley floors relatively extensive – especially in Breckland, but also in the district of dry, heathy soils extending northwards from Norwich to the coast – scattered late Saxon farmsteads were too widely dispersed to fuse into sizeable villages. Most simply expanded *in situ*, usually acquiring a church in the course of the eleventh and twelfth centuries. In the area around Bodney in Breckland a detailed fieldwalking survey by Alan Davison revealed a very thin scatter of late Saxon farms strung at intervals of between one and three kilometres along the margins of the low marshy ground formed by the floodplain of the river (Davison 1994, 61–3). Each expanded in the twelfth and thirteenth centuries to form a loose girdle of settlement along the edge of the low lying ground (Davison 1994, 63–5). Similar developments can be traced at Hargham on the eastern edge of the Breckland, another area fieldwalked by Davison (Davison and Cushion 1999).

There was thus much variation in the development of medieval settlement in these sheep-corn lands, but some common themes emerge. Romano-British and early Saxon farms were sometimes quite widely scattered but middle Saxon settlements were fewer in number and tended to cluster beside areas of damp ground: around patches of boulder clay, at the margins of more extensive deposits of till, or near pockets or ribbons of low-lying marshy or peaty land, watered by springs, streams or rivers. In late Saxon times loose girdles of farmsteads developed around the margins of such areas, which usually acquired the status of common land. Where land was fertile, populations dense and/or the area of damp ground relatively compact, neighbouring farmsteads fused, during post-Conquest times, to form villages exhibiting varying degrees of nucleation. Where the areas of damp ground were small and scattered, the settlement pattern was more dispersed; and where population levels remained low, Saxon farms were more thinly scattered and villages more usually developed from the expansion of single foci.

Conclusion

On close inspection it is evident that the character and early development of the fields and settlements of the 'champion' districts within the region examined in this book displayed considerable variation. It was in the far west – in Northamptonshire, Leicestershire, and north Buckinghamshire – that the landscape approximated most closely to the familiar Midland norm, with nucleated villages farming two or three great open fields in which the holdings of the tenants were evenly, and often very regularly, scattered. Here, the dispersed and relatively unstable pattern of early Saxon times was abandoned in the eighth and early ninth centuries. Settlement stabilised at places which are still, for the most part, occupied by villages. Some of these middle Saxon sites were large hamlets or villages *ab initio*, some perhaps developed as such over time. These nucleated settlements underwent a variety of changes in the course of the late Saxon and post-Conquest periods, but for centuries villages remained the dominant form of settlement in this region: it was rare for farms to move away from them, until the enclosure of open fields in late medieval or post medieval times. Some powerful factor, or factors, ensured the perpetuation of an essentially nucleated pattern of settlement, as population rose, and manors divided. The 'regular' open fields which were, by the thirteenth century, ubiquitous in this region have uncertain origins. In the forms in which we first encounter them, in documents from the thirteenth century, they were perhaps no older than late Saxon but open fields of a kind – in some places laid out in the form of 'long furlongs' – seem to have existed since the middle Saxon period. Either way, these landscapes were usually quite unrelated to the countrysides they replaced. Furlong boundaries seldom coincided with the boundaries of Romano-British or early Saxon fields. Fields were usually ploughed in ridges, and arable often occupied 80 per cent or more of the land by the thirteenth century, although areas of wood-pasture and woodland, often associated with royal forests, survived on the high interfluves.

On the light, 'sheep-corn' lands of the Chiltern escarpment and western East Anglia, in contrast, field systems usually remained more 'irregular' in character, and where 'regular' forms developed this was often at a comparatively late date. Here, as in the Midlands, the middle Saxon period saw the abandonment of a scattered pattern of settlement, as settlements moved to the margins of damp ground. But instead of remaining close together farms dispersed away from the old sites during later Saxon times, to form loose girdles of settlement around areas of damp pasture. Villages then emerged, often as late as the twelfth century, through the expansion and fusion of these separate foci, sometimes as the intervening areas of damp ground were divided into meadows and closes, and built on. But many remained very poorly nucleated and in some eastern districts might even boast two or more churches, while in all districts minor hamlets often remained as subordinate elements of the settlement pattern.

In between the light lands of the Chiltern escarpment and the clayland 'core' of the Midlands lay a third distinctive landscape region, albeit one with indistinct boundaries. This embraced west Cambridgeshire, south Huntingdonshire and much of Bedfordshire. Here the landscape displayed many 'woodland' characteristics. In some places large areas of common land survived into the middle ages and, to varying extents, villages existed within a matrix of dispersion. Nucleated settlements were probably established in middle Saxon times, but as population rose in the tenth, eleventh and twelfth centuries new farms and hamlets were created on the periphery of vills, often close to common edges, frequently on top of former open-field furlongs. Although by the late middle ages two- or three-field systems were the norm in many vills this was often the consequence of comparatively late remodelling, in the post-Conquest period. As in the sheep-corn lands, some furlong patterns appear to have perpetuated elements of earlier landscapes. Some vills, especially in Bedfordshire, retained highly irregular field systems up until the time of enclosure.

I have over-simplified a complex picture; time and space would allow this simple three-part division to be broken down still further. Nevertheless, enough has been said to make it clear that not all 'champion' landscapes were the same. They displayed many variations in the character both of their field systems and their settlements, and they evidently developed in rather different ways. We must now see whether this was also true of the dispersed settlement patterns, 'irregular' field systems and enclosed fields of the 'woodland' districts.

CHAPTER FOUR

Woodland

....

The 'ancient countryside' or 'woodland' areas – as usually defined, and as discussed in this chapter – form an extensive but continuous block of territory lying to the south and east of the champion, sheep-corn lands of the Chiltern escarpment, Breckland, and northern and western Norfolk. The boundaries of this landscape region are sometimes sharp but in many cases distinctly fuzzy. The main 'core' of this zone of dispersion corresponds with three principal geological formations, and with the intermediate areas of lighter land lying between them: the boulder clay plateau which extends from central Norfolk, through the middle of Suffolk, into north Essex and east Hertfordshire; the Chiltern dipslope; and the London clays and associated Eocene deposits found in south Hertfordshire, south Essex and Middlesex (Figure 22, p. 63). All are areas largely dominated by clay soils, often very poorly draining. Nevertheless, to the east of this broad band of clayland territory a strip of lighter land – fertile loams in the north, infertile sands to the south – runs down the coast of East Anglia, and this – somewhat surprisingly – was also characterised by landscapes of 'irregular' open fields, and varying degrees of settlement dispersion.

Even within this relatively compact block of territory several quite different kinds of landscape could be found in the middle ages. In some districts, irregular open fields occupied quite extensive areas, in others they were only a minor feature in landscapes dominated by enclosures, while in a few localities they were absent altogether. In some areas substantial, compact nucleations of settlement existed within a matrix of dispersion, but in others 'villages' as commonly understood were entirely absent. The character of the dispersed elements in the settlement pattern also displayed much variation by the time the earliest maps were made, although the profound demographic and economic changes of the later middle ages had doubtless often altered their size and form: as Harold Fox was able to demonstrate in the case of Devon, what appears on early maps as a series of isolated farms might, in the high middle ages, have been a scatter of hamlets (Fox 1983). In many places, areas of common grazing formed important foci for settlements. The larger commons were generally referred to as 'common', occasionally 'moor' (if on clay) or 'heath' (if occupying an area of sand or gravel). Smaller areas were normally called 'green', but in central and eastern Essex, and in south Suffolk, the term 'tye' was also often employed (Martin 1995, 82). Like all commons these were, at least by the thirteenth century, regarded by law as the property of the lord of the manor in which they lay. They were 'common' by dint of the fact that a defined group of people had rights to use them, primarily for grazing. Usually such rights were restricted to the farms clustering at the margins of the common or green, but sometimes they were more widely shared.

As we shall see, most green- and common-edge settlements developed in the course of the eleventh, twelfth and thirteenth centuries. Located, in many cases, in areas of poorly draining soils, many have experienced a high degree of subsequent contraction, allowing their early history to be recovered through field walking. The origins of smaller and more compact forms of settlement – isolated farms and non-greenside hamlets – is often less clear. It is usually assumed that the majority are of post-Conquest origin: that they were pioneer settlements established away from older sites, represented by village nucleations, as population expanded in the course of the twelfth and thirteenth centuries. But this view is largely based on negative evidence. Few such sites have been excavated and, as the majority have remained in existence and on the same site since the middle ages, the archaeological evidence for their origins often remains hidden beneath gardens, buildings and paddocks. Documentary evidence is also problematic. It is true that many isolated farms and hamlets are only first mentioned by name in the twelfth or thirteenth centuries. But this does not necessarily mean that they only came into existence at this time: only that the kinds of documents that were made in earlier periods do not name them, subsuming them within some wider territorial unit, manor or estate. Stray references in wills and charters provide tantalising flashes of light into the darkness of pre-Conquest geography. The obscure hamlet of Cockernhoe in the parish of Great Offley in Hertfordshire is typical of many on the edge of the Chiltern plateau, first mentioned in a document of 1221. But the will of the Lady Æthelgifu, drawn up in *c.* 980, shows that it had then been in existence for more than two centuries, for this ordered that following her death a slave named 'Wulfestan of Cockernhoe' was to be freed (Whitelock 1968, 10). Several other small hamlets in Hertfordshire are mentioned in Æthelgifu's will but are omitted from Domesday and only appear again in the documentary record in post-Conquest times, such as the lost settlement of *Acersce* in Aldenham.

In certain districts, especially on the dissected dipslope of the East Anglian heights – in north east Hertfordshire and north west Essex – idiosyncrasies of tenurial development have ensured that a relatively large number of small Saxon settlements were recorded as distinct vills in Domesday, rather than being subsumed within the returns for some neighbouring settlement: places now represented by farms, moated halls and small hamlets (Williamson 2000a, 142–3). Many (although not all) must presumably, like the hall-church complexes and associated villages found nearby, occupy their Domesday sites. It is not unreasonable to assume that many other farms or hamlets, occupying similar situations and with names incorporating Old English elements, are of comparable antiquity, or at least were established relatively soon after the

Norman Conquest. In contrast to these settlements are farms or hamlets which bear names suggesting that they came into existence at a rather later date: those, in particular, featuring the names of medieval owners or occupiers, or incorporating Middle English place name elements, and which thus probably originated after *c.* 1100. It is true that some of these might have equally early origins – might have been renamed in the course of the twelfth or thirteenth centuries. But the fact that there may be some degree of overlap between these two categories does not of itself invalidate the proposed distinction. It should be noted in passing that the presence, or absence, of moats associated with these dispersed sites is of little or no help in ascertaining their origins. Moats were a fashion which began in the twelfth century but they were often added to existing sites. Many Domesday manors subsequently acquired them.

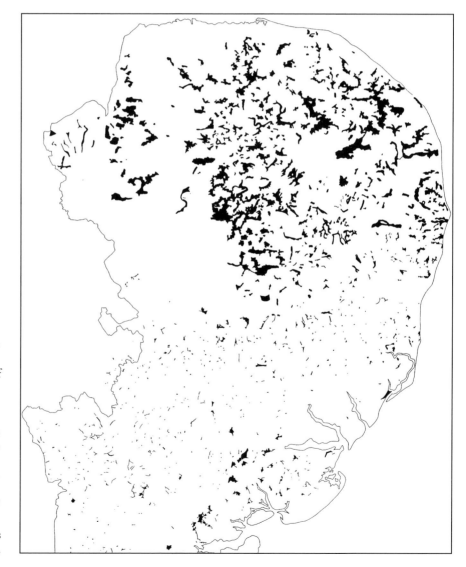

FIGURE 30.
Common-edge settlements in East Anglia and Essex in the eighteenth century. The map does not show all commons, only those which attracted a significant numbers of farms and cottage to their margins. Note how both their size, and number, increase markedly towards the north. Based on William Faden's map of Norfolk (1797); Hodskinson's map of Suffolk (1783); and Chapman and André's survey of Essex (1777).

93

Northern East Anglia

Bearing these and other variations in mind the 'ancient countryside' areas under consideration here may be divided into a number of separate landscape zones. Perhaps the most distinctive embraces central, eastern and southern Norfolk, and northern and eastern Suffolk. Its most striking feature was the ubiquity of common-edge settlement, and the large size of many of the commons themselves (Figure 30). Churches often stood alone, some way away from any common or in a marginal position relative to one of them (Figure 31). Eighteenth- and nineteenth-century enclosure has served to remove, wholesale, these extensive commons but churches often still remain quite detached from the main focus of settlement in a parish.

This settlement zone has at its core the northern end of the East Anglian till plateau. The level surface of this formation is characterised by poorly draining stagnogley soils of the Beccles 1 Association, but where the terrain is dissected by wide, gentle valleys the lighter clay loams of the Burlingham 1 and 3 Associations are found (Hodge *et al.* 1984, 117–19, 132–8).[2] Most of the larger commons were located on the Beccles soils, often occupying slight depressions in the plateau surface or damp areas beside minor watercourses. Some could also be found on the floors of major river valleys, which in this region were generally characterised by deposits of peat (Williamson 1993,

FIGURE 31.
Isolated churches, like this one at Carleton Forehoe in Norfolk, are a familiar feature of the East Anglian countryside.

2. See above, p. 63, for an explanation of the terms used to describe different types of soil.

Map labels (as visible): FLYAR CLOSE, PARKE WOOD, STVBBENMEDOW, STVD WOOD, PARKE MEADOW, ONE YARDE, THE BRICK YARDE, HORSEGATE, KILL FEILD, THE MOORE, GVNBALLS MEDOW, BROOME CLOSE, BROOME, BROOME GROVE, WHEATE CLOSE, POND CLOSE, CHVRCH FEILDE, WARNERS GROVE, KILLEWOOD, Little Dove Croft, GREEN, Mr HOBERTS HOME CLOSE, Mr HOBERTS CLOSE, GVSSINGE COMMON

168–9). Commons were generally less extensive on the lighter Burlingham soils, other than along floodplains, but here too they were the key feature in the medieval settlement pattern, as at Morley in mid Norfolk (Figure 32).

By the time the earliest maps were made the larger commons were sometimes settled all around their margins but more usually farms tended to cluster near to the entrances, where roads funnelled in (Figure 33). Smaller commons generally had more continuous settlement around their peripheries. All had characteristic curving, concave outlines, narrowing towards the entrances. Much enclosure of commons took place – especially in river valleys – from late medieval times, but they remained extensive even at the end of the eighteenth century. When William Faden surveyed his map of Norfolk in 1794–95, great strings of commons, linked end to end, rambled across the clay interfluves, and it was still possible to walk for twenty kilometres or more in central Norfolk without leaving one.

Although commons and their attendant settlements were particularly characteristic of the clay soils of northern East Anglia they were also an important feature of the landscape on the lighter lands to the east – on the fertile Wick soils in east Norfolk and Lothingland, and on the poor infertile soils of the

FIGURE 32.
A section from a map of an estate in Morley St Peter and Morley St Botolph, surveyed by Thomas Waterman in 1629, showing isolated churches, residual open fields, and common-edge settlements.

95

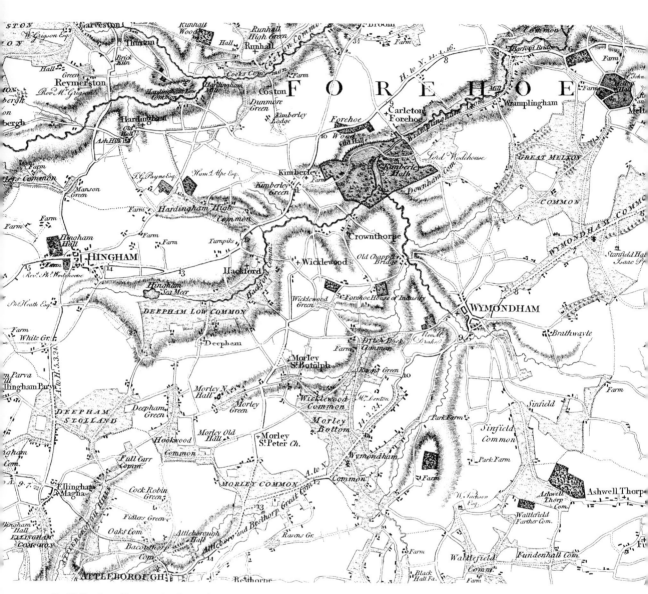

Suffolk Sandlings. Such soils are all, for the most part, freely draining: the majority of commons thus occupied restricted areas of damp ground, mainly low-lying deposits of peat in the floors of the numerous valleys, although some were associated with sporadic patches of upland clay. In this district, too, the majority of churches stood and often still stand alone, or on the edge of settlements.

It should be emphasised that the large number and size of commons, and the ubiquity of common-edge settlements, in northern East Anglia did not simply or directly reflect the fact that particularly extensive areas of unploughable ground existed in this region. It is true that the topography ensures that there were many areas which medieval farmers would have found hard to cultivate – the clay plateau has many poorly draining concavities. But in many

FIGURE 33. Common-edge settlements in mid Norfolk, as shown on William Faden's county map of 1797. Most of the commons shown were enclosed by parliamentary act during the following twenty-five years.

96

cases the boundaries of commons appear quite arbitrary, in the sense that there is no obvious reason why land on one side of the line should have remained as pasture while that on the other was ploughed. Indeed, even where obvious topographic imperatives determined the configuration of a common – where, for example, it occupied a shallow depression in the surface of the clay – this does not in itself 'explain' its size or even existence. Equally intractable areas in the Midlands were commonly ploughed. But even if we accept that environmental factors did indeed determine the ubiquity of clayland commons in this region, this does not explain why medieval settlements clustered around their margins, or around the edges of the 'low' commons found in the peat-filled floors of many valleys.

As a consequence of numerous fieldwalking surveys – most notably those carried out by Alan Davison, Andrew Rogerson, Peter Wade Martins, Mike Hardy and John Newman – we now have a fairly clear idea of the way in which this distinctive pattern of settlement developed (Davison 1990; Rogerson 1995; Wade-Martins 1980b; Hardy 1989; Hardy and Martin 1986; Hardy and Martin 1987; Newman 2001). Most of this work has concentrated on the claylands and it is evident that Roman settlement was extensive here, and that even the heaviest soils were, in some places at least, under arable cultivation. As in the clayland areas of the Midlands, early Saxon settlement continued the dispersed character of the Roman period, but on a reduced scale. Farms retreated from the main plateau areas, concentrating in or around the lighter Burlingham soils of the principal valleys, or on the islands of glacial sand and gravel which sporadically occur on the clay plateau. During the middle Saxon period – probably during the eighth century – settlement became more concentrated. Fieldwalking surveys usually reveal only one settlement per parish, generally located beside what is now the site of the parish church. These sites remained the principal settlement foci at the time when later Saxon pottery – Thetford Ware – came into use in the area in the later ninth century. Some secondary vills were established in late Saxon times – fieldwalking beside some parish churches reveals only Thetford Ware – but the majority of church sites have scatters of middle Saxon pottery beside them.

As in the Midlands, not all these middle Saxon sites were necessarily of the same size or status. Those located on or beside the more extensive areas of better-drained clays seem to have mostly been nucleated villages and excavations at North Elmham in central Norfolk have shown that some at least had a planned layout, although this site may have been atypical, due to its association with a possible cathedral site. 'By far the most prominent of the middle Saxon features were the eleven boundary ditches ... laid out in straight lines carefully orientated to create a regular pattern to the early settlement' (Wade-Martins 1980b, 37). In contrast, middle Saxon settlements in more remote locations, in areas dominated by heavier soils, often lie in parishes with names suggesting that they began life as small grazing farms, or places for the exploitation of woodland resources: Hardwick, Woodton, Stockton and the like (Williamson 1993, 85). These probably only later expanded into true villages as, in late Saxon times, these heavy but fertile soils fell to the plough. Many such places contained high percentages of free men, *liberi homines*, at the time of Domesday, perhaps suggesting the creation of patrilocal lineages as isolated farms developed into larger communities (Williamson 1993, 120–6).

Less fieldwork has been carried out on the strip of lighter soils running down the coast of Suffolk and Norfolk, but here a similar pattern is apparent. Scattered and short-lived early Saxon sites were replaced by middle Saxon settlements, usually one per parish, located beside parish churches – as at Witton near North Walsham in Norfolk (Wade 1983). Numerous variations in soils and topography make it more difficult to generalise about the location of these places but many were on well-drained sites overlooking, at no great distance, a ribbon of damp ground in one of the many valleys that dissect these generally arid soils.

The movement of settlement away from these middle Saxon sites, to the edges of greens and commons, evidently began in pre-Conquest times. Although Peter Warner's suggestion that it had started in north-east Suffolk as early as the ninth century does not appear to be supported by the available archaeological data, Andrew Rogerson's detailed survey of Great and Little Fransham in Norfolk recovered scatters of Thetford Ware along the margins of some of the commons (Warner 1987; Rogerson 1995), suggesting movement there by the start of the eleventh century and certainly by the time of the Conquest. Two large, nucleated late Saxon settlements – associated with the parish churches of Great and Little Fransham – were supplemented by a further sixteen small sites (presumably single farmsteads), twelve of which were certainly and two very probably on common edges. Around 1100, the nucleated settlements were themselves abandoned, leaving their churches isolated within the fields. This pre-Conquest chronology for the movement to common edges is probably typical. Indeed, some Domesday manors, and even some Domesday vills, were located on common edges, such as Honingham Thorpe in Norfolk. Nevertheless, the move to the commons seems to have accelerated in the post-Conquest period. By the thirteenth century the majority of farms and cottages in this extensive area lay beside a green or common, or on the roads leading to them (Ridgard 1988). Most moated sites, representing large freehold farms or secondary manors, lay on common edges. Some settlement, it is true, remained close to parish churches, especially towards the south of the region under discussion; and some isolated manorial sites are known; but the prominence of common-edge settlement was unquestionably the most distinctive feature of the medieval landscape of northern East Anglia.

Of course, we should note again the conceptual difficulties involved in distinguishing settlement *movement* from settlement *dispersion*: between the actual drift of settlement away from the parish church, and the growth of new settlement foci suppressing the development of a nucleation there. The quantities of middle and late Saxon pottery found by fieldwalking beside some

FIGURE 34.
Hales Green in
Norfolk, one of
relatively few clayland
commons in northern
East Anglia to survive
the enclosure
movement of the
eighteenth and
nineteenth centuries.

isolated churches, especially in north Suffolk, suggests that these were only ever associated with a small cluster of buildings, perhaps an isolated manorial complex (Martin 2001, 5). Nevertheless, even where isolated or near-isolated churches are not actual evidence of settlement migration, they do indicate that particularly powerful forces were at work preventing the development of sizeable settlement nucleations on old, pre-Conquest sites. Whether the consequence of settlement shift, or of the expansion of subsequent settlement on to new sites, the isolated or peripheral churches so typical of northern East Anglia attest a significant change in the priorities of settlement location in the course of the early medieval period.

Although many manors with bond populations could be found throughout northern East Anglia, on heavy clays and lighter loams alike, the region's most striking feature at the time of Domesday was its tenurial complexity. There were many small manors and numerous free men and sokemen, circumstances which may explain the fact that a number of villages in this district can boast two or more parish churches, sometimes standing in adjacent or shared churchyards (Warner 1986). It was also a very densely populated region and, to judge from the number of plough teams, an intensively cultivated one. Yet there was still room for expansion, and the population continued to increase, and the area of ploughland to expand, in the course of the twelfth and thirteenth centuries (Campbell 1981, 20–1). Population growth and the expansion of cultivation were considerable even in areas already densely populated, in relative terms, by the time of the Conquest. A list of plough teams in 28 vills in the Waxham Deanery, on the light loams of east Norfolk, drawn up in 1234, suggests that their number had virtually doubled since the time of Domesday (Campbell 1981b, 20). But this extension of the cultivated acreage was not enough to keep up with the growth in population and, under the impact of partible inheritance, farm size declined steadily. By the later thirteenth century there were few holdings of more than 30 acres in this district and ones of less than five were in the majority (Campbell 1981b, 17). Population growth was also rapid on the clay soils, and much assarting took place, especially on the high interfluves where Domesday suggests the largest areas of woodland were to be found (Rogerson 1995).

By the twelfth century open fields were widespread throughout the region. They were most extensive and continuous on the light soils of the coastal strip, especially in north east Norfolk, where they normally covered the whole land area, exclusive of the commons. But even on the lighter clays of the Burlingham Association open fields often occupied the vast majority of the land area (Campbell 1981b; Rogerson 1995; Skipper 1989). Morley in south Norfolk, for example, was mapped in 1629 and almost all the parish was then either open field, or lay in fields clearly created by piecemeal enclosure. The principal exceptions were the large deer park in the south west of the parish, associated with Morley Hall, and the commons which formed the main foci for settlement (NRO PD3/108(H)) (Figure 32). Where the clay plateau was more extensive and continuous, and dominated by the poorly draining stag-nogley soils of the Beccles Association, open arable was less extensive, and interspersed with enclosed fields farmed in severalty, parks, and areas of managed woodland (Addington 1982; Skipper 1989). Nevertheless, even on the heaviest plateau soils areas of common arable were generally extensive. Shelf-hanger in south Norfolk, for example, lies almost entirely on Beccles soils but a survey drawn up in 1589 describes numerous open fields, albeit evidently in an advanced state of attrition and interspersed with hedged closes: Nab-bers Field, Westfield, Netherwood, Southend, Millfield, and the 'Field of Shelfhanger', as well as numerous 'furlongs' and 'wents' (NRO PD 80/90).

Open fields were always irregular in character and field nomenclature was often highly complex. In Hemsby in east Norfolk thirteenth-century surveys make no mention of 'fields' as such, but instead record the location of strips in terms of no fewer than 100 divisions, of which the largest covered less than 30 acres (Campbell 1981b, 16). Holdings – usually described as *tenementa* or *eriungs* –were often tightly clustered. So too were the actual farms, which by the thirteenth century bore little relationship to them, due to the working of an active land market. On the more fertile soils virtually no communal controls were maintained over farming. Cultivators planted what and when they wanted, and even fallowing was a matter for informal agreement between neighbours – when it happened at all, for by the thirteenth century the adoption of a number of innovations, including the widespread cultivation of legumes, had often removed the need for year-long fallows altogether (Campbell 1981b).

On the clays, the situation was more complex. Where open fields were of limited extent and intermixed with land held in severalty regulation might be largely limited to the organisation of fallowing and communal grazing. But where – on the lighter clays – they were extensive, more detailed controls were often enforced, sometimes involving 'fold courses' of the kind we have already met on the light lands to the west (Wade Martins and Williamson 1999, 28).

The southern clay plateau

The medieval landscape of the East Anglian till plateau in the area to the south west of the Gipping valley displays subtly different characteristics: the boundary is vague and permeable, more of a broad zone than a firm line, but the change is clear enough. The character of the natural topography, and of the principal soils, both change significantly as we move into south Suffolk, and on into northern and central Essex and east Hertfordshire. The Beccles and Burlingham soils give way to those of the Hanslope Association, the principal constituent series of which are better drained and more calcareous (Hodge *et al.* 1984, 209–12). True, where the plateau is most level the poorly draining stagnogleys of the Ragdale Association occur; but such areas are seldom very extensive because the plateau is much more dissected than it is further north, by numerous closely spaced but relatively narrow valleys. The areas of level plateau soil are thus seldom more than two kilometres across, and even the major valleys of the principal rivers are rarely separated by more than five kilometres. Indeed, in many places the terrain is gently rolling, presenting a picture very different from the wide, level interfluves of the northern claylands. In their higher reaches the sloping sides of the valleys are occupied by soils of the Stretham series, calcareous, fertile and fairly freely draining clay loams. But where they are wider, a range of well-drained soils, formed in chalk, head or glaciofluvial deposits can be found (principally the Melford and Ludford Associations: Hodge *et al.* 1984, 237–41, 245–7). In addition, the soils of the valley floors are different from those found to the north and east of the Gipping. Instead of peaty, poorly draining deposits, here the floodplains are characterised by soils formed in alluvium. Further to the east and south east the clay plateau gives way to lighter soils, formed in glacial outwash deposit and cover loam, which comprises a narrow band lying between the till to the north, and the London clays to the south.

The most striking difference between the medieval landscape of this extensive district, and that of the area to the north of the Gipping corridor, is that there were far fewer large commons here, and few isolated churches (Figure 30). Most parishes contained a recognisable 'village' clustered near a parish church, usually located beside the principal manorial focus, and sometimes (as at Long Melford in Suffolk or Finchingfield in Essex) ranged around a large green. But there were in addition numerous outlying settlements which took the form either of isolated farms – some moated, and many with 'early' names – or hamlets, often clustered around small greens and tyes (Figure 35). The

main nucleations and hall/church complexes were usually associated with the lighter soils and were located on the margins of the till plateau – beside the major valleys – or on the valley floors themselves, close to major watercourses. Many isolated farms and small hamlets are also found in these locations but others, especially those grouped around small greens, were scattered across the level interfluves (Figure 36).

The small greens and tyes occupied, and often still occupy, distinctive locations. Like the larger clayland commons to the north of the Gipping, most lie in slight concave depressions in the plateau surface, or in marshy areas, often associated with springs, at the headwaters of minor streams. But, in striking contrast to the situation further north, there were few valley-floor commons and, by the twelfth century, both minor streams and major rivers were generally bordered by meadow land, rather than by areas of common grazing.

Less fieldwalking has been carried out in this region than in northern East Anglia but the main lines of settlement development are tolerably clear. Settlement was particularly dense on these fertile and relatively tractable soils in the late Iron Age and Roman period, with an average of between 1 and 2 sites per square kilometres (Williamson 1986; Hunn 1996, 52). The largest and most prosperous sites – including 'villas' – were usually located in or beside the principal valleys, like the main nucleations of medieval and later times. Smaller and, for the most part, lower-status establishments were scattered across the level interfluves between, although even these were more than just isolated ranches, or places involved solely in the exploitation of woodland

FIGURE 35.
Bridge Green, Elmdon in Essex: one of the many diminutive greens found scattered across the boulder clays of Hertfordshire and Essex.

FIGURE 36.
The landscape around Thaxted in Essex, as depicted by Chapman and André in 1777. Typical Essex boulder clay countryside, with some large nucleations of settlement like Great Bardfield or Thaxted in the main river valleys, and a scatter of isolated farms, some located beside small greens, on the surrounding clay plateau.

102

Woodland   resources: most sites are surrounded by a 'halo' of sherds evidently derived from the manuring of arable land (Williamson 1984, 156–8). The extent of post-Roman abandonment and retrenchment remains obscure, largely because early Saxon settlements are not easily recovered in this district through field walking surveys. Nevertheless, much evidence suggests continuity of occupation and exploitation, at least within the major valleys cutting through the plateau. Indeed, evidence for settlement continuity from Roman through to medieval times is much stronger here than in districts to the north of the Gipping. The Rodwells' excavations at Rivenhall in Essex, beside the Cressing Brook, towards the southern edge of the till plateau, revealed clear evidence for continuous occupation from Roman villa through to medieval hall-church complex (Rodwell and Rodwell 1986). At Saffron Walden in the Cam valley,

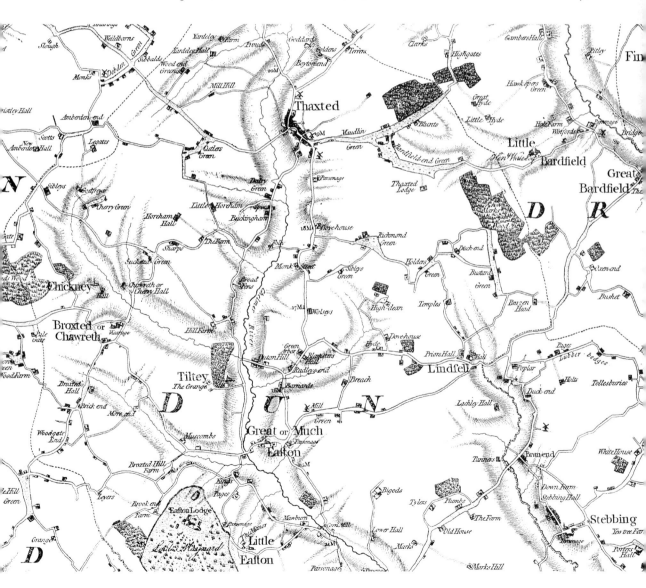

in the north west of the same county, excavations in the 1970s similarly suggested continuity of occupation from Roman through to medieval times (Bassett 1982, 4–15). Perhaps of greatest interest is the site at nearby Wicken Bonhunt, again situated on light soils, in the valley of the Wicken Water (a tributary of the Cam). The important middle Saxon settlement excavated here in 1971–73 was not established on a virgin site. Earlier Anglo-Saxon pottery was recovered from pits and ditches, while a number of Roman features indicate substantial occupation nearby – apparently in the field to the west, to judge from the results of exploratory trenching here (Wade 1980, 96). The middle Saxon site itself was probably occupied from the early eighth to the mid ninth century and, to judge from the quality and quantity of the pottery recovered, was a high-status residence. Occupation evidently continued on or near the excavated area in the form of a manor, demesne farm and associated buildings, into the post-Conquest period and beyond: a manorial chapel was erected in the twelfth century which, for a while, achieved parochial status (Wade 1980, 102).

The frequent proximity of Roman villas to parish churches or major manorial sites – in Essex especially – is noteworthy in this context (Rodwell 1988, 137). So too is the close association of Romano-British and early medieval settlements recovered by field walking. In north-west Essex, Iron Age, Roman, and late Saxon settlements often lie within a few hundred metres of each other, on the floors of the principal valleys, or on their upper margins, at the junction with the clay plateau, suggesting short-range mobility of settlement over the long centuries. Away from the main valleys in contrast the heavier plateau soils were evidently abandoned to woodland and pasture in the post-Roman period, and a number of known Iron Age and Roman settlements now lie beneath areas of 'ancient' woodland (Williamson 1984, 255, 264). At Stansted airport, similarly, the only evidence for Saxon occupation was found in the south of the survey area, towards the lighter land of the Stort valley. The level clays to the north, farmed as arable in Roman times, had regenerated to woodland by the middle ages (Hunter 1999, 67).

By late Saxon times settlement was once again extensive throughout the area, although still largely restricted to the light valley soils or their margins. Settlements mentioned in Domesday, bearing probable pre-Conquest names, or with other evidence (archaeological or documentary) for late Saxon occupation, are scattered at intervals of two kilometres or so along, or above, all the principal valleys (Figure 37): only a proportion of these became villages with parish churches, the rest remaining as subsidiary settlements, isolated farms or hamlets. Many, like Wicken Bonhunt, probably had middle Saxon or earlier origins. The average settlement density was thus probably greater than in the less dissected claylands to the north and east of the Gipping, although interestingly the population densities recorded by Domesday were noticeably lower. Evidently, by late Saxon times – and probably earlier – this was a district of smaller, more dispersed settlements.

As population increased in the course of the twelfth and thirteenth centuries

FIGURE 37.
Late Saxon settlement on the Hertfordshire/Essex border. Domesday Book and place names suggest that numerous settlements existed in this district by the start of the twelfth century, mostly located in or beside the principal valleys cutting through the boulder clay plateau. Sources: Bassett 1982; Williamson 1984; Reaney 1935; Gover *et al.* 1938).

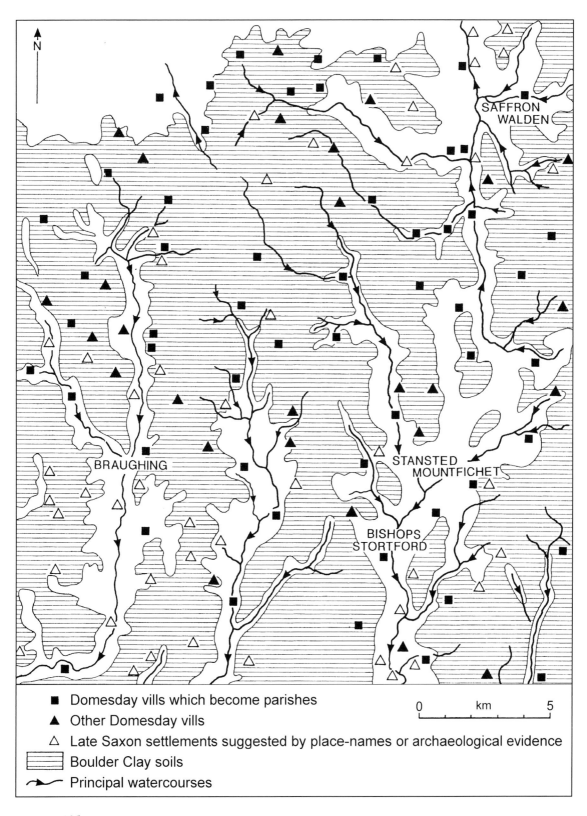

■	Domesday vills which become parishes
▲	Other Domesday vills
△	Late Saxon settlements suggested by place-names or archaeological evidence
▭	Boulder Clay soils
～	Principal watercourses

N

SAFFRON WALDEN

BRAUGHING

STANSTED MOUNTFICHET

BISHOPS STORTFORD

0   km   5

this pattern developed in a number of ways. Loose nucleations of settlement emerged, generally through the fusion of neighbouring settlements in the by now familiar 'polyfocal' fashion: many 'villages' remained poorly nucleated and some, like Aspenden in north east Hertfordshire, appear to have expanded around the margins of low, valley-floor commons. And at the same time, settlement expanded once more out onto the interfluves (Williamson 2000a, 142–4, 185–7). Here, however, there was no wholesale migration to the margins of extensive commons. Instead, existing occupation normally remained close to parish churches as new settlement overflowed on to the plateau: small hamlets clustered around diminutive greens, and isolated farms and sub-manors, often moated, set within their own fields (Figure 34). Some were evidently established within areas newly assarted from woodland but others were in places already cleared and divided into fields, which had presumably been farmed – as pasture or arable – from old valley-edge settlements (Williamson 1984, 128).

As we have seen, farms began to congregate around the extensive commons found in northern East Anglia before the Norman Conquest. But the rather smaller greens and tyes characteristic of this district were evidently settled rather later, in the twelfth or thirteenth centuries (Martin 1995, 82; Martin 1988). Moreover, there are fewer examples in this district of manorial or moated sites on common edges, and many green-edge farms appear to have been quite lowly affairs. These smaller commons evidently did not form such powerful magnets for settlement as those found further north. They were settled later, often by lower-status establishments, as a kind of 'overspill' from older-established settlements in the principal valleys.

By the twelfth century the landscape of this district was characterised by complex mixture of small open fields, enclosed land, deer parks and woodland. Early charters, like those relating to the property of the Knights Hospitallers in northern and central Essex, make numerous references to intermixed arable. As early as 1152 the order received four acres of land 'in the field of Leurichesheye' at Norton in Finchingfield (Gervers 1982, 216). In the following century the charters provide more detailed descriptions and some suggest the existence of 'subdivided' closes, small enclosed fields divided into strips of unequal size rather than small open fields in the usual sense. In 1270 for example Simon Cosin of Hawkes Hall in Toppesfield granted three acres to William of Toppesfield 'lying in the croft called Myddelcroft between the land once Lord Raddulph's on the one part and the land of John de Neville on the other part, abutting at on end the land of [illegible] and at the other the land of William Cosyn ...' (Gervers 1982, 7). References to assarted land also occur, as in 1186, when the order was granted seven acres on land in Little Leighs 'and 2 acres of woodland, now cultivated'; or in 1199, when they received 'six acres of assarts' in Finchingfield (Gervers 1982, 36, 44).

For the most part, the distribution of field systems mirrored that of soils and settlement. The largest areas of open arable lay in the major valleys (Hunter 1999, 95–104; Roden 1973, 338–9; Williamson 1984, 46–8). Thaxted in Essex, for example, had five common fields in 1393 – Northefelde, Asshefelde, Worthens, Boxstede, and Newefelde – all mainly located on the light soils of the Ludford Association on the slopes of the Chelmer valley. On the heavier, higher ground lay enclosed fields, woodland, and two substantial deer parks. As well as the manor of Thaxted – associated with the main nucleated settlement in the parish, and the parish church – two pre-Conquest manors lay beside the light soils of the valley sides: Priors and Yardleys, the latter accounted a separate vill in Domesday. By 1393, when a detailed survey of the parish was made, Yardleys' land lay in enclosed fields but there are signs that originally it had had its own separate set of open fields. The lands of Priors, in contrast, still lay in the open fields to the south of Thaxted village. In post-Conquest times two subsidiary manors were created in the vill. Richmonds, a tiny property, was held by the keeper of the parks but Horham, first mentioned in a document of 1263, was a more substantial estate. Its lands were separate from the open fields: they lay mainly in hedged closes on the heavier soils of the uplands in the west of the vill. Also on the uplands, more than two kilometres from the main village, were three small green-edge settlements – Cutlers Green, Bardfield End, and Richmonds Green (Newton 1960).

Where the topography was more broken, vills often comprised a rather larger number of discrete hamlets or manorial foci, often with demonstrable pre-Conquest origins, each farming its own group of fields (Roden 1973) (Figure 38). As late as 1814, for example, when the common fields of Arkesden in north west Essex were enclosed, the holdings of some of the main properties were still clustered in restricted areas of the open arable, associated with particular hamlets or named sections of polyfocal villages (ERO D/Dy 01) – a pattern replicated, as we have seen, on the more extensive areas of light soil found on the escarpment of the East Anglian Heights, a little to the north (above, p. 82). Fields were often associated by name with an adjacent hamlet: in Elmdon the hamlet (and Domesday manor) of Lea lay on the clay plateau above Lea Field (ERO Q/RDc26) while in Arkesden, even at the time of enclosure, Minchins Field bore the old medieval names of the settlement known for centuries as Becketts (ERO D/Dy01). In nearby Chrishall, similarly, the field book of 1597 (ERO Vm 20) shows that the inhabitants of Buildings End held much of their land in the adjacent ten-acre common field called 'Bilden Hill Feylde als Bulls Herne' (ERO Vm 20, fol. 18).

Where, as was usually the case, townships included both open fields and enclosed land, tenants often had a share of both, at least by the thirteenth century, although customary holdings composed entirely of enclosed land were also common (Roden 1973, 343–4). Whatever the precise mixture, the normal customary holding throughout this region – even in parts of southern Suffolk – was the virgate or half-virgate. Various forms of rotation were imposed on the fields – communal regulation was generally more rigorous and pervasive than in the areas to the north of the Gipping, and sheep were often close-folded on the fallows – but cropping was generally flexible and fallowing was often by

individual furlongs rather than by fields. Enclosed fields were often thrown open
to communal grazing when fallow but could otherwise be cultivated as the
tenant saw fit. Demesne land was often, as at Thaxted, intermixed with that
of the tenants in the open fields, but where it was not it sometimes took the
form of very large closes. At Cressing in Essex the demesne North Field covered
77 acres (31 hectares), Bannerley 111 acres (45 hectares), and Whistocks no less
than 299 acres (121 hectares) (Hunter 1999, 116). Not all areas of 'woodland'
countryside, in other words, even when enclosed directly from the waste, were
as densely hedged in the middle ages as they appear on the earliest maps.

Throughout east Hertfordshire and north Essex, and less clearly in south
Suffolk, this same set of contrasts can be seen: pre-Conquest manors and
settlements associated with the main areas of open-field arable on the lighter
soils, and later manors, isolated farms and green-edge settlements associated
with enclosed fields, smaller areas of subdivided arable, parks and woods on
the 'uplands'. Woodland, in general, was a more prominent feature of the
landscape than it was on the level clays to the north, and deer parks were

generally more common, and often occupied a considerable area of land (Rackham 1988; Rackham 1986, 124) (Figure 38).

The distinction between the medieval landscape of the clay plateau to the north, and to the south, of the Gipping has been sharply drawn for convenience. In reality, some of the key characteristics of the former district, while not dominant in the latter, were nevertheless fairly common. While small greens and tyes were thus a more frequent feature of the landscape than large commons, the latter could certainly be found; and while, for the most part, churches were found close to sizeable nucleations, there is often evidence for settlement drift and movement, especially around the margins of flood-plains, so that the church is located in a relatively marginal position. In some places, large 'upland' commons seem – in true East Anglian fashion – to have acted as powerful magnets for settlement, leaving churches like those at Sacombe, Tewin or Digswell in Hertfordshire quite isolated (Williamson 2000a, 187).

The Chilterns and the London clays

Moving to the south and west further variations on the essential 'ancient countryside' themes become apparent. Both the Chiltern dipslope, and the area of London Clays and associated Tertiary deposits in the far south of the region, were thinly settled in pre-Conquest times, certainly in comparison with the districts so far discussed. As we have seen, soil acidity seems to have been a major factor limiting the expansion of cultivation and settlement in the early middle ages and all these formations give rise to soils which are, to varying degrees, base-poor.

In the Chilterns, ribbons of light chalky soils were found in the major valleys but the interfluves between, although often much dissected by dry valleys, were occupied by leached soils formed in clay-with-flints and pebbly clay – easier to work than the boulder clay soils further to the east, but considerably less fertile (Munby 1977, 30–3). Moreover, these soils were on the whole less impervious than those formed in the boulder clays, the perched water table less reliable and less continuous, a further discouragement to the spread of settlement away from the major valleys. Nevertheless, the area appears to have been quite densely settled in Iron Age and Roman times. Large villas were found in the major valleys, smaller settlements on the interfluves, and although the extent of arable was apparently less than on the boulder clays to the east clearance was evidently extensive (Hunn 1987; Hunn 1994, 44–56; Brannigan 1967; Brannigan 1973). The fact that the Iron Age linear earthwork known as Grim's Ditch runs across the level plateau between major valleys in a series of ruler-straight lines, up to six kilometres in length, strongly suggests that its builders did not have to contend with a landscape excessively cluttered with trees. But here, too, the immediate post-Roman period witnessed large-scale abandonment of the interfluves. Iron Age and Roman sites thus survive as earthworks within areas which came to be occupied by woodland and wood-pasture in the middle ages and after – as in the area around Ashridge,

FIGURE 38.
Field and settlement patterns in north-west Essex at the start of the nineteenth century. On the lighter soils exposed on the sides of the principal valleys, extensive areas of irregular open fields still survived. On the heavier soils there were some small areas of open arable, but mainly enclosed fields and areas of ancient woodland. The area of Clavering Park, created in the twelfth century, can be seen. Some of the hedged fields were created by the early piecemeal enclosure of small open fields but others were enclosed directly from the waste. The settlement pattern features poorly-nucleated, polyfocal villages, isolated farms, and green-edge settlements. Source: pre-enclosure maps for Arkesden (*c.* 1819: ERO D/Dyo1); Chrishall (*c.* 1808: ERO T/M 144); Elmdon (*c.* 1824: D/Dqy 33); Langley (1851: Q/RDc 41); and Littlebury (*c.* 1805; ERO D/DQy 27). Estate maps for Langley, 1733 (ERO D/DQy 2) and 1767 (ERO D/DSs P1).

to the north of Berkhamstead on the Hertfordshire/Buckinghamshire border (Morris and Wainwright 1995). Few early or middle Saxon settlements are known from the region, and they are entirely restricted to the major valleys: examples include Broadwater Farm near Knebworth in Hertfordshire; the recently discovered site at The Grove, near Watford, beside the river Gade; and that at Latimer in Buckinghamshire, beside the Chess, where several phases of post-Roman occupation are recorded from the villa site (Wingfield 1995; Brannigan 1971).

Matthew Paris, writing in the thirteenth century, believed that the entire area of the Chiltern dipslope had been an impenetrable forest, harbouring only wild beasts, until the extensive clearances carried out by the Abbey of St Albans in the eleventh century (Riley 1867, 39). While he certainly exaggerated, Domesday shows this as a well-wooded district (vills like Chesham, Wendover or Wycombe had woodland for 1000 swine or more) and twelfth- and thirteenth-century documents suggest extensive clearance of woodland and waste (Levett 1938, 180–1). This was also, at the time of the Conquest, an area of large estates, often conterminous with equally extensive vills. Many places which were later accounted separate vills or parishes do not appear in Domesday: places like Bovingdon or Flaunden in Hertfordshire, located on the high interfluves. Place name evidence and early documentary sources, like the tenth-century will of Æthelgifu already referred to, make it clear that many of these places, and also some minor hamlets, were already in existence by this time (Williamson 2000a, 128–9). Nevertheless, it was only in the course of the twelfth and thirteenth centuries that settlement really spread across the interfluves (Hudspith 1995; Levett 1938; Lewis *et al.* 1997, 112–13).

Yet in spite of these large-scale clearances the medieval landscape of the Chilterns continued to be characterised by vast areas of managed woodland, open commons and common wood-pastures, like that which still survives at the Frith in Berkhamsted in Hertfordshire. As late as 1576 Wycombe Heath in south Buckinghamshire was said to extend over some 2,000 acres (809 hectares) (Reed 1979, 101). Extensive commons like this were usually inter-commoned by several communities: in this case the inhabitants of Penn, Hughenden, and Great and Little Missenden could all pasture their livestock there, and remove thorns, 'bushes', holly, hazel and willow (Reed 1979, 103). The larger commons usually became foci for settlement, with girdles of farms and cottages strung around their peripheries, similar to those fringing the extensive commons in northern East Anglia. Occasionally, as at Sarratt or Little Gaddesden in Hertfordshire, they appear to have sucked (in familiar fashion) settlement away from older, valley-edge sites, beside parish churches, leaving the latter isolated or marginalised (Figure 39). In some cases, as at Harpenden in Hertfordshire, these common-edge agglomerations might become so populous that, in the course of the twelfth century, they attained separate parochial status (Williamson 2000a, 188). There were also large numbers of isolated farms, often associated with sub-manors established in the course of the twelfth century; and numerous straggling lines of farms and

FIGURE 39. Sarratt, Hertfordshire: typical countryside on the Chiltern dipslope. The river Chess flows through the middle of the picture, and just right of centre stands the parish church, flanked by a small group of houses, occupying high ground overlooking the valley. Most of the farm and cottages are clustered around a large common some way to the north (top right). The slightly sinuous shapes of many of the field boundaries, especially those around the church, indicates early piecemeal enclosure from open arable. To the east (right) of the church, traces of medieval strip lynchets can be seen, indicating the former existence of open-field strips on the steep valley sides.

cottages along roadsides, usually described as 'Ends' or, in a reflection of the abundant dry valleys which dissect the plateau surface, 'Bottoms'. Moated sites were rare, probably because of the difficulties of constructing such features on the relatively porous soils formed in the clay-with-flints.

In a pattern which will by now be familiar, the principal areas of open arable on the Chiltern dipslope occupied the sides of the valleys, while the heavier soils of the plateau were, by the thirteenth century, characterised by enclosed fields, woods, parks and commons. The open fields were mainly associated with settlements bearing place names containing Old English elements, referred to in pre-Conquest documents, or appearing as vills in Domesday. In the Hertfordshire parish of Kings Walden, for example, the village itself, and the hamlets – separate Domesday vills – of Wandon and Flexmere, each had their own separate field systems, interspersed with areas of woodland, commons and pockets of enclosed fields (Roden 1973, 329).

Throughout the area of the Chiltern dipslope peasant holdings, and the organisation of open fields, were much as in the boulder clay districts lying to the south and west of the Gipping, described in the previous section. Communal controls were usually imposed over the management of the open fields, often involving the close folding of sheep on the fallows, but rotations were usually flexible and peasants often held portions of both open and enclosed arable. Here, too, immense demesne closes covering 99 acres (40 hectares) or more could be found (Roden 1973, 333–4). Both open furlongs and enclosed fields often exhibited marked brick-work like patterns and had evidently developed within older co-axial frameworks, defined by tracks and boundaries running at right angles to the floors of the principal river valleys – frameworks which, in some cases at least, were probably of late prehistoric origin (Williamson 2000a, 144–52).

On the London clays and associated deposits in Middlesex, south Hertfordshire and south Essex, we encounter similar but more pronounced patterns. The London clay soils were even less attractive to early farmers than those formed in the pebbly clay and clay-with-flints of the Chiltern dipslope: they suffer from severe seasonal waterlogging, as well as being leached and acidic. Those derived from the sands and pebbly gravels of the Claygate and Bagshot Beds are better-drained but even more acidic and infertile. In addition to all this, the principal areas of Eocene deposits were comparatively undissected by valleys in which more amenable, and more calcareous, soils were found – the interfluves are generally wide. All this made for peculiarly inhospitable terrain.

Our knowledge of the development of settlement in this region is poorer than in any of those so far discussed. The number of field surveys carried out has been limited, in part because much of the district is now occupied by urban and suburban sprawl, in part because much of the rest lies under pasture and woodland. Prehistoric and Roman occupation appears to have been extensive towards the margins of the main clay masses and in some of the major valleys cutting through them: on the Thames gravels in Essex, for example, where extensive spreads of early settlement are revealed by aerial photography; and in the valleys of the Colne and the Lea in Hertfordshire (Couchman 1980; Drury and Rodwell 1980; Hunter 1999, 58–9). Late prehistoric and Roman settlement was also dense in the area around the great oppidum and Roman town of Colchester. But in the interiors of the clay-covered uplands prehistoric settlement appears to have been comparatively sparse and Romano-British occupation largely limited to small farms and industrial centres – particularly pottery kilns, presumably making use of extensive reserves of woodland (Niblett 1995, 74). Early medieval settlement

Woodland   displayed similar patterns. Numerous early and middle Saxon settlements are known from the Thames terraces in Essex, especially to the north east of Heybridge around the Blackwater estuary or (most famously) at Mucking (Hamerow 1993; Wallis and Waughman 1998; Tyler 1996). Examples are also known from the major valleys, as at Old Parkbury or Brickett Wood, beside the Colne in Hertfordshire; and numerous small settlements with probable 'early', pre-Conquest names are also found in these locations, a few of which are mentioned in Saxon wills and charters, although only a relatively small proportion appear in Domesday Book (Wingfield 1995, 39; Niblett 1995, 70; Williamson 2000a, 135–44). Occasional early Saxon sites are found on the uplands, but only where pockets of well-drained sands or gravels occur – like that at Foxholes Farm near Hertford Heath, excavated by Partridge in 1987 (Partridge 1989). A scatter of farms and outstations for the exploitation of woodland may well have existed here throughout the Saxon period, but even at the time of Domesday the clay uplands remained a largely empty landscape of woodland and waste. In south Hertfordshire in particular, a large number of settlements (now mostly engulfed in the outer suburbs of London) which later in the Middle Ages grew into sizeable communities, often separate vills or parishes, are not mentioned in the Survey, although some at least probably already existed, as outstations of estates lying on the better soils, in the Vale of St Albans to the north or the Lea valley to the east (Williamson 2000a, 126–30). Most have names with clear woodland associations: Borehamwood, Northhaw, Barnet, Monken Hadley and Arkley. Many, like Arkley, only appear in documents as late as the thirteenth century (Gover *et al.* 1938, 69, 75).

By this time the situation was changing rapidly, in part because of the expansion of London and the market it provided for agricultural commodities (Bailey 1998, xxi–xxiv): by 1300 both clearance and settlement were extensive. A landscape of mixed farmland and managed woods, not dissimilar to that which existed here by the eighteenth century, had come into existence in a remarkably short period of time. Nevertheless, extensive tracts of open heath-land and wood-pasture commons remained, especially where the poor, thin soils of the Bagshot and Claygate Beds, or patches of glacial outwash gravels, were prominent. Notable examples include the great interconnected commons of Bushey Heath, Northaw Common, and Cheshunt Commons, on the high ground between Hertfordshire and Middlesex; Epping Forest; and Tiptree Heath in Essex. The latter was intercommoned by the inhabitants of seventeen parishes and still carried extensive stands of pollards into the modern period (Hunt 1999, 105). Many of the larger commons in Essex fell within the bounds of Writtle and Waltham Forests, the latter comprising the three physical forests of Epping, Wintry and Hainault (Rackham 1980a, 49–62).

Phrases in fines for places like Havering, Rocheford and Rawreth in south Essex make it clear that many small open fields existed in this district; common arable is recorded around Lawling, for example, between the Crouch and Blackwater estuaries, in 1309 (Roden 1973, 344). In a few places open fields could be quite extensive – in the valley of the Lea in Hertfordshire, for example, where large areas survived until enclosure in the early nineteenth century at Cheshunt, Wormley and Hoddesdon (HRO B1444; HRO DSA 4 120/2). But for the most part they were limited in extent, like the areas of valley soil with which they were generally associated. A survey of Shenley in Hertfordshire, drawn up in 1276, thus describes three open fields in the north of the parish – on well-drained soils towards the river Colne, associated with the church-hall complex (Barton 1981). But the majority of the parish lay on heavy soils, apparently enclosed directly from the 'waste'. 'Descriptions of land in feet of fines, charters of such religious bodies as Hornchurch Priory and Beeleigh Abbey, and rentals and extents … suggest that this was above all a country of hedged crofts, private woods, heaths and open forest' (Roden 1973, 340). Nevertheless, 'the pre-eminence of enclosed land did not mean that the economy was based primarily on woodland or pastoral activities … most closes were in tillage about 1300' (Roden 1973, 341).

As in the Chilterns, the open fields in the valleys, and the mainly enclosed fields on the clay-covered interfluves, often developed within earlier frame-works. In parts of Hertfordshire these take the form of co-axial patterns, originally defined by tracks and large enclosures, which are partly at least of prehistoric date, to judge from the evidence from the area around Wormley, Cheshunt and Broxbourne, where major axes of such a system continue, in earthwork form, beneath an extensive area of ancient, semi-natural woodland (Bryant *et al.* forthcoming). In the usual fashion, the parallel tracks led from the principal valleys into the interior of the main clay masses. In south Essex more 'grid-like' patterns are found, partly perhaps of Romano-British date, but in part perhaps early medieval (Rippon 1991). Everywhere, settlement was highly dispersed in character, with many small 'hall-church complexes', numerous hamlets strung out along the sides of roads, and isolated farms. Green-edge settlements, in contrast, were relatively rare, certainly by comparison with the boulder clays to the north, although where extensive heaths occurred their margins were often quite densely settled, to judge from the evidence of the earliest available maps.

The blurring of boundaries

I have managed to adhere so far to a fairly simple dichotomy between 'woodland' districts and 'champion'. But as I have already intimated on a number of occasions the reality is more complex. We have already seen how some districts with markedly 'woodland' characteristics could be found deep within the Midlands. But equally important is the fact that the division between 'two countrysides' has, and always has had, distinctly fuzzy edges – many 'frontier' districts display intermediate characteristics, and different authorities place them on different sides of the dividing line. I have treated north-east Norfolk as a 'woodland' area on account of its fairly dispersed settlement pattern and chaotic field systems. But the very extent of its open fields, usually covering the entire parish, except for the greens and commons, together with the fact that many parishes were enclosed only in the eighteenth or nineteenth centuries, have led others to consider it as an extension of the 'champion', 'planned countryside' region (e.g. Rackham 1986, 3). Similarly, the light soil areas of western East Anglia have been treated as 'champion' areas here, because of the extensive and rigidly organised character of their field systems. But certain features aligned these districts more with the 'woodland' areas to the east, most notably the tendency for medieval settlement in some parishes to be fairly scattered in character, sometimes around the margins of low-lying, flood-plain commons. Perhaps the largest 'indeterminate' district, however, was the Fenland of Norfolk, Suffolk and Cambridgeshire.

The area now loosely referred to as 'Fenland' was, and is, two distinct regions. The *Black Fens* comprise those areas furthest from the North Sea and consist of deposits of peat, overlying silts and marine clays. Until the post-medieval period this was a vast damp common, exploited by communities living on its margins (or on islands of older rock within it). Grazing occurred for some of the year but large areas were principally mown for hay or litter, or cut for thatching materials and peat (Darby 1940). The northern and eastern *Silt Fens*, or Marshland, in contrast, comprise higher, firmer ground, on the drier parts of which settlements were first established in middle Saxon times. By the late Saxon period a number of small villages had emerged here, associated with a pattern of small, irregularly shaped fields (Silvester 1988, 160). The wealth and population of Marshland grew rapidly in the course of the twelfth and thirteenth centuries, as expansion occurred inland, onto the lower silt ground, with the new land being protected by 'walls' or banks. The new fields comprised bundles of long strips, seldom more than twenty metres in width yet in some cases as much as 2 kilometres in length, although they were often subdivided in the course of the middle ages (Silvester 1988, 161; Silvester 1999, 127–30) (Figure 39).

Most if not all of these strips were under the plough but they nevertheless differed in a number of important respects from the 'lands' found in Midland vills. They were wider; they were dyked, rather than ridged; and only limited rights of common grazing, and few communal controls, were imposed upon them (Hall 1999, 40). But it was the pattern of settlement which diverged more from Midland norms. Archaeological fieldwork has revealed a massive increase in the number of farms and cottages during the later twelfth and the thirteenth centuries. In a pattern by now familiar from areas further to the east, in East Anglia proper, settlement spread out from old sites, on roddons and *levées*, clustering instead along the edges of commons and greens, and in particular beside the long, wide drove ways which ran through the fields, southwards, to the great peat common of Smeeth Fen (Silvester 1988, 160–3).

The diversity of landscape

I have described above, in rather broad and general terms, the settlement patterns and field systems of the main landscape regions within the zone of

MARSHLAND   The Medieval Landscape

King's Lynn

Wisbech

'ancient countryside' extending northwards and eastwards from London, into East Anglia. A more detailed study would also include some account of smaller sub-regions, such as the band of relatively light land which lies between the till plateau and the London clay belt in south Essex. But enough has been said to allow us to identify some of the main ways in which 'woodland' landscapes varied in medieval times.

The most important observation has already been made, but deserves repetition. Dispersed settlement was certainly a feature of districts in which Domesday population levels were low, and which experienced considerable expansion of settlement in the course of the twelfth and thirteenth centuries

116

– the Chilterns, and the London clay area in the far south of the region. But most 'ancient countryside' areas possessed population densities which were, by late Saxon times, equal to or greater than anything found in the champion Midlands. Their landscapes simply followed a different path of development, although the reasons for this are not immediately apparent. As population increased in the course of the late Saxon and early post-Conquest periods, furlong was not simply added to furlong, to create ever larger open-fields, the normal Midland practice. Instead, relatively extensive areas of woodland and pasture survived into the post-Conquest period, and settlement became increasingly dispersed. Yet while the main areas of 'ancient countryside' had this much in common, there were important differences in the way that the landscape developed in areas to the north, and to the south, of the river Gipping.

To the south of the Gipping late Saxon settlement appears already to have been noticeably more dispersed than in the Midlands, with numerous small hamlets and individual farms scattered along the principal valleys, associated with areas of open arable. In post-Conquest times sizeable villages often developed in these same locations, as hamlets grew and coalesced. But most new farms were established on virgin sites, among the woods and pastures of the clay plateaux. Some stood alone, within their own fields, but others were clustered around small green and tyes. The 'wastes' recorded by Domesday thus dwindled, but where they were most extensive, numerous fragments were preserved as parks or managed woods. In the area to the north of the Gipping, in contrast – more densely settled than any 'champion' region – developments took a different turn. From the eleventh century a substantial proportion of farms and cottages came to congregate on the margins of commons: small greens, large upland moors and low, valley-floor fens. In many places settlement migrated away from parish churches, leaving them marginalised or isolated. Here rather larger areas of the common 'wastes' thus survived into medieval times, although most degenerated steadily to treeless common pastures, and fewer areas were preserved as parks and manorial woods. Open fields were, for the most part, more extensive than in the areas to the south of the Gipping, and less restricted to the lighter soils.

The diversity of 'woodland' landscapes – 'ancient countrysides' – is perhaps their most striking feature, and to discuss them as a single undifferentiated group is clearly misleading. But such diversity poses hard conceptual questions for students of landscape. Some historians and archaeologists, aware that 'woodland' landscapes cannot simply be written off as a consequence of 'late assarting', have suggested or implied that dispersed settlement patterns are survivors from earlier, pre-nucleation arrangements: that regions of dispersal are ones in which the 'great replanning' of the landscape in middle or later Saxon times failed to occur, or else failed to occur to the same extent, as in Midland, champion districts (e.g. Roberts and Wrathmell 1998, 103–5). But the available evidence suggests a more complex picture. In districts to the south of the Gipping – and especially in east Hertfordshire or north Essex, where extensive areas of light clay loams occur – elements of an early pattern of dispersion probably did survive into the medieval period. But even here the vast majority of scattered settlements are of late Saxon or post-Conquest date. And in the districts to the north of the Gipping very few if any settlement foci lying at any distance from parish churches appear to have existed before the later Saxon period, and fewer still of these can be related to the scattered sites occupied in pagan Saxon times. Here the character of the archaeological evidence (especially the existence of Ipswich Ware) allows us to track the evolution of settlement during the early and middle Saxon period with some clarity: and what is most striking is the marked similarity with developments in the champion Midlands. In both areas, scattered and shifting early Saxon settlements were replaced by a more stable and nucleated pattern in middle Saxon times. Divergence came later, for while in the Midlands most settlements simply expanded on the old sites, in East Anglia farms drifted inexorably away, to the edges of greens and commons. Most if not all of the areas considered in this study thus appear to have experienced the same basic changes in settlement patterns in the eighth or ninth centuries – with the stabilisation of farms in the landscape, and the emergence of the first nucleations. And it is this most important of all changes which must be first explained, before the reasons for the subsequent divergence of landscapes are explored.

The technological revolution

Glenn Foard and others have argued cogently that the 'middle Saxon shift' (Arnold and Wardle 1981) was related to the development of a more hierarchical society, with the incorporation of relatively egalitarian tribal groups into multiple estates and early kingdoms (Brown and Foard 1998, 91–2). But we might also emphasise other, and complimentary, developments which seem to have occurred during the eighth and ninth centuries, of the kind suggested by Eric Kerridge (Kerridge 1992, 48–9). One was the probable move from jointly held property – with land and resources exploited by extended families, kin groups or tribes – to individual holdings. In this context it is important to note that changes in settlement patterns were accompanied by significant changes in settlement *morphology*. Early Saxon settlements like Mucking in Essex, or Upton or Brixworth in Northamptonshire, comprised loose collections of timbered 'halls' and sunken-floored buildings, laid out with little obvious plan and usually with few, if any, internal boundaries (Hamerow 1993; Brown and Foard 1998, 73). Middle Saxon sites like North Elmham in Norfolk or Pennyland in Buckinghamshire, in contrast, have more substantial internal boundaries and appear more organised – sometimes 'planned' – in layout (Brown and Foard 1998, 77; Wade-Martins 1980b, 37). This may well reflect the emergence of new forms of tenure, with individual holdings – and the burdens, in tax or rents, which they owed – now being allocated more carefully to individual tenants, whether bond or free, rather than being considered the property of larger social groups. In Hodges' words, 'property was no longer considered in tribal terms but designated as belonging to individuals' (Hodges 1989, 61). We might note in this context that open fields of all kinds were, by definition, associated with individualised forms of tenure – with landscapes of separate holdings, rather than with jointly held land – and it is thus probable that the first examples emerged as part of this same process.

Once properties had been allocated to particular individuals – especially if these took the form of intermingled strips – it may have been harder for settlements like Mucking or West Stow to drift unhindered around the landscape. But a more important reason for the increasing stability of settlement in the eighth and ninth centuries – and one again emphasised by Kerridge – was the development of more stable and intensive forms of agriculture, as population rose and as new forms of farming were adopted (Kerridge 1992, 38–9, 47–9). We must be careful not to exaggerate the extent to which early Saxon farmers practised primitive, 'shifting' modes of husbandry. Nevertheless, settlement drift and instability certainly suggests a periodic need to break in new land, as existing fields became exhausted or, more plausibly, weed-choked. But agricultural innovation in middle Saxon times is more strikingly evident in the fact that settlement and cultivation now spread away from the permeable geologies onto the heavier but more fertile land which farmers had hitherto avoided.

The fact that the stabilisation and nucleation of settlement, and expansion onto heavier land, both occurred at around the same time suggests that they were connected: and the most likely connection was the widespread adoption of a heavy plough, equipped with mouldboard and coulter. A number of writers, most notably David Hall, have emphasised the importance of changes in plough technology in the evolution of Saxon fields and settlements, and to several early researchers, notably Seebohm and the Orwins, the development of ploughs and ploughing techniques lay at the very centre of any understanding of open-field origins (Hall 1981, 37; Seebohm 1890, 120–5; Orwin and Orwin 1938, 37–44). Such an emphasis is not unreasonable: after all, early medieval documents, most notably Domesday, place ploughs and teams at the centre of agrarian life, while early terms for land measurement such as *carucate* and *bovate* derive from words for ploughs or teams.

Yet surprisingly little is known about early medieval ploughs. There are no surviving illustrations earlier than the eleventh century, and the significance of these has been the subject of debate, some historians contending that they are representations – direct, or via other manuscripts – of continental rather than native implements (Millar 1926, 20; Wilson 1962) (Figure 41). Moreover, because ploughs were constructed of materials either perishable or recyclable, they are poorly represented in the archaeological record. Most archaeologists believe that early prehistoric ploughs came in a variety of forms which all lacked either coulter or mouldboard: all were *ards*, or breaking-ploughs, which when pulled through the soil threw the earth symmetrically on both sides of the ploughshare (Payne 1957, 76–7). The coulter, which cut the soil into slices, was widely adopted in Iron Age times, and the mouldboard – which

FIGURE 41.
'January', from the
Cotton Tiberius
calendar, showing
fields being ploughed
with a heavy wheeled
plough (redrawn by
Della Hooke).

turned the slices over – together with an asymmetrical share, were in widespread use in Roman Britain. Unfortunately, subsequent developments remain uncertain: 'Evidence for the development of British ploughs during the Dark Ages and the Middle Ages is scanty' (Payne 1947, 79). Payne implies that the technological improvements of the Roman period were maintained throughout subsequent centuries, but as David Hall has argued the distribution of early Saxon settlements suggests otherwise. The abandonment of heavy clays in the immediate post-Roman period, the retrenchment onto lighter sands and gravels, 'implies settlements with primitive agricultural techniques, incapable of utilising the heavy clays that had been ploughed by Iron Age and Roman peoples' (Hall 1981, 35).

There is no direct archaeological or historical evidence for when heavier ploughs, with coulters and mouldboards, came back into widespread use. Late Saxon ploughshares – such as those from St Neots in Huntingdonshire, Westley Waterless in Cambridgeshire, or Nazeing in Essex – have the asymmetrical form expected on ploughs supplied with mouldboards (Hill 2000, 12–13); eleventh-century illustrations in the Caedmon MS in the Bodleian Library, and the Cotton MS in the British Library, show a heavy wheeled plough with a mouldboard (Hill 2000, 7); and the existence of a plough equipped with share and coulter are explicitly stated, the existence of the mouldboard very strongly implied, in a number of late Saxon sources (Hill 2000, 8). No direct evidence testifies to the existence of such ploughs before the tenth century, but there can be little doubt that they had come into widespread use in middle Saxon times simply because, by the eighth century, settlement had expanded once more onto the kinds of heavy soil which could not be easily cultivated without them.

Heavy ploughs of this kind were pulled by oxen: Domesday both assumes that plough teams are composed exclusively of oxen and records their numbers on each manor meticulously. The dominance of oxen is also clear in pre-Conquest literary sources, such as Aelfric's *Colloquy* of *c.* 1000, which describes the ploughman and his boy driving the oxen to a field, yoking them to the plough, and ploughing. They also feature as ploughbeasts in all pre-Conquest illustrations, and are almost the only kind of draft animal listed in late Saxon estate leases and inventories (Langdon 1986, 22–3), vastly outnumbering horses. In so far as the latter were employed in the field it was probably for harrowing, rather than ploughing, and even the majority of haulage work was undertaken by ox teams. Domesday assumes, moreover, that eight oxen made up a normal team: 'plough' was in effect the survey's shorthand for eight oxen, as innumerable references made clear. The number of oxen listed in late Saxon rentals and inventories are likewise generally divisible, at least roughly, by eight (Langdon 1986, 27), while twelfth-century extents also suggest teams of this size. While larger (ten or twelve oxen) or smaller (five or six) demesne teams are recorded, the average is around eight. In Langdon's words, 'soil and terrain had to be somewhat out of the ordinary to push a particular demesne off the eight-animal standard' (Langdon 1986, 66). True, an eight-ox team may not necessarily have involved eight oxen all harnessed together and working at the same time. Two might have been kept in reserve, to allow some change during the course of a day. Moreover, such large teams may not have been used in all circumstances, but only in the spring, when stock were weakest after the long winter, during which fodder was often in short supply (van Bath 1963, 69; Postan 1973, 17; Eyre 1953, 93). But large *working* teams are nevertheless implied in a variety of late Saxon sources, as Hill has recently pointed out (Hill 2000, 8). In the late Saxon poem known as the *Gerefa*, for example, the master asks the ploughman whether he has any companion in his work. He replies: 'I have a boy driving the oxen with a goad, who is now also hoarse of the cold and the shouting' (Liebermann 1935, 455). As Hill noted, such an arrangement would only have been necessary with a large ox team: the boy would lead and direct the team at the front, while the ploughman would devote all his attention to the plough itself, the large distance between them necessitating repeated shouting. 'The direction of the team was left to the ox-driver. The ploughman saw to it that the furrow was turned: the ox-driver helped to ensure that it was a straightish one' (Hill 2000, 17).

On heavy soils, as all agree, heavy mouldboard ploughs were essential. Simple breaking ploughs were not substantial enough to slice through heavy clay, while successful cultivation of such land required the cutting of deep furrows, in order to expose as much ploughsoil as possible to the elements, so that it could be broken down by frost and rain. A heavy mouldboard plough also allowed fields to be ploughed in ridges, thus assisting drainage. But it is important to emphasise that even on lighter land the impact of this new technology would have been profound. A plough with a mouldboard turned the soil over completely and thus allowed weeds to be thoroughly buried. Without this, even with repeated working, fields would eventually have become so choked with perennial weeds that it would be easier to break in new land, on which regular grazing had allowed grass – more easily killed by ploughing – to out-compete more serious infestations. At Yarnton, on the Thames gravels to the west of Oxford – and just outside the area studied here – recent excavations revealed important differences between the crop residues from early and middle Saxon settlements. 'On the ninth-century settlement site the seeds of perennial weeds brought in with the harvest declined dramatically in favour of annuals', something which the excavator cautiously attributed to the use of a mouldboard plough (Hey 2001, 224). The use of such a plough also allowed some of the lime and nutrients, leached from the surface by rain action, to be brought to the surface. In a variety of ways, larger and heavier ploughs would thus have allowed more regular and intensive forms of cultivation, encouraging settlements to become fixed in the landscape.

But the adoption of a heavy plough also had implications for the way that fields were laid out. It has long been argued that simple breaking-ploughs could most easily be used in fields of relatively square shape, while heavier ploughs encouraged the cultivation of narrow strips. This is because ploughs of the former type were relatively inefficient, and the ground needed to be cross ploughed; while a heavier mouldboard plough, pulled by larger teams, was less easy to turn and was therefore most efficient if it could run forward for long stretches (Hill 2000, 12). These arguments should not be pushed too far – heavy mouldboard ploughs could be efficiently used in fields of whatever shape, if large enough – but they do help explain, as the Orwins noted long ago, why the subdivision of arable land into small portions, through partible inheritance or whatever, took the form of strips rather than small squares.

Yet the spread of the new technology – itself encouraged, presumably, by population pressure, as well as by increasing demands of an emergent élite – had a number of other effects, of crucial importance in the shaping of the medieval landscape. Where fields were in more regular and continuous cultivation, especially on light land, they had to be more systematically manured than when ground was cultivated for several years and then fallowed for a long period. This might have important implications for the management of livestock. Larger ploughs required larger teams, and these needed to be fed, on grass and fodder, throughout the year, significantly changing the relative importance of these resources in the agrarian economy. Moreover, large ploughs were expensive to construct, large teams were expensive to maintain, and yet they were only used at intervals. Ways of pooling resources might therefore be important to farmers and this, as we shall see, could have important effects on settlement patterns. In the following chapters we shall explore how the impact of the new technology – coupled with population growth, and the adoption of more stable and intensive forms of cultivation in a landscape of small, individual holdings – was mediated through different natural environments to produce the complex kaleidoscope of medieval landscapes which I have described in the previous chapters.

CHAPTER FIVE

Field and Fold

....

Farming and settlement on light soils

Within the area studied in this volume, clayland districts came to be characterised by 'champion' landscapes, and by 'woodland' ones, in more or less
equal measure. But most areas of light, freely draining soil had landscapes
approximating to the former type and featured settlement patterns which were
usually more nucleated than otherwise, extensive areas of intermixed arable,
and – for the most part – tightly regulated forms of communal agriculture.
True, there were some, principally in east Norfolk and east Suffolk, which
displayed characteristics which aligned them more with 'woodland' districts.
But by and large light land was champion land, both in the Middle Ages,
and for long after. Indeed, on the chalk escarpment of the Chiltern Hills and
the East Anglian Heights, on the sands of Breckland, and in northern and
western Norfolk, many parishes remained almost entirely unenclosed at the
start of the nineteenth century. Some, like Bygrave on the rolling chalklands
of north Hertfordshire, retained their open fields into the early twentieth
century (VCH Hertfordshire II, 329). It is also noteworthy that within
many 'woodland' districts, where fields were a mixture of open arable and
enclosures, the former were very closely associated with the light soils found
in the principal valleys, a relationship particularly marked on the Chiltern
dipslope, but also evident across much of the boulder clay plateau of East
Hertfordshire and Essex. To understand this broad connection between light
land, and open-field farming, we must first examine the particular characteristics of freely draining soils, and the particular challenges which they
posed for early cultivators.

   It is often hard to translate modern accounts of soils, written primarily for
farmers equipped with a modern agricultural technology of tractors, artificial
fertilisers and the rest, into terms which are useful for studying medieval
agriculture. But the fundamental properties of the principal soil types have
not altered significantly since the early middle ages (even if in earlier times
their character may have been profoundly modified by human action) and
farmers' reactions to them have changed in detail, but not in kind. The
majority of light soils in the region studied here can be divided into two main
groups: those which derive principally from chalk, and which are calcareous,
at least below the top few centimetres; and those which are formed in sands
and gravels, and which are acid in character. Most of the latter are associated

with glacial drift, although in parts of the Suffolk Sandlings region, and in a few localised Midland districts, the parent material comprises earlier, 'solid' formations. There are considerable differences in the agricultural potential of these two broad categories of soil, but both are relatively easy to work and both were attractive to farmers from early prehistoric times.

Most areas of sandy soil were deforested by later prehistoric times and their inherent acidity favoured the development of heathland, with a characteristic undershrub vegetation dominated by heather or ling (*Calluna vulgaris*), bell heather (*Erica cinera*), gorse (*Ulex europaeus*) and broom (*Sarothamnus scoparius*). This is turn encouraged the development of the characteristic soil of the heathlands, the *podzol*, in which grey upper levels, leached of humus and iron, overlie hard layers of humus pan and iron pan, where these have been redeposited (Rackham 1986, 282–3; Dimbleby 1962). In the Bronze and early Iron Ages the heathlands and their margins often formed core areas for settlement. But improvements in plough technology ensured that their relative importance subsequently declined and by Roman times they seem to have carried lower population densities – or at least, fewer numbers of settlement sites – than heavier and more fertile clays and loams. The post-Roman recession saw some reversal of this trend: known pagan Saxon cemeteries and settlements are clustered markedly on such land, in Breckland in particular. But as population levels rose again during the later Saxon period the relative import-ance of the heathland districts again declined, and by the time of Domesday Breckland, the Suffolk Sandlings, and the areas of light heathy soils extending northwards from Norwich to the sea, were all among the more sparsely settled districts in the study region (Darby 1971).

The principal soils formed in sands and gravels – the Methwold, Worlington, Barrow and Newport Associations – are, as already noted, highly acidic in character (Hodges *et al.* 1984, 107–11, 249–53, 270–2, 368–70). High soil acidity inhibits plant growth, and reduces yields, in a whole host of ways (see above, p. 33). But in addition, the principal soil nutrients required for plant growth are rapidly leached from such soils, due to their large particle size and extreme porosity. These were *hungry* soils, in the parlance of early agricultural writers, and needed to be constantly fed with nitrogen and other necessary chemicals: 'when you put humus into it the humus does not last long. In fact, to make sandy soil productive you must put large quantities of organic manure into it ...' (Seymour 1975, 14). Sandy soils bring some advantages to farmers. In particular, sandy land is 'early' land, which warms up much more quickly than soils formed in clay. But such soils also tend to dry out quickly, parch, and suffer from drought during the summer months, restricting the growth of both grain crops and grass.

Chalk soils are different in a number of respects. Within the region studied these are principally found along the scarp slope of the Chiltern Hills and the East Anglian Heights, and on the more gentle escarpment running down the western side of East Anglia. It is possible that the character of chalk soils has changed over time, and that intensive land use in prehistoric and Roman times served to erode thin but fertile loess deposits, thus producing the thin calcareous soils – *rendzinas* – which we encounter today (Bell 1981, 84). Either way, the soils which had developed here by early medieval times – classified as the Newmarket 1 and 2, Swaffham Prior, Upton and Wantage 1 and 2 Associations – were generally more fertile than those formed in sand and, by the late Saxon period at least, carried higher population densities (Hodge *et al.* 1984, 265–9, 316–19, 333–5, 341–4). These soils seldom suffer from acidity, being calcareous almost to the surface. But, light and freely draining, leaching of soil nutrients is again a perennial problem. So too is the parching of grass, and crops, in mid and late summer.

There was only one way in which early farmers could maintain reasonable crop yields on all these light soils: by constantly pouring large amounts of organic manure into them. But they had only one major source of manure – animal dung – and only one animal which could thrive on the thin grazing afforded by chalk downs, and the coarse grasses, and heather and ling, of the heaths – the sheep. By the time the earliest documents allow us to see the working of agriculture on these light lands, complex management systems had evolved to make the most efficient use of the dung, and/or to ensure that a high proportion of it ended up on the land of the lord's demesne. Early modern farmers referred to the light lands as areas of *sheep-corn husbandry*: large flocks were grazed on extensive heaths or downs by day, and folded by night on the arable fields, when they lay fallow or after harvest. This ensured a constant flow of nutrients from the one to the other which allowed the poor, leached soils to be kept in heart. The heaths and downs, far from being under-utilised 'wastes', functioned as nutrient reservoirs, essential for keeping the thin soils in cultivation (Kerridge 1967, 42–5; Kerridge 1992, 74–86). On all these light lands versions of sheep-corn husbandry generally survived until enclosure in the eighteenth or nineteenth centuries. Sheep-corn husbandry, and open-field agriculture, were intimately connected.

The centrality of sheep to light land farming cannot be exaggerated. Indeed, until the various agricultural changes of the post-medieval period – the adoption, in particular, of new rotations featuring clover and turnips – it was difficult to keep large numbers of other animals, especially dairy cows, bullocks, or draft oxen, in these districts. Cattle are more demanding in their requirements than sheep, which could scratch a living on the barest heaths even during the winter months (Kerridge 1973, 17–20). They require, in particular, lusher grass growth. This was especially true of draught oxen, when they are working hard, ploughing or harrowing the fields. Yet because the grass growing in sandy or chalky soils tends to die back by mid summer, and then provides meagre pickings through to the following spring, for a large part of the year cattle needed to be fed on hay, or grazed on pockets of damper ground.

In the prehistoric and Romano-British periods some small settlements could be found scattered across the wide, dry chalklands or heaths, presumably associated with minor springs (Williamson 1984, 133, 146; Rogerson 1997, 6–18); while early Saxon settlements can be found in almost every conceivable

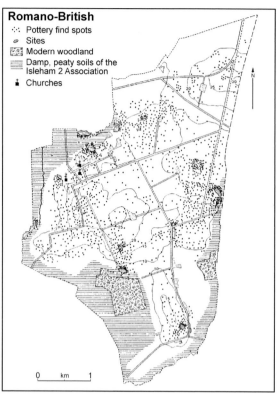

Romano-British

- ∴ Pottery find spots
- ⌀ Sites
- Modern woodland
- Damp, peaty soils of the Isleham 2 Association
- ⚐ Churches

0   km   1

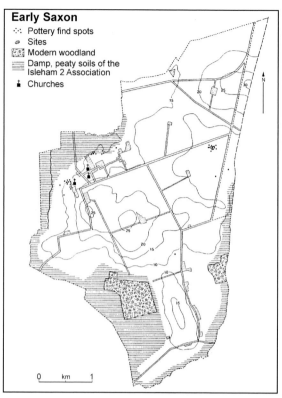

Early Saxon

- ∴ Pottery find spots
- ⌀ Sites
- Modern woodland
- Damp, peaty soils of the Isleham 2 Association
- ⚐ Churches

0   km   1

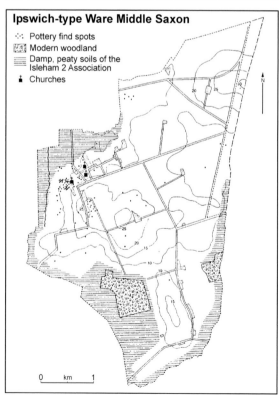

Ipswich-type Ware Middle Saxon

- ∴ Pottery find spots
- Modern woodland
- Damp, peaty soils of the Isleham 2 Association
- ⚐ Churches

0   km   1

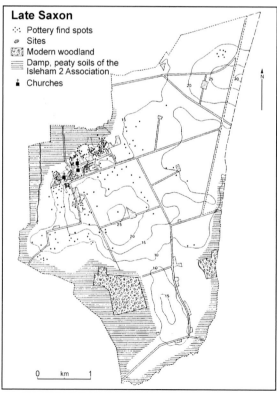

Late Saxon

- ∴ Pottery find spots
- ⌀ Sites
- Modern woodland
- Damp, peaty soils of the Isleham 2 Association
- ⚐ Churches

0   km   1

126

location. But as a more stable settlement pattern developed in middle Saxon times more obvious and comprehensible locational considerations came into play. Most farms were now placed near streams and rivers, and in particular beside areas of damp alluvium, peat, or deposits of impervious clay. All were places which afforded better grass growth in late summer and early autumn than the surrounding areas of chalk or sand (Figures 42 and 43). They also provided more reliable water supplies, not only for human consumption but also for dairy cows and, in particular, plough oxen (these need much more water than sheep which, indeed, consume little except when lactating). As more intensive forms of husbandry were adopted in the course of the Saxon period – as larger ploughs, pulled by larger teams, came into widespread use – pockets of damp ground thus formed increasingly important magnets for settlement. But in addition, it is possible that the more understandable, 'rational' location of sites in the middle Saxon period was also associated with the kinds of social developments I suggested earlier, with the development of more individualised forms of land tenure. Each landholder now needed to have access to those things necessary to sustain a farm, rather than relying on other members of some extended social group for the performance of particular tasks, or the exploitation of particular resources. Each farm now had to find pasture for oxen throughout the year. Whatever the precise explanation for the congregation of farms in such places, wide areas of chalk scarps and uplands and arid heaths were quite devoid of settlement. And from this simple fact, much else follows.

FIGURE 42.
The development of Saxon settlement at Barton Bendish in Norfolk. Andrew Rogerson's field-walking survey revealed how intensive Romano-British settlement was succeeded by a much sparser early Saxon pattern. By middle Saxon times a single settlement existed, beside one of the parish churches in the village, overlooking an area of damp, peaty soils to the north. In late Saxon times a number of discrete farms appeared, strung around the margins of this low-lying, peaty area.

The development of intermixed holdings

We do not know when intermixed holdings first emerged on the light lands, or what form they originally took, but by the thirteenth century we meet everywhere arrangements similar to those depicted on the earliest available maps – landscapes largely occupied by varying proportions of subdivided arable, and – usually on the more distant areas of ground – heaths or calcareous grassland (Figure 44). As we have seen, these open fields were not, in most cases, like those of the Midlands. In some districts, especially those of poorest soil, periodically cultivated 'outfields' existed in addition to the main areas of arable. In most districts 'fields' were unimportant as cropping units, and in many places the holdings of particular farms were clustered in restricted areas of the arable, rather than being more extensively intermingled. But such holdings nevertheless took the form of standard customary units, although their structure had frequently been obscured by the effects of the land market by the later thirteenth century, when we first see them clearly in extents and surveys. Along the Chiltern escarpment and the East Anglian Heights these were, as on the Midland clays, usually called yardlands or virgates (with subdivisions called *ferlingates* or *cotlands* (Roden 1973, 333)). But in Breckland and north-west Norfolk, as elsewhere in northern East Anglia, they were normally called *tenementa*, although virgates were also more common than many authorities imply (Bailey 1989, 49). *Tenementa* usually comprised either 12 or 24 customary acres, divided into strips, and were named after (and were presumably once occupied by) a particular family although, by the time we see them clearly in thirteenth century documents, they were actually occupied by a variety of other landholders. One in Redgrave in Suffolk, for example, was split between 34 tenants (Bailey 1989, 49). Although they had ceased to exist as units of landholding they had survived as notional entities because they formed the basic structure for levying manorial dues and for electing manorial officers.

Gray, writing in 1915, believed that the earliest *tenementa* had been discrete blocks of enclosed land, and these had fragmented under the impact of partible

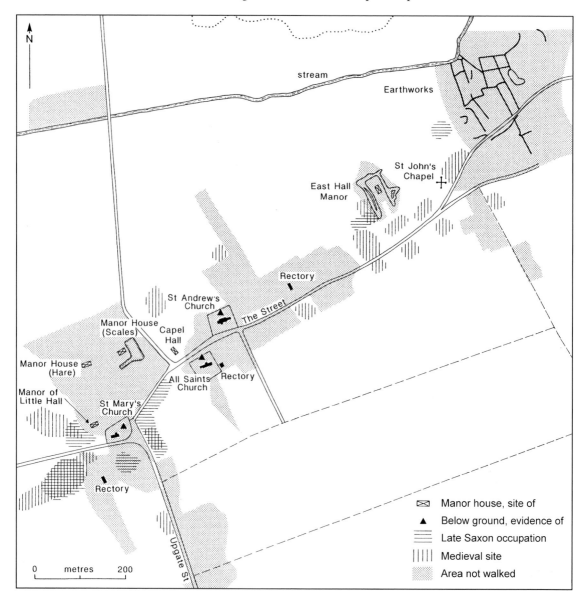

FIGURE 44.
A surviving fragment
of the Breckland
heaths: Knettishall in
Suffolk. Vast areas of
open heathland
existed in western East
Anglia before
enclosure and
reclamation in the
nineteenth century,
and large-scale
afforestation in the
twentieth.

FIGURE 43 (*opposite*).
The development of
medieval settlement at
Barton Bendish in
Norfolk. The loose
scatter of late Saxon
farms expanded and
fused to form a linear
village, but echoes of
the earlier
arrangement were
maintained in the
three separate parish
churches with which
the village was
endowed.

inheritance (which was widespread, for both free and customary holdings, in this region), as well as by the active market in customary land which was such a notable feature of East Anglia by the twelfth and thirteenth centuries (Gray 1915, 333–41; Homans 1941, 117–18; Dodwell 1967). Recent research suggests, however, that these tenurial units were not very ancient when first recorded in the thirteenth century and all had in fact probably originated as subdivided, rather than discrete, holdings. Mark Bailey has suggested that they were imposed on peasant cultivators as late as the later twelfth century, when labour services were re-asserted, or increased, following a period in which there had been much leasing of demesnes (Bailey 1989, 49).

Although Gray's suggestions about the origins of *tenementa* have not stood the test of time, it remains probable that – not only in East Anglia, but in other light land districts – many areas of subdivided arable first developed though the division by partible inheritance of land which has once been held in severalty. Free tenants were still numerous in many of these areas at the time of Domesday, and the kind of loose cluster of farmsteads seen developing in late Saxon times at places like Barton Bendish could be plausibly interpreted as the residences of groups of co-heirs, a patrilocal kin group (Faith 1997, 130) (Figures 42 and 43). As farms proliferated, family land would have been subject to repeated division, and some archaeological evidence, as we have seen, hints at the development of subdivided arable through the progressive division of fields originally held in severalty, with furlong boundaries apparently perpetuating earlier field patterns (above, p. 81). But it is unlikely that all subdivided fields originated like this. Although the light lands were often areas of complex and confused manorial organisation, especially towards the east, demesnes were everywhere present, villeins and bordars usually formed the majority of the population and many open fields may have been created by lords allocating land to dependent tenants. Certainly, ordered systems of strip fields seem to have existed in some places from the ninth century. At Brandon in Suffolk a sale of land in the mid ninth century refers to *omnem octvam acram in Brandune* – 'every eighth acre in Brandon' (Hart 1966, 227).

It might be useful to consider for a moment why the proliferation of holdings – whether through partible inheritance, or from the allocation of land to bond tenants – should have led to landscapes of intermixed strips, rather than to a scatter of ring-fence farms exploiting land held in severalty. There were a number of reasons. In many places the limited availability of water, and of well-watered grazing land, militated against any significant dispersal of settlement. But environmental circumstances in these districts often permitted a greater scattering of farmsteads than actually occurred, and of equal importance was probably the fact that the land nearest the settlement was more valuable, and more valued, than that more distantly located. When land was being divided by inheritance there would thus be some resistance to the idea that one heir should establish a new home on the outer fringes of the ancestral holding. And for the same reasons, when land was being so divided – or, indeed, being allocated in such a way that tenants who were being settled around an existing hall, owing similar rents and dues, received land of roughly equal value – it would be difficult to lay out holdings in the form of fields occupied and exploited in severalty, as opposed to scattered and intermixed shares.

A number of factors ensured that land nearest the settlement was more valuable than that lying at a distance. The most important was that it was more fertile, because over previous years it had been more intensively manured – not only by the dung from the sheep flocks, but also with the manure of cattle overwintered in yards, and household rubbish, collected in middens and carted out to the fields. Archaeological field surveys regularly show a marked fall-off in the density of the stray sherds in the ploughsoil, derived from manuring, with increased distance from the settlement. At Barton Bendish, for example, Rogerson noted how the distribution of pottery fragments around the Late Saxon and medieval settlement displays an inner zone of density, indicating frequently manured crofts and inner furlongs, and an outer zone, exhibiting a much sparser sprinkling of sherds (Rogerson 1997, 26–7).

In addition to this, in many places the arable land located near the settlement was *naturally* more fertile than that found at a distance. Thus in west Norfolk most of the larger settlements were sited close to valley floors, with well-drained calcareous loams on the lower ground but more acidic soils, formed in sandy drift, on the uplands. In Breckland similarly the better arable soils – those of the Methwold and Newport Associations – are generally concentrated on the sides of the valleys cutting through the plateau, with the truly abysmal Worlington Association covering the higher ground, some distance from settlements. Differences in fertility, whether arising from natural factors or resulting from the treatment and management of the land over previous decades, were of crucial importance in certain light land districts – those of poorest, least fertile soil – simply because nutrients were in particularly short supply. The differences in fertility may often have been marginal, but in a marginal landscape they mattered all the more.

Lastly, we should remember that land nearest settlements was more conveniently reached than that found at a distance. Men and equipment could be got on to it with greater speed. Although this was a less important consideration than on clay soils – where, as we shall see, the timing of cultivations was often of profound importance – it was nevertheless a significant factor at certain times of the agricultural year, especially at harvest, when in some years the interval of time between successive wet spells, and thus the window of opportunity available to the farmer and his men, might be limited indeed.

A range of considerations thus ensured that land near to the farm was more highly valued than that lying at a distance; and, where properties were being split by partible inheritance, or otherwise divided equitably, there would be strong pressure to allocate land in scattered parcels, rather than in the form of ring-fence farms. In the first case a pattern of intermixed holdings would develop over several generations; in the latter, intermixed holdings might be created at a stroke. But either way, both the end result, and underlying causes, were much the same.

To such cores of subdivided arable further areas were added as heaths and sheep-walks were ploughed and incorporated into the open fields. The early, pre-Conquest stages of this expansion of cultivation are poorly documented, not least because the paucity of pottery in use in Saxon times makes it hard to use the distribution of stray sherds to plot areas of arable land-use with any confidence. But its latter stages are clear enough. At Barton Bendish, for example, an extensive, low-density scatter of late Saxon sherds was recorded beyond the area of the settlement, representing its arable fields. 'This zone is bordered by low meadow and pasture ground to the north and west, but to the south and east its relatively well-defined boundaries are not marked by any topographic feature. These edges represent the outer margins of arable cultivation reached during the currency of late Saxon pottery'. Twelfth and thirteenth-century pottery, in contrast, was found across 'most of the upland areas of the parish' (Rogerson 1997, 25–6). Field name evidence frequently attests the expansion of open fields onto less fertile and more distant grounds in early medieval times. Harrison has suggested how, in south-east Cambridge-shire, encroachments on the heaths at a distance from the villages were often given the name Heath Field (Harrison 2000); while in north Essex fields in the middle of the chalk escarpment – midway between settlements at the scarp foot, and on the edge of the clay plateau above – sometimes have names implying reclamation, such as Breach Piece (OE *brec*, 'land newly broken') in Littlebury. At Sawston in south Cambridgeshire, similarly, the open field lying furthest from the village was known as The Brack, or Breach Field (Taylor 1973, 98). Documentary studies of particular light-soil parishes provide addi-tional evidence. It has been suggested that the area of arable in the Chiltern scarp parish of Watlington in Oxfordshire, for example, grew by as much as 50 per cent between 1086 and 1289 (Emery 1974, 78).

There is little doubt that land reclaimed from the downs and heaths would usually have been shared amongst groups of farmers, in the form of strips, at the outset. This was common practice in early medieval England (above, p. 74). It was not so much that reclamation was an arduous process which was best carried out by a team of men, rather than by an individual – although this may have been a consideration. It was rather that prior to reclamation the areas in question did not represent portions of virgin wilderness, up for grabs, but common land, used to graze the livestock of the community and a source of fertility for the fields of that community. Their conversion to a block of several land would have represented unilateral enclosure. All who had once enjoyed the benefits of the heath or down would, of necessity, have received a share when it was being brought into cultivation.

In some places, as I have noted, subdivided arable may have developed from an earlier pattern of fields enclosed by ditches and, by implication, hedges. But once repeated division had reduced each portion of land below a certain size – once relatively narrow strips had been produced – hedges would have been removed or neglected, eventually succumbing to the effects of grazing. And where virgin land was being allocated in strips for individual occupancy, similarly, the various portions were unlikely to be hedged. There are simple and obvious reasons for this. As the area of parcels fell, so the proportion occupied by enclosing hedges increased. Moreover, as the number of such parcels rose, and as they became more scattered, the amount of labour required for the maintenance of hedges would have become unsustainable. A dense mesh of hedges or fences would have interfered with the turning of the large ploughs which had now come into general use: and, in particular, with the movement of the flocks.

Folding

The importance of folding in the genesis and development of open-field systems has been emphasised by a number of historians, but most eloquently by Eric Kerridge in *The Common Fields of England* (1992). Archaeologists and landscape historians, in contrast, have paid remarkably little attention to this matter. In part this is because most research has focused on the open fields of the Midlands, where folding was nothing like as important as it was on the light lands of the south and east. As already emphasised, light land had to be heavily mucked in order to coax reasonable crops from it, and the quantities required would have increased in proportion to the frequency and intensity of cultivation. Although muck from yards and cattle sheds was evidently carted and spread on the fields by early medieval farmers, the sheep provided the vast majority of the necessary manure. The sheep fold was thus central to the operation of agriculture before the innovations of the seventeenth and eighteenth centuries. Indeed, once these innovations – most notably, the cultivation of turnips and clover in regular rotations with grain crops – had been widely adopted, open fields lost much of their *raison d'être* and were rapidly enclosed.

The precise operation of folding varied from district to district and from region to region, but in all the practice involved moving sheep, grazed on

FIGURE 45.
'The Sheep Fold', by George Linnell. This nineteenth-century painting shows clearly the practice of close-folding sheep, so vital to ensure the fertility of arable land – especially on light, porous soils.

downland or heath by day, on to areas of uncropped arable by night. Here they 'tathed' the land, to use the common East Anglian term: that is, they both dropped dung there, and trod it into the soil. The most efficient way of organising this was to pen the sheep tightly together in moveable folds, constructed usually of hazel hurdles (Figure 45).

But folding would have been prohibitively expensive in labour and time if each farmer had moved his own diminutive flock every day to a fold erected on his own land, especially where holdings were splintered and intermingled. As Kerridge observed, the farmer, as well as driving his sheep daily from grazing to tillage and back again, 'would also have had all the lambing and shearing to attend to. All this would have preoccupied him to such an extent as to leave him little time for growing cereals' (Kerridge 1992, 26). In landscapes of small farms and intermingled parcels, held by individual households, it was inevitable that common flocks, controlled by communal shepherds, would develop. To quote Kerridge again:

> In the absence of evidence, it is impossible to see exactly what was done in the early common fields; but as soon as the evidence becomes available it proves beyond doubt that in permanent common fields, while some small and easily accessible parts were mucked with farmyard manure, most of the tillage was usually close-folded by joint flocks according to strict regulations (Kerridge 1992, 27).

The institution of the common fold was a powerful agent in the development of the open fields. Firstly, as already intimated, the need to allow the easy movement of the flocks across the arable would have ensured that the strips would not have been hedged or fenced when intermingled holdings were laid out, and that they would have been removed or neglected as farms attained this form through progressive subdivision. Certainly, in post-medieval times the reversal of this process – the spread of such physical barriers, through piecemeal enclosure – wrought havoc with folding arrangements and was usually opposed by manorial courts (Wade Martins and Williamson 1999, 34–43, 105–7). Common folding may even have been another factor encouraging the division of holdings into strips in the first place, as new land was being brought into cultivation, as existing arable was divided by inheritance, or as land was allocated to bond tenants. This was because the fold was normally moved fairly slowly over the area of the township, remaining for several nights in each place, in part to allow the full benefits of the tathe to be realised, in part because of the time and labour involved in erecting it (Kerridge 1992, 34). A fold would usually contain several hundred sheep and would therefore embrace a number of strips at once. As it was gradually moved across the field, each farmer would have had his land dunged in turn, strip by strip. Intermingling of holdings in small parcels allowed an obvious equity in the receipt of manure on the part of all who had contributed to the common flock. 'Only by intermingling could each man be assured he would be neither the first nor the last to enjoy the fold passing over his land' (Kerridge 1992, 30).

134

Yet of more importance was the role of the fold in developing the communal management of the arable land of a township. For obvious reasons, folding could only be carried out if numbers of contiguous strips were cropped, harvested and fallowed in concert. Communal rotations – and the management of sheep-corn farming more generally – took a number of different forms. In some districts the flocks were under the control of the cultivators, albeit administered through the medium of the lord's court. But across much of the region studied here rather different arrangements prevailed. In Kerridge's words, 'where common field farmers were rather less numerous or less influential, there was a marked tendency ... for common flocks and folds to be subordinated to those of the demesne farmers or lords of manors' (Kerridge 1992, 80). The latter might come to exercise rights of *faldage* – that is, compel tenants to accept the duty of fold-soke, and place their sheep in the demesne flock or fold. In the east of the region studied here such arrangements took an extreme form to which modern historians have given the name *fold course system*.

The fold course is a complex institution, which varied from place to place, changed its character over time and has not always been fully understood by historians. Under such a system, by the late Middle Ages the grazing on the fallows and much of that on the heaths and downs was reserved for the flocks of the manorial lord. Tenants usually contributed their sheep to these flocks, and the demesne lands had first call on the fold, and received a majority of the dung, although various arrangements were made to ensure that tenants, too, received a proportion. Commonly, for example, they were allowed the dung dropped by the sheep as they roamed across the fallows after harvest, while the intensive night-folding was the preserve of the lord. Most East Anglian townships were divided between more than one manor and each was allotted its own fold course, comprising open arable, heaths and commons, and occasionally areas of coastal marsh. In the words of one sixteenth-century Norfolk document, 'Within eury Towne and vyllage is most commonly ii or iii manors or more and to eury manor a Shepps Course or ffouldcourse belongyng' (Allison 1957, 16). Each 'course' had defined boundaries, delimited by both natural features and artificial markers, such as 'doules' or mounds of earth. In some cases, such was the complex confusion of East Anglia's tenurial system, manorial boundaries crossed those of townships or parishes, and fold courses did likewise.

Although the fold course is often described as a peculiarly East Anglian institution it could be found in many vills outside Suffolk and Norfolk. Thus in the thirteenth and fourteenth centuries the Cambridgeshire vills of Fulbourn, Sawston, Snailwell and Oakington all possessed fold courses (Postgate 1973, 318). Something similar seems to have operated in Saffron Walden in north Essex. The fields of the town, as described in fifteenth- and sixteenth-century surveys, were divided into three folding sectors, one for each of the principal manors (Cromarty 1966).

The fold course system as we encounter it in fifteenth- and sixteenth-century documents – and as described by historians like Allison or Postgate – had not remained unchanged since early medieval times. As Mark Bailey has shown, in the twelfth and thirteenth centuries something more flexible, and perhaps less hostile to the interests of peasant cultivators, had generally existed. In particular, some peasant folds had been maintained – generally granted by seigniorial license for a year at a time, but sometimes permanently attached to particular tenements (Bailey 1989, 43–4). Nevertheless, even in this earlier period most folds were restricted to demesnes, and the right to create them remained with the lord.

The fold course was associated with cropping systems which involved not large, continuous areas of spring- and winter-sown crop and fallow – 'fields' in the Midland sense – but discontinuous 'shifts'. In other words, a certain proportion of the arable would lie fallow, under a regular sequence, but this would take the form of a collection of disconnected furlongs rather than a single continuous 'field'. To some extent such arrangements were the necessary consequence of the fact that holdings were clustered in particular areas of the fields, rather than being widely distributed. But even where a more even distribution is recorded – as in some Breckland parishes – some form of shift system was generally imposed (Bailey 1989, 41). Evidently, when field systems were laid out in medieval times – when standard 'tenementa' were being created or reorganised – a wide and even scattering of strips, in regular sequence, had not been attempted in many townships, either because it could not be easily achieved, or because it was deemed unnecessary, or both. While folding arrangements might thus encourage the common management of intermixed holdings, and might even be a contributory factor in the development of such holdings, they did not necessarily lead to the reorganisation of townships along familiar 'Midland' lines.

It is noteworthy in this context that such irregular arrangements were more prevalent in eastern light soil districts than in western. Fold courses and 'shift' systems could be found, as I have noted, in north west Essex and south Cambridgeshire, but in general moving south-westwards along the chalk escarpment arrangements more akin to the 'Midland' system were found, albeit often the consequence of remodelling in the twelfth century or later. The reasons for this east-west difference are not entirely clear. The distinctive character of East Anglian field systems has often been ascribed to the complex tenurial patterns found there – the dominance of multi-manorial vills and the high proportion of free tenants – both of which militated against a more comprehensive reorganisation and regularisation of field layout. The density of free tenures is unlikely to have been a major factor in all this, however, given that the fold course was itself a symptom of seigniorial strength rather than weakness: it was a system in which

> The entire grazing of a township's lands was usually the prerogative of the manorial lord or his lessee, irrespective of the occupance of the land. The practice was in contrast to Midland townships where pasturage

rights inhered in the community as a whole and were jointly exercised by all its landholding members (Postgate 1973, 314).

At the time of Domesday, *liberi homines* were relatively thin on the ground in these parts of East Anglia and not, in all probability, very wealthy or powerful. These poor soils were instead characterised by populations of sokemen and villeins. In the post-medieval periods this was, quintessentially, the land of large estates, like Holkham, Houghton or Raynham. Poor soils, in other words, made for weak tenants, and the communities which inhabited these districts in early medieval times were evidently less able to resist manorial domination in the vital matter of folding than those more favourably located. But this in itself does not explain why manorial lords insisted on maintaining their own flocks and grazing grounds, rather than combining together with tenants and other lords in a vill to organise folding; nor, indeed, why they were so keen to monopolise manure supplies in a way that lords of Chiltern manors, for example, were not. Once again, the explanation lies in the marginal nature of these light, sandy soils. Control of manure was likely to have been a matter of particular concern in such districts, and rights to fold therefore jealously guarded. On the more fertile and calcareous lands to the south west, in contrast – along the Chiltern escarpment – tenants were more numerous and perhaps more powerful, monopolisation of control over folding less essential to manorial lords, and their rights to the fold therefore less jealously guarded. Here it was more likely that a single flock, under communal control, would develop, and that the various lords within each vill, and their tenants, would re-organise the landscape so as to ensure its most efficient movement across the fields – leading, in many cases, to the adoption of a regular two- or three-field system.

Nevertheless, it is clear that there were other factors encouraging, or discouraging, the adoption of 'Midland' arrangements on these light lands, for highly 'irregular' field systems could be found in many places where fold courses never developed and land was moderately fertile, on the calcareous soils of the Chiltern escarpment and the East Anglian Heights. One factor was the pattern of settlement. There was a close correlation between places with irregular field systems, and places which displayed markedly polyfocal or dispersed patterns of settlement. Great Shelford and Sawston in south Cambridgeshire, for example – where irregular and dispersed settlement was noted in Chapter 3 – thus maintained multiple field systems throughout the middle ages and beyond. Sawston still had six fields in 1802. Great Shelford had ten named fields in 1222 and there were still seven at the time of enclosure in 1834 (Postgate 1964, Appendix II, ix, x).

Settlements on these calcareous soils displayed very varying degrees of nucleation, in large measure a reflection of topographic factors. Where population levels were high but areas of damp, well-watered ground were of limited extent, then tightly nucleated villages often developed in the course of the middle ages, as we have seen at places like Thriplow or Bassingbourne. But where damp ground was extensive, a wider dispersal of farms might occur, especially as – on these comparatively fertile soils – there was less pressure on the part of heirs to remain close to well-manured ancestral acres. This presumably explains the markedly polyfocal villages and small hamlets clustered at the junction of the chalk scarp and clay plateau in north Hertfordshire and north west Essex. Elsewhere, dispersal might be encouraged by the *paucity* of damp ground, and by the fact that it was scattered in a number of small parcels – as across much of south west Cambridgeshire or south Bedfordshire, at the foot of the chalk escarpment. Where farms remained relatively scattered in these ways, holdings became intermingled to only a limited extent. But where they became increasingly clustered, land would have become more extensively intermixed. In the latter circumstances, more 'regular' layouts could be created with relative ease, because the necessary re-allotment of holdings could be effected without any relocation of individual farmsteads. Conversely, in other circumstances the advantages to be gained from the maintenance of a single communal flock were not so overwhelming that lords or communities were prepared to completely re-organise existing patterns of settlement in order to achieve it.

In the last chapter I emphasised the 'fuzziness' of regional landscape boundaries, and the dangers of positing too hard a dichotomy between 'woodland' and 'champion' districts. The vast majority of light land areas developed 'champion' landscapes along the kinds of lines which I have just described. But not all. Across much of east Norfolk – an area I have already noted for its display of both 'woodland' and 'champion' characteristics – communal regulations of any kind were usually limited. In contrast to other areas of East Anglia, fold courses either did not develop at all, or disappeared at an early date. There are references to the institution in medieval and early modern documents, at Aylsham or Cawston, for example. As late as 1728 a farm at Oulton was leased with 'liberty of sheep walk over land in other's possession' (NRO BUL 11/310). But it was never deeply entrenched. Much of this was light yet fertile land, dominated by rich loams of the Wick 1 and 3 Associations, and there was an abundance of damp pasture in the numerous valleys cutting through the region. This was also, for the most part, a landscape of weak and divided lordship in which free tenants had been particularly thick on the ground at the time of Domesday. As we have seen, complex and extensive open fields developed in this area but, given the social and environmental circumstances, their organisation generally remained chaotic. On the Suffolk Sandlings the fold course was also poorly entrenched (Wade Martins and Williamson 1999, 43–4; Burrell 1960, 20–5). Here the sandy soils were very poor but most vills extended, eastwards or westwards or both, onto rather different soils – the rich heavy clays of the Beccles 1 Association, or the damp alluvial soils of the coastal marshes. The abundance of good grazing offered by these soils, and also by the many damp valleys cutting through the arid sands, again lessened the need for strict management of folding and fallowing.

Conclusion

Although the development of field systems and settlement patterns in light soil 'champion' areas thus displayed a fair degree of variation, a number of common themes emerge. The need to provide cattle, especially draught oxen, with good supplies of pasture or hay and the need to obtain reasonable supplies of drinking water for both men and beasts ensured that from middle Saxon times farmsteads clustered beside areas of damp ground, with their arable extending away across the lighter land. As population expanded, and bond tenancies and free holdings proliferated, areas of intermixed arable were created, and these increased in extent as the frontiers of cultivation expanded. At the same time, nucleated 'villages' often developed as the spaces between neighbouring farms were filled in by further areas of settlement, often at the expense of areas of low-lying common land. The overwhelming need to supply the arable with regular supplies of dung from the flocks led to the regularisation of cropping and sometimes, where clusters of farms developed into nucleated villages and soils were moderately fertile, to the reorganisation of holdings along 'Midland' lines. Elsewhere, on the poorer soils and/or where topography ensured a more scattered pattern of settlement, more clustered patterns of landholding were the norm, across which discontinuous cropping shifts were imposed. This account, it must be emphasised, is only a *model*: a description of a process which accounts for most of the observed phenomena, but which cannot itself be directly demonstrated from the available evidence. This is simply because, as I have already emphasised, direct evidence concerning the origins and early development of open fields is simply unavailable. The model may not explain all aspects of open-field formation on light soils but it does account for much of the observed data. But what it does not do, of course, is explain the development of open-field agriculture within its principal heartland – the Midlands.

As already noted, there are a number of areas of comparatively light soil in this extensive district, most notably in the valleys of the Nene and the Ouse; in the area to the north of Bicester; or between Stamford and Peterborough. In some of these districts the kinds of developments outlined above may well have occurred, and – in particular – folding may have been an important factors in the development both of landscapes of intermingled strips, and of highly communal forms of agriculture. But for the most part, the Midlands are characterised by heavy, water-retentive soils, and on these the proposed model simply cannot be applied for it depends, crucially, on the existence of clustered farmsteads, and on social and environmental factors which discouraged their dispersion as population increased and cultivation expanded. In these districts, water was widely available in the form of surface ponds or shallow wells, and numerous damp areas, suitable for grazing draught oxen, existed. Moreover, on these less 'hungry' soils there would have been less difference in fertility and value between land near to, and distant from, established settlements. Farms could thus have spread out across the landscape as population expanded, each farming its own set of fields, or sharing in limited areas of open arable. And while folds, and communal folding arrangements, were a feature of vills on the Midland clays, they lacked there the crucial importance that they possessed on the light lands, simply because these heavier soils were less in need of such regular and recurrent inputs of manure. More importantly, because the land was moisture-retentive, the flocks could not be close-folded on the arable for large parts of the year (Fox 1984, 130–3). On damp land the animals were likely to contract foot-rot; while close folding would have 'poached' and compacted the soil, making it harder to cultivate in the spring (Kerridge 1992, 77–9). Folding was thus often limited to the period from late summer into late autumn. Moreover, in most Midland districts the area of common grazing was relatively restricted – commonly less than *c.* 15 per cent of the area of the vill – very different from the situation on the downs and heaths, where extensive tracts of unploughed ground usually survived into the high middle ages and beyond. The organisation of the fold doubtless had an impact on the development of these landscapes, but it is unlikely to have possessed the kind of central significance which it had in light land districts. In short, while partible inheritance and the proliferation of bond tenancies might have encouraged the development of intermixed arable on the Midland clays, and while the need to organise folding might have encouraged the development of intermingled strips, as well as the adoption of communal rotations; these things cannot have been major factors in the emergence here of 'champion' landscapes. Some other factor, or factors, must in particular have militated against the dispersion of farms across the landscape as population rose, and as holdings and sub-manors proliferated. And this immediately brings us back to soils, and to the practicalities of farming life in early medieval England.

CHAPTER SIX

Plough and Furrow

....

Co-aration

The adoption of a heavy plough, equipped with a mouldboard, was a major factor in the development of the champion landscapes in light soil districts. But it was on the heavy clay soils that the new technology must have had the greatest impact. The regular and successful cultivation of such areas would simply have been impossible without a plough able to slice through heavy earth, cut a deep furrow, and lay down parallel furrows together in order to form a ridge which could assist drainage. The use of such a plough, as we have seen, everywhere encouraged the laying out of small parcels of land in the form of strips, rather than squares. But on heavy soils it was particularly necessary to maintain the momentum of the plough in order to keep the ploughshare from riding high and lifting out of the furrow: a heavy plough was 'efficient only if it ran forward for long stretches, and the turning areas (the 'headlands') were not too high a proportion of the field' (Hill 2000, 12). The 'long furlongs' which, it has been suggested, were the initial form of open field in some Midland townships were an extreme form of land-division suited to a cumbersome plough, although one which evidently went out of fashion at an early date. 'Long furlongs' were also a feature of the field systems which emerged on the silt clays of the northern Fens in the twelfth century (Silvester 1988, 161; Silvester 1999, 127–30; Hall 1999, 40). And they may once have existed in some 'woodland' areas. In this context attention might be drawn, for example, to the infamous 'reave-like' field patterns around the South Elmham and Ilketshalls group of parishes in north Suffolk (Rackham 1986, 156–8), a pattern which has more in common with the long furlongs of the Fens than with the normal forms of co-axial field layout known from the eastern claylands (Martin 1999, 57). The long axes of this 'field system' are laid out parallel to a probable Roman road, and it covers an area suspiciously co-terminous with the probable bounds of the Bishop of East Anglia's ancient estate. It is possible that here, a major Saxon landowner attempted to replan the landscape along lines more suitable for a heavy plough: but if so, changes were soon made. Greens and commons were intruded into the system, interrupting the long ploughlands, and settlement dispersed across the landscape.

There are, however, a number of other and more important connections between the genesis of open fields in the Midlands, and the adoption of a heavy mouldboard plough. Both Seebohm, and the Orwins, saw an intimate association between the development of 'regular' open fields and the practice of joint ploughing, or *co-aration*. Specifically, they argued that because individual farmers were unable to maintain, all the year round, eight ploughing oxen – nor afford the luxury of their own individual plough – they were obliged to combine with their neighbours, supplying parts and beasts to a shared plough and team. Ease of organisation encouraged joint ploughers to live in close proximity, in nucleated villages. And the equal contribution which each made to the plough was reflected in the equal distribution of their holdings across the landscape, on good and bad, near and distant, land (Seebohm 1890, 105–25; Orwin and Orwin 1938, 12–14, 51–2).

This theory has a number of attractions but on closer inspection has always raised more problems than it solves. This is because Domesday implies that eight ox teams – and therefore, presumably, the practice of co-aration – were found throughout England. Why, then, did regular open fields and nucleated villages only become the usual mode of agrarian organisation in some districts and not in others? Moreover, as Homans pointed out in the 1940s, farmers could surely share teams, and ploughs, without farming their land in intermingled strips or living, cheek-by-jowl, in tightly clustered settlements. It was, in his words, 'a matter of indifference whether a villager had his land as a single parcel or in scattered strips: the common plow had in any case to move about from the land of one of the partners to those of the others' (Homans 1941, 81), a view supported by a number of subsequent writers (e.g. Dodgshon 1980, 31–3). To understand how plough-sharing might be linked to open-field genesis, and to the development of nucleated villages, we need to examine the particular environmental circumstances in which these things occurred. And this in turn demands a more detailed discussion of clay soils, and their cultivation, than is usually provided in books on the early medieval landscape.

Farming clay soils

Clay soils presented medieval farmers with both opportunities and problems, but both are usually treated in a vague and cavalier fashion by historians and archaeologists. We learn that such soils are 'heavy', 'intractable', 'difficult yet fertile': but little more. In fact, clay soils within the area studied display considerable variation, in structure and mineral content, and this is further compounded by significant differences in climate. Some of these variations have already been touched on: in particular, the contrast between leached, acid soils of the kind found on the Chiltern dipslope and in Middlesex, south Hertfordshire and south Essex, soils which invariably carried, in early medieval times, low population densities; and the more fertile clays found across much of East Anglia and the Midlands (above, pp. 33–4). Other aspects of variation, however, are more subtle: so subtle in fact that although apparent enough to modern soil scientists they have not previously been called as evidence in the great open-field debate.

Clay soils do not suffer from a chronic shortage of nutrients, like those of the light lands. Nitrates, phosphates and the rest are not rapidly leached away as they are on the poor 'hungry' lands of down, wold and heath (Seymour 1975, 14). Instead they suffer from two equally severe problems; problems intimately connected, but which are nevertheless both theoretically, and practically, distinct. One is seasonal waterlogging. Most clay soils have sub-strates which are only slowly permeable, and where drainage is most impeded they have profiles which are *gleyed* – that is, mottled for the upper 40cm (Hodges *et al.* 1984, 49–50). Soil scientists refer to such soils as *stagnogleys*. More evocatively, early modern farmers called this 'cold' land, for fields which lie wet in early spring do not warm up so rapidly as those on drier soils and germination and plant growth are both delayed (Cook 1999). In addition, waterlogged crops do not take up nutrients well, and their root structure is poorly developed. The removal of stagnant surface water allows root systems to develop to a greater depth (Robinson 1949, 36–7). Drainage also helps soil structure: the pore space within the soil is increased, and aeration improved. Paradoxically, this increases the amount of water which can be taken up by the plant during the dry summer months, because the roots can derive moisture from a greater depth (Robinson 1949, 37).

The second main difficulty with clay soils would have been particularly acute before the advent of the internal combustion engine and efficient forms of under-drainage. This is their tendency to *puddle*: that is, form a sticky mass which adheres to ploughs, harrows and other implements when wet, and which dries to a hard, brick-like mass. Where soils are most prone to this tendency they can be almost impossible to cultivate with the kinds of technology available to medieval farmers. Such soils therefore require particularly careful, and carefully *timed*, cultivation. The aim of the farmer is to encourage *flocculation*: that is, to get the microscopic particles of clay to coalesce together in larger grains.

> When this happens the clay is more easily worked, drains better, allows air to get down into it (an essential condition for plant growth), and allows the roots of the plant to penetrate it more easily (Seymour 1975, 14).

The propensity for clay soils to flocculate can be encouraged by careful management. Exposure to air and frost, incorporation of humus, and improved drainage all encourage the process. Conversely, and more importantly, working clay soils when they are wet encourages puddling: 'Clay must be ploughed or dug when in exactly the right condition of humidity, and left strictly alone when wet' (Seymour 1975, 14).

The particular characteristics of different clay soils are important here. Some are naturally more prone to puddling than others. One factor is the nature of the parent materials – those formed from calcareous parent materials, notably chalky boulder clay, tend to be more tractable and easier to flocculate than those derived from the Jurassic and Cretaceous clays found across much of the Midlands. But another is the character of the local climate. In general rainfall is lower in the centre and east than in the west of the region studied here, although the close relationship between relief and precipitation means that in detail the pattern is rather more complex. Moreover, levels of transpiration as well as levels of precipitation affect the amount of water in the soil, and agricultural scientists often combine the two in the measure of *median field capacity* – conveniently defined as the number of days during which the soil is saturated, and field drains flow with excess water (Smith 1967; Smith and Trafford 1976). Again, in general there is a tendency for variation to fall into an east-west pattern but complexities of relief complicate the picture. The duration of field capacity is longest both in the west of the region, on the uplands of Northamptonshire, and towards the east, on the high ground of west Norfolk (Figure 46). It must be emphasised, however, that field capacity is a theoretical, meteorological concept, and can only be used to understand the limitations posed by precipitation on farming practice when account is also taken of the physical properties of particular soils. The cultivation 'of well drained coarse textured soils is often possible within the field capacity period without harmful effects whereas clayey … soils are usually impassable' (Hodge *et al.* 1984, 33–4).

FIGURE 46.
Map of *median field capacity* within the study area (after Hodge *et al.* 1984). The map provide a useful measure of soil moisture content: field capacity is defined as the number of days during which the soil is saturated, and field drains flow with excess water.

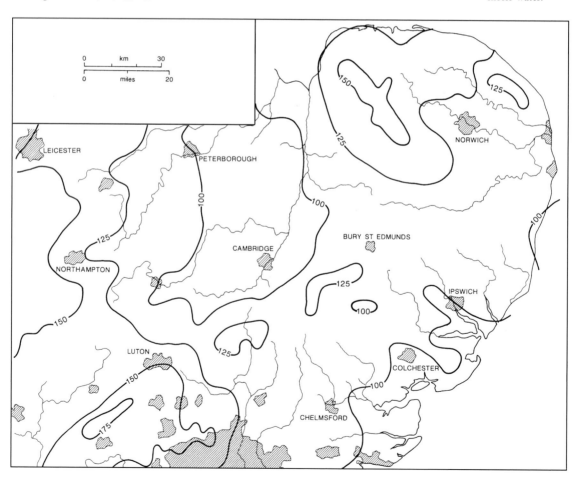

In terms of clay soils, the most important distinction is that between *pelo* and *non-pelo* soils. The former have clayey horizons throughout, the latter have upper horizons which are loamy or silty above an impermeable or slowly permeable lower level (Thomasson 1975). Soils of the former kind are often waterlogged for longer periods than the latter; but this is not invariably true, and most of the relevant soil associations are classified as having wetness class III (i.e., the soil profile is waterlogged within 70 cm of depth for between three and six months in the year) or IV (waterlogged within 70 cm for more than six months). More important is the fact that *pelo* soils are much more prone to coalesce into a sticky, intractable mess, and much less ready to flocculate.

There are five main associations of *pelo* soils in the region studied, of which three are particularly intractable. These are the so-called *pelo-stagnogleys*: that is, soils which are waterlogged for long periods in the winter months (wetness class III or IV), and which are clayey to the surface. One of these, the Windsor Association, has already been mentioned in chapter 2 and will not concern us further here: formed in London clay and associated Eocene deposits in south Hertfordshire, south Essex and Middlesex, the soils of this association are not only highly intractable but also acid and infertile. In early medieval times these characteristics ensured, as we have seen, low population densities and a comparatively late chronology of settlement. The other two associations are of more importance in the present context, however, because while hard to work they were at least moderately fertile, and they occur widely within areas of average to high Domesday population density, in which open-field farming was well entrenched by the twelfth century.

Soils of the Denchworth Association are found over extensive tracts of Buckinghamshire, Northamptonshire and Leicestershire. Formed in Jurassic and Cretaceous clays, they consist of a variety of wet clayey soils (Hodge *et al.* 1984, 155–8). Those of the dominant series, the almost stoneless, clayey Denchworth, are strongly mottled and are waterlogged for long periods in winter, especially as most soils of this type occur in districts in which median field capacity is in excess of 125 days. They are particularly prone to puddling and compaction:

> Even with drainage improvements there is little opportunity to work the land in spring … Because the topsoil takes a long time to dry out, timing of cultivations is critical and measures to reduce ground pressure, such as cage wheels, are desirable to protect against structural damage (Hodge *et al.* 1984, 157–8).

The number of days on which Denchworth Association soils can be worked without serious damage, even under modern conditions, is around 44 in autumn in a normal year, and no more than four in the spring, falling in a wet year (one year in four on average (Hodge *et al.* 1984, 73)) to fourteen and zero respectively (*ibid*, 158). It is hard to relate such figures to the medieval situation but there is little doubt that the period of working would have been

145

similarly restricted: ploughs pulled by oxen, even the heavy wheeled plough adopted in late Saxon times, may have caused less compaction than modern tractors and ploughs, but on the other hand the absence of under-drains would have increased the degree of surface waterlogging, and hence compaction, considerably.

The soils of the Ragdale Association are also pelo-stagnogleys, in spite of the fact that they are derived from deposits of chalky till (Hodge *et al.* 1984, 293–6). The dominant series are 'difficult to cultivate because of their slowly permeable clayey and fine loamy horizons'. More importantly:

> When cultivations are carried out under wet conditions, the resulting structural damage reduces the already low porosity and causes prolonged waterlogging, often to the soil surface, and the death or retardation of seedlings due to lack of oxygen (Hodge *et al.* 1984, 295).

The period of time available for cultivation is, once again, often severely restricted, particularly as the majority of such soils occur towards the west of the region, in areas of high field capacity.

The other associations of *pelo* soils found within the region take the form, not of pelo-stagnogleys, but of *pelosols* – clayey soils which crack deeply in dry seasons, but which are generally more permeable when wet than the kinds of stagnogleys just discussed, and which are not in general prominently mottled within 40cm of depth. The most important are those of the Hanslope Association, formed in chalky boulder clay, which cover some 1,393 square miles (3,610 square kilometres) in Essex, Hertfordshire, Cambridgeshire and Bedfordshire (Hodge *et al.* 1984, 209–12). The principal constituent series – Hanslope and Faulkebourne – are stiff and hard to work. But they are at least moderately calcareous and seldom seriously waterlogged (wetness class II/III, following drainage). Nor do they suffer from problems of compaction and puddling to anything like the same extent as the soils just discussed. True, the Association includes areas of the pelo-stagnogleyic Ragdale series, especially in Hertfordshire and Essex, but these are generally of limited extent, restricted to level plateau areas, and often occur next to extensive areas of well-drained, calcareous soils characteristic of another component of the Association, the Stretham Series. Only in the far west of the region – where rainfall levels are appreciably higher than in most eastern districts – can Hanslope Association soils suffer from significant problems of compaction and puddling, and from longer periods of winter waterlogging. This can limit the period of time during which they can be worked, especially in the spring months, but seldom to the same extent as with soils of the Ragdale or Denchworth Associations.

The other pelosols found in the region, however – the Evesham 1, 2 and 3 Associations – can pose more serious difficulties (Hodge *et al.* 1984, 186–92). Although the dominant series are again calcareous in character, they are less easily drained and more prone to puddling. Those of the Evesham 1 Association 'are sticky and plastic when wet and harden quickly on drying' (Hodge *et al.* 1984, 187); while the Evesham 2 and 3 Associations include significant proportions of the pelo-stagnogleyic Denchworth Series, hard to drain even with modern technology, and (as we have seen) particularly prone to compaction.

The other forms of clay soils found in the region are of the non-pelo variety: that is, they have upper horizons which are loamy rather than clayey. Although many such soils are stagnogleys – that is, suffer from seasonal waterlogging – they are not as prone to puddling and compaction as most pelo soils. The most important association of this type is the Beccles 1, which covers extensive tracts of ground on the East Anglian till plateau. Once again, included within this association are areas of the pelo-stagnogley Ragdale Series – particularly prone to compaction – but these are of relatively limited extent and the easterly location, and generally dry climate, ensure that the problems these pose to farmers are limited. In contrast, where non-pelo stagnogley associations include significant proportions of pelo-stagnogley series, *and* where these occur in the wetter west, then more serious difficulties are encountered – not least because the extended duration of waterlogging often enforces cultivation in less than optimum conditions. The Oxpasture and Wickham 2 Associations are the principal examples of this. These associations include soils of the pelo-stagnogley Denchworth Series, and the argillic pelosols of the Holdenby Series, both of which are waterlogged for long periods in the winter, dry out slowly in the spring, and are very prone to structural damage (Hodge *et al.* 1984, 285–8, 351–4).

Some of the other clay soils found within the study area – most notably those of the Ashley Association – can suffer from compaction and puddling but Figure 46 shows only those which, to judge from modern soil survey data, would have presented the most serious difficulties to medieval farmers: that is, the principal pelo-stagnogleys (the Denchworth and Ragdale Associations); those pelosols suffering from serious problems of waterlogging (Evesham 1, 2 and 3 Associations); and associations dominated by non-pelo series, but which include significant proportions of pelo-stagnogley soils (the Oxpasture and Wickham 2 Associations), where these occur in areas with a long field capacity period (in excess of 125 days). Together, these represent the areas in which the problems of puddling and compaction would have been most severe and, conversely, where the timing of cultivations would have been most critical.

It will be immediately apparent that these areas are markedly concentrated towards the west, within the champion belt of the Midlands. Moreover, within this broad band of territory such difficult soils are generally less significant towards the east, in west Cambridgeshire, Bedfordshire and south Huntingdonshire: districts which, as we have seen, in some ways represented a distinct zone exhibiting both 'woodland' and 'champion' characteristics (above, pp. 74–9). The correlation is powerful and persuasive: but some readers may not be convinced. It is, as I have already intimated, difficult to evaluate the problems posed by different kinds of clay soil to medieval farmers on the basis of modern soil survey data. But some further light can be thrown on this matter by examining the ways in which medieval and post-medieval farmers actually farmed and exploited these difficult soils.

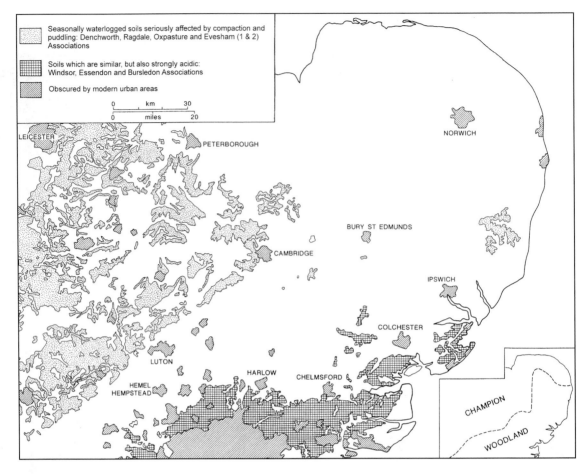

Ridge and furrow

Agricultural underdrains appear to have been an innovation of the post-medieval period and medieval farmers instead employed various forms of surface drainage (Hall 1999; Williamson 1999). In areas dominated by enclosures, the lateral flows in waterlogged soils were encouraged by the presence of deep perimeter ditches, usually associated with hedges: sometimes flows at surface level were aided by ploughing in impermanent ridges or 'stetches'. Where open fields were extensive, however, the land was cultivated in wide, permanent ridges, thus producing the distinctive form of earthwork generally known as 'ridge and furrow' or 'broad rig' (Figure 48). Even today some large areas of ridge and furrow survive in Midland districts, generally on pelo-stagnogley soils of the Denchworth or Ragdale Associations, especially along the border of Warwickshire and Northamptonshire, in southern Leicestershire and in north Buckinghamshire. But in the 1940s, when the RAF conducted an invaluable aerial survey of the country, vast areas of the Midland clays were carpeted with these earthworks (Harrison *et al.* 1965).

FIGURE 48.
Ridge and furrow at
Padbury in
Buckinghamshire.
Vast areas of 'broad
rig' survived in the
Midlands until the
second half of the
twentieth century.

The process of ridging is described by a number of early agricultural writers, such as Walter of Henley (Oschinsky 1971, 321), and has been discussed in detail by David Hall (Hall 1999). Medieval ploughs cut a single furrow and the mouldboard turned the soil towards the right. Each strip or 'land' was ploughed in a clockwise direction: the ploughman began in the middle, and then went round and round, in an outward spiral, until the perimeter of the land was reached. As a result, each ploughing served to move soil towards the middle of the strip, and over a period of several years this led to the build-up of a marked ridge (Hall 1999, 55). But if strips were ploughed in this way year after year very high, sharply sloping ridges would have been produced, bounded by deep, wide furrows cutting into the infertile subsoil. It was thus normal for strips to be 'ploughed out', in an anticlockwise direction, during the fallow season, in order to displace soil towards the edge. Although some early historians seem to have believed that ridging was simply a by-product of using a heavy plough with a fixed mouldboard, this was evidently not the case. By ploughing in a clockwise and anticlockwise direction in alternate years – that is, alternatively starting at the outside, and at the centre, of the strip – land could have been kept virtually or entirely level and indeed, in areas of light thin soil, as we have seen, ridging was generally avoided. On such land, even shallow ridging might expose the infertile subsoil, and was anyway unnecessary due to the freely draining character of the soil.

Bylaws and other records make it clear that manorial courts took very seriously the problems posed by poor drainage. Ridging of strips was the business of the individual farmer, but the water so displaced had to be conducted to natural watercourses, without simply causing flooding elsewhere. Where the free flow of water was impeded by the banks of soil which accumulated on the 'headlands' at the ends of furlongs, for example, outlets were regularly cut using a trenching spade or trenching plough. Nevertheless, after protracted rain the water often stood for long periods in the furrows. John Clare described the 'mire and sludgy' winter fields of his native Helpston in Northamptonshire, with the shepherds picking their way across the furlongs, and having 'oft to ford the sloughs that nearly meet/Across the lands' (Robinson and Powell 1984, 139).

I have described the ploughing and management of open field strips as it is usually presented in books on medieval agriculture or landscape history: and, in particular, I have concurred with the general assumption that each strip was ploughed individually. But there are grounds for doubting whether this was indeed the case, at least in the period in which open-field farming first developed. An eight-ox team and its plough would together have had a total length of at least 12 metres. This ensemble could not have been easily turned at the end of a narrow strip, in order to come down its opposite side. It is quite possible that groups of strips lying in the same furlong were ploughed at the same time, the plough travelling up the side of one strip but down the side of another, and so on, thus providing a much wider and more convenient turning circle on the headland. Indeed, it is particularly hard to see why, *if* tenants were sharing a plough and team, they would not prefer to plough in this manner. A team of oxen could plough at least an acre each day; in many Midland townships, strips with an area of a quarter or less than this were common. I have also assumed that ridging was entirely carried out to aid drainage. But again, there are reasons for doubting whether this was the case. Ridging increased the area of ploughsoil exposed to the wind and frost, albeit to a limited extent, and so may also have been intended to encourage flocculation. Either way, ridging continued to be normal practice in Midland townships well into the post-medieval period, largely because it was hard to adopt new forms of underdrainage in a landscape of intermingled strips. Even villages enclosed and put down to grass in the later eighteenth century are (or were until recently) usually carpeted with ridge and furrow (Williamson 2002, 54).

The distribution of ridge and furrow, as recorded on aerial photographs taken in the middle decades of the twentieth century, was heavily biased towards the west of the region studied here and closely mirrors that of the 'difficult' clay soils already defined and discussed (Figure 49). Evidence for ridging is rare in the long-enclosed countrysides of Essex, Hertfordshire, and south Buckinghamshire, and also in East Anglia. It fades in intensity somewhat before the edge of the 'champion' belt is reached: although there is a fair scatter of ridge and furrow in Bedfordshire, Huntingdonshire and western Cambridgeshire, its density here is noticeably less than in Leicestershire, Northamptonshire, and north Buckinghamshire. The latter counties were, and indeed still are, the real home of ridge and furrow.

FIGURE 49.
The distribution of ridge and furrow in the study area in 1946 (source: Harrison *et al.* 1965; RCHME 1984; Liddiard 2000; the Suffolk, Essex, Hertfordshire and Leicestershire Sites and Monuments Records).

This westerly distribution is susceptible to two distinct explanations, both of which have an important bearing on the issue under discussion here. Most historians and archaeologists have assumed that it reflects, in broad terms, the areas of medieval and post-medieval England in which the technique of ridging was most widely adopted; and conversely, that areas from which ridge and furrow is absent represent those in which other modes of land drainage were adopted, or in which soils were comparatively freely draining and ridging

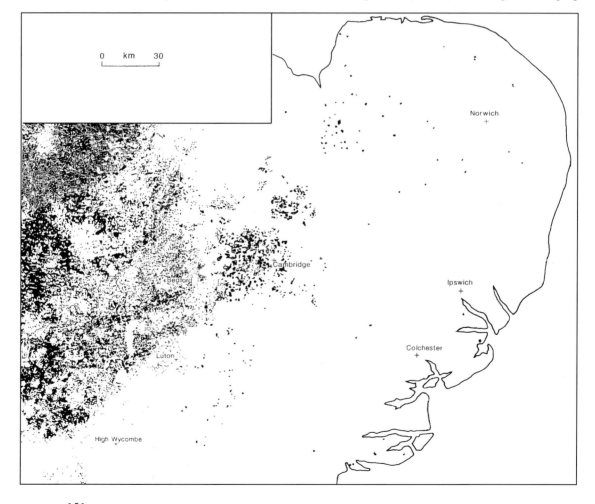

therefore unnecessary. This is not an unreasonable contention. Ridge and furrow is extremely rare on light chalk or sandy soils. And on heavier soils its distribution does broadly correlate with that of open-field arable, as opposed to districts in which the arable lay largely or entirely in enclosed fields. But only very broadly, for open fields were widespread on the heavier soils of northern East Anglia but very little ridge and furrow has been recorded from this district, implying that ridging was here unnecessary. Taken at face value, the distribution of ridge and furrow might thus be taken as a confirmation of the modern soil survey data, suggesting that the clay soils in the west of the region were, in general, more difficult to cultivate, and more in need of ridging, than those in the east (compare Figures 47 and 49).

However, the distribution of ridge and furrow has recently been re-examined in an important article by the landscape historian Robert Liddiard (Liddiard 1999). After close examination of the Norfolk evidence, he concluded that the twentieth-century distribution of ridge and furrow was, in large measure, a consequence of post-medieval developments. For a comparatively short period in the sixteenth and seventeenth centuries large areas of clay soil in East Anglia were laid to pasture and used for grazing cattle: a form of agricultural specialisation easily adopted here, as a more sophisticated and regionally specialised farming economy emerged in the post-medieval period, because much common grazing land and land held in severalty existed, while the irregular character of the local open fields ensured that they could be enclosed with relative ease. From the eighteenth century, however, the East Anglian claylands became a more and more intensively *arable* region (see Figure 12, above, p. 36). Ridge and furrow, formerly preserved in fields of permanent pasture, was thus steadily erased. Indeed, by the late nineteenth century the extent of arable land use was so great in Norfolk and Suffolk that there were precious few places where ridge and furrow (or indeed, any other kind of medieval or earlier earthwork) *could* have survived. The few exceptions, where pasture was maintained right up to the twentieth century, are precisely those places where islands of ridge and furrow are recorded on early aerial photographs (Liddiard 1999).

Liddiard's argument is an elegant one – this brief summary hardly does it justice – but it can, perhaps, be criticised on a number of grounds. In particular, it is hard to believe that eighteenth- and nineteenth-century arable land use was on such a scale that ridge and furrow would have been so completely eradicated from eastern regions, and its virtual or total absence from particular terrains and locations is difficult to explain in these terms. In particular, we might legitimately expect to find more evidence for ridging in some of the numerous landscape parks, such as Ickworth in Suffolk or Melton Constable in Norfolk, laid to grass in the seventeenth or early eighteenth centuries and not subsequently ploughed; or beneath areas of woodland, for ridge and furrow is a moderately common discovery within ancient, but secondary, woodland in areas like west Cambridgeshire. In all probability, the truth lies some-where between the 'traditional' explanation, and Liddiard revisionism. Ridging probably was never as ubiquitous on the East Anglian clays as in the Midlands, partly because the area under open-field cultivation was less, partly because environmental factors made ridging less necessary. But in addition, subsequent patterns of land use have served to remove, wholesale, this form of earthwork from Norfolk and Suffolk, thus increasing the dichotomy between the east and the west of the region studied here.

Looked at in this way, the distribution of ridge and furrow has a rather different, and arguably more important, relevance to the present discussion. This form of earthwork was created when arable open fields, ploughed in ridges, were enclosed and put down to grass; and it only survived for as long as the land in question remained under grass. In other words, the distribution of ridge and furrow tells us as much about the history of regional farming in late medieval and post-medieval times as it does about the management of open arable in the early middle ages. It shows us, very vividly, that the single most important development in the west of the region studied here in the period after *c*. 1400 was the steady expansion of the area under pasture. Large areas of the East Anglian clays, as I have noted, were under grass in the sixteenth and seventeenth century. But the shift to pasture in Midland counties, although it began more slowly, continued later, was more complete, and was not significantly reversed until the twentieth century (Williamson 2002, 56).

The contraction of tillage on the Midland clays began in the fourteenth century, with the drastic demographic decline following the Black Death. Small villages, often in upland 'wold' locations, were depopulated by manorial lords, often following a period of voluntary desertion, and their land was laid to grass (Fox 1989, 96–100). Depopulating enclosures of this kind came to an end in the early sixteenth century, but enclosure *per se* – now usually achieved through the agreement of the principal proprietors in a village – continued right through the sixteenth and into the seventeenth century, in spite of demographic recovery and a consequent rise in grain prices. Almost always, enclosure was directly associated with the expansion of pasture – a point seldom lost on contemporaries (Allen 1992, 32). Where landowners wanted to create farms suitable for grazing sheep or cattle in these champion landscapes, they had to enclose. It was impossible to run large-scale livestock enterprises in a landscape of scattered, unhedged strips. And while complete abandonment of villages was now rare, many continued to contract in size and population (Reed 1983, 142).

Enclosure for pasture continued through the late seventeenth and early eighteenth centuries. Thus the Verney family enclosed Middle Claydon in Buckinghamshire in 1654–56, and East Claydon ninety years later: in both cases, the entire parish was laid to grass (Broad 1980, 83). By this time landowners were, once again, responding to obvious economic incentives. Cereal prices were relatively low in this period because population growth was again sluggish. But what is striking and superficially surprising is that even in the second half of the eighteenth century, as demographic growth resumed and grain prices rose steadily, the expansion of pasture on the Midland clays proceeded apace. In particular, the conversion of arable to pasture in North-amptonshire, Leicestershire, and north Buckinghamshire was the almost invariable consequence of parliamentary enclosure, which peaked in this district in the 1770s and 80s. The vicars and rectors who replied to the government enquiry of 1801 – the 'Crop Returns' – were in no doubt about the nature of the changes in the landscape around them. The vicar of Breedon on the Hill in Leicestershire remarked how:

> Within the last 30 years almost all the country north-west of Leicester to the extremity of the county has been enclosed: by which means the land is become in a higher state of cultivation than formerly; but on account of a great proportion of it being converted into pasturage much less food is produced than when it was more generally in tillage (Turner 1982, II, 53).

In Kegworth in the same county only 580 acres were said to be under cultivation, around a quarter of the parish, and the vicar noted how this was 'considerably diminished since the Inclosure which took place about twenty-two years ago' (Hoskins 1949, 131). At Twyell in Northamptonshire the vicar noted that 'less corn is grown since the enclosure ... the land being laid down in grass' (Turner 1982, II, 151). Almost the entire area of Clipston parish – some 2,000 acres – was now 'good grazing land', but 'before the enclosure most of the field was ploughed' (*ibid*, 142). To judge from this same source, by the start of the nineteenth century a mere 22.3 per cent of Northamptonshire (excluding fallow) was devoted to arable crops (Turner 1981, 294); 'the great breadth of upland, laid down, in ancient and modern times, to permanent grass' (Pitt 1813b, 113). In Leicester, only 16 per cent of the total land area was arable in 1801, and in Buckinghamshire north of the Chiltern scarp, around 20 per cent. The Vale of Aylesbury in the latter county was described in 1851 as being

> celebrated for the excellence of its pastures, for which it is better adapted by nature than for tillage. In three parishes which we visited, the proportion of tillage to pasture was very small, there being in the first only 8 acres in 2000 under the plough; in the second 90 acres in 900; and in the third no tillage whatsoever (Caird 1852, 1).

The great swathes of ridge and furrow which survived in the Midlands into the twentieth century were thus a graphic, physical testimony to a profound change in the agrarian economy of this extensive region in the period between the fifteenth and early nineteenth century. Interestingly, the only area left out of this steady drift to grass – the only part of the Midlands which maintained a largely arable economy – was that area towards the eastern edges of the conventional 'champion' belt, embracing much of Cambridgeshire and Bedfordshire (Allen 1992, 32–3), in which medieval settlement and field systems diverged markedly from Midland 'norm', and displayed many characteristically 'woodland' features.

The slow but steady drift of the Midland clays into pasture has important implications for our understanding of the agricultural character of these districts in much earlier periods: we can learn much about the genesis of these champion landscapes, that is, by examining the reasons for their decline. A number of scholars, as we have seen, have suggested that open-field landscapes reached their most developed form in the Midlands because this was the prime arable area of Roman and early Saxon England (Roberts and Wrathmell 2000a). Yet this area's suitability for cereal production was much less evident to late medieval and post-medieval farmers and landowners, whose universal opinion appears to have been that it was better laid to grass. It was the clay soils of the 'woodland' districts, lying further to the east – in Norfolk and Suffolk, north Essex and east Hertfordshire – that, as an integrated national economy developed, became the prime wheat-growing areas of England.

Windows of opportunity: co-aration revisited

Post-medieval sources make it clear that one of the main reasons why arable gradually contracted on the Midland clays was that ploughing costs were significantly higher here than on the eastern clays (Chambers and Mingay 1966, 65). This was not because the soils were in general terms more prone to waterlogging, or were waterlogged for a longer period of time – although to some extent they were. It was mainly because of the dominance here of land on which cultivations had to be timed with particular care, to avoid damage to the soil structure. This necessitated the maintenance of a greater number of plough teams, idle for much of the year. This simple observation has an obvious relevance when we come to examine the development of the Midland landscape in a much earlier period. To Homans, and to a number of more recent writers, there was no obvious connection between the nucleation of settlement and the intermixture of properties on the one hand, and the sharing of ploughs and teams on the other (Homans 1941, 81; Dodgshon 1980, 31–3). Ploughs could be shared by neighbours living in scattered farms as much as by those in nucleated settlements. But the recognition that classic 'champion' clayland landscapes were closely correlated with areas in which relatively few days were available for cultivating the land, especially in spring, throws a shaft of new light on this old problem. Where cultivations needed to be carefully timed, and where full advantage had to be taken of every hour in which the soils were suitable for ploughing or harrowing, ploughteams needed to be assembled with particular rapidity; and this was obviously much easier to achieve where farms were in close proximity, rather than scattered across the landscape. In areas of dispersed settlement it might take an hour or more of vital time to send a message to a neighbouring farm, and for the farmer to arrive with his plough beasts. Co-aration on certain kinds of clay soil was thus more likely to encourage settlement nucleation than on others.

If a short 'window of opportunity' thus encouraged farmers to dwell together in compact villages, it might well have had additional effects. Where the time available for cultivation was limited it was a matter of some importance whether land was located near to, or far from, the farms clustered in a village. Moreover, variations in slope, aspect, and in the mineralogical qualities of the soil itself ensured that some parts of the land might be available for cultivation for a longer period of time than others. When, in early times, bond tenants were being allotted land according to some equitable scheme then intermixed properties, widely and evenly scattered, would be an obvious choice. And where farms were being divided by inheritance there would be an understandable desire to divide the property within each field, rather than *by* field, again leading in time to the development of scattered and intermixed holdings. Such 'organic' layouts might themselves be recast in more regular form at a later date, perhaps following a period in which assarting had added further areas of subdivided arable. Vinogradoff and other early writers, as we have seen, viewed the intermixture of holdings in open fields as a manifestation of some primitive concept of 'shareholding', a partial survival from some archaic, tribal period when the land had been viewed as the common property of the inhabitants of the vill. But it is possible that the shares represented by virgates, bovates and the rest originated as shares in *ploughteams*, and the intermixture of properties reflected the fact that each shareholder expected to benefit as much from the joint team as his neighbours. In *certain environmental circumstances*, in other words, it is easy to see how co-aration could have encouraged a nucleated pattern of settlement, the development of extensive areas of intermixed arable, and the eventual re-working of these into more ordered and regular layouts. It is noteworthy in this context that where the demesne land was not scattered and intermingled with the holdings of the tenants, but was instead concentrated in a single block, this always lay close to the village, often occupying the majority of the most easily accessible land.

Because settlement nucleation and open field genesis occurred well before the advent of abundant written records this suggested pattern of development is, once again, only a model, based on an interpretation of the archaeological record, coupled with a consideration of the particular characteristics of the clay soils found in the 'core' areas of the champion Midlands. But in the areas further to the east – in the more varied and complex landscape of west Cambridgeshire, and upland Bedfordshire – it is apparent that some 'regular' field systems only came into existence in post-Conquest times through the remodelling of earlier, more irregular layouts. One important case – that of Dry Drayton in Cambridgeshire – lends some support to these arguments. As described in an earlier chapter, the fields of the vill were reorganised around 1150, by the agreement of its five manorial lords. The stated reason was that the land, or parts of it, had been 'for long uncultivated' on account of being 'dispersed in certain minute parts'. As the result of the reorganisation, the village acquired a regular three-field system. Harold Fox, who discussed this important document in some detail, suggested that there must have been a 'fundamental flaw' in the previous arrangements, although he was unclear about its precise character. The most likely explanation, he suggested, was that there was 'a lack of adequate arrangements for grazing in order to keep the land in good heart: strips may be cultivated if they are inconveniently located but not if they are inadequately manured' (Fox 1981, 95). But shortage of nutrients was seldom a major obstacle on the rich Evesham Association soils, and livestock were hardly in short supply in this vill, to judge from the fact that the extensive commons were stocked with over 600 sheep in 1285. Indeed, between 1258 and 1315 3,600 sheep were being grazed in the parish, clearly suggesting that by this time, at least, pasturage was more than adequate (Taylor 1973, 112). A more likely explanation is that, as a consequence of the expansion of cultivation and an active land market, some farmers were cultivating a disproportionate proportion of land lying remote from the village, inconvenient and in some years impossible to cultivate. A redistribution of lands was necessary, in order to provide a reasonable share of far and distant land for those contributing to the common ploughs.

The clustering of farms in nucleated villages was thus intended to allow rapid assembly of plough teams, in order to take full advantage of the narrow windows of opportunity available to cultivate these heavy soils. But it may also have ensured a more efficient use of teams generally, so that fewer had to be maintained, as Nick Higham has suggested (Higham 1990). Certainly, the density of plough teams at the time of Domesday was generally lower in the Midland counties than it was in, say, East Anglia, a region in which rather less land was in tilth. Of course, not everywhere in the Midlands was characterised by heavy, intractable clay soils, prone to puddling and compaction. In the valleys of the major rivers, in particular, lighter soils, derived from sandstone or limestone, were often extensive. Nevertheless, most vills in the Midlands contained a significant proportion of such soils, and these were steadily brought under cultivation in the course of the early medieval period.

Conclusion

The argument that the development of champion landscapes in the Midlands was connected with the practice of joint ploughing on particular kinds of clay soil, those on which the opportunities for cultivation were limited, has a great deal to recommend it. In particular, it helps to explain why strongly nucleated villages, and field systems featuring a wide and even dispersal of holdings, became progressively less important features of the medieval landscape moving from west to east. Climatic conditions – not only lower rainfall and higher transpiration rates, but also, perhaps, the incidence of sharp, late frosts, together with the mineralogical properties of the relevant soils, ensured that towards the east the land could be cultivated over a more extended period of time, reducing the need for ploughs to be rapidly assembled. Not only might this help explain the differences between the medieval clayland landscapes of the Midlands on the one hand, and of East Anglia, Essex and Hertfordshire on the other. It also helps explain the contrast *within* the champion belt, between the highly nucleated settlement patterns of north Buckinghamshire, Northamptonshire and Leicestershire, and the more variable arrangements encountered in much of Bedfordshire and Cambridgeshire. Nevertheless, it is evident that the theory, as stated rather simply and baldly above, has a number of problems.

The first is that some historians doubt whether farmers in early medieval England really ploughed with teams of eight oxen. Late Saxon and early post-Conquest illustrations always show much smaller teams – usually of two or four animals – and while this might be artistic convention it has been argued that large teams were really only a feature of demesne agriculture, and that peasants often made do with smaller ones (Richardson 1942, 288–9). Domesday certainly makes it clear that smaller teams were in use. In Kirby Bedon in Norfolk, for example, 'there are two sokemen and a half with twelve acres. Then as now they plough with three oxen' (Langdon 1986, 32). References in many twelfth-century extents can also be interpreted in this way. Thus the *Kalendar* of Abbot Sampson records how Galant Blunt and his heirs, holding some twenty to thirty acres from St Edmunds Abbey, owed ploughing services 'with as many animals of his as he will have in his plough' (Davis 1954, 130). Langdon, in his discussion of the problem, concluded that 'the evidence seems to imply that the peasant very often managed to get away with ploughing with much smaller teams than the eight-animal standard' (Langdon 1986, 72), in part because they had a relatively small area of land under cultivation. Against this, however, it can be argued that while some peasants all of the time, and all peasants some of the time, made do with smaller teams, at certain times of the year, and in certain environments, they would be forced to use large ones. In particular, small teams could only be employed where soils were light and/or where the oxen could be worked at a leisurely pace, in small bursts. On the difficult clay soils of the Midlands, needless to say – especially for spring ploughing – neither of these conditions applied. The short window of opportunity and tenacious soils demanded rapid ploughing with a large team. In short, eight-ox teams probably were the norm, on peasant as on demesne farms, at least for spring ploughings on the heavy soils with which we are here concerned.

A second and more serious objection is that the available evidence suggests that villein farmers, in late Saxon times at least, owned on average around three oxen (the actual figure is 2.9: Lennard 1946, 256). There is, therefore, no obvious reason why joint ploughing should have led to the development of anything more than small hamlets, each comprising perhaps three or four farms, rather than large villages containing ten or more households. True, some allowance would need to be made for animals falling lame or being otherwise incapacitated – especially, once again, at time of spring sowing, following the cold and lean winter months. But even so, it is hard to see why such large nucleations should result from this cause. This is an important point, and one to which I shall return in the final chapter.

But a yet more serious objection, perhaps, is that while the clay soils of the Midlands were, and are, more tenacious than those in East Anglia, Essex or Hertfordshire, the difference does not appear so great that it should have produced quite such divergent patterns of landscape development. The Beccles

158

Association soils which cover much of East Anglia are, in particular, workable over only a slightly longer period in the spring months than the various pelosols and pelo-stagnogleys found in the Midlands. Moreover, large areas of the 'champion' Midlands are characterised by clay soils – most notably those of the Hanslope Association – no different from those found in 'woodland' districts of north Essex or east Hertfordshire. In addition, variations in the character of clay soils would not appear to offer any obvious explanation for the differences in landscape which we have discussed *within* the 'woodland' zone – between, in particular, the clayland countrysides of northern East Anglia, with their sprawling common-edge settlements, and the rather different versions of 'ancient countryside' found on the boulder clay soils to the south and west of the Gipping corridor. Above all, while the demands of co-aration on the difficult Midland soils might go a long way towards explaining the divergent development of settlement patterns and field systems in 'champion' and 'woodland' areas, it cannot so easily explain that other key difference between them – the way in which Midland farmers had, by the thirteenth century, generally extended their arable almost to the limits of their land, whereas in 'woodland' districts large areas of woodland and pasture generally survived. Co-aration, mediated by particular environmental influences, is a vital part of our story. But the divergent development of the various clayland landscapes under discussion here was evidently the consequence of additional factors.

CHAPTER SEVEN

Meadow and Green

....

Greens and commons

Historians, geographers and others have paid considerable attention to the organisation and management of arable land in medieval England: to the origins of, and variations in, field systems. Much research has also focused on private managed woodland. But the exploitation and management of pasture and other forms of grazing have in comparison been rather neglected, in spite of the fact that these were crucial to the sustenance of the flocks and herds upon which the maintenance of the arable depended – and in particular of the teams of oxen which provided the traction for the plough. One notable manifestation of the importance of grazing in the landscape is the ubiquity, in woodland districts, of settlements clustered around the margins of greens and commons.

Some historians and archaeologists have suggested that greens originated as clearings in forested country, spaces within which livestock could be safely corralled against predators, human or natural. As Hoskins and Stamp put it:

> The commons and small greens of Essex and Kent ... pretty certainly originated as clearings in densely wooded country, either as natural glades in an old forest or as deliberately cleared ground. In such circumstances the natural thing to do was to build the houses of the new settlement round the edges of the small clearing rather than at random all over it (Hoskins and Stamp 1963, 32).

Other authorities – more plausibly – have seen the larger commons, in particular, simply as the last areas of 'waste' to which settlement gravitated in the final stages of colonisation. The dominance of green-edge settlement in East Anglia, and the vast numbers and large size of commons there, would thus reflect the social and economic idiosyncrasies of that region: the dense population, complex manorial structure, and high proportion of free tenures, which encouraged more individualistic solutions to the problems posed by dwindling reserves of pasture which also brought about settlement nucleation and the emergence of 'regular' open field in the Midlands. Because tenurial complexity precluded the possibility of reorganising arable land in order to maximise grazing on fallows or the harvest aftermath, that is, farms simply migrated to the margins of the remaining areas of grazing, in part because of the convenience of exploitation which this afforded, in part simply to stake a claim. I have myself suggested something like this in the past (Williamson 1993, 167–71). But closer inspection suggests a more complex explanation.

In order to understand the real significance of this important form of settlement we need first to reiterate some essential points about its chronology and distribution. Hamlets grouped around greens and commons are quint-essentially a feature of ancient countryside areas but were also found in places within the Midlands, especially in that distinctive area of Bedfordshire which we have already noted for its combination of 'woodland' and 'champion' characteristics. Within ancient countryside districts common-edge settlements are most numerous on the boulder clay plateau extending from east Hertford-shire through to Norfolk (above, p. 93). In the northern section of this broad topographic zone – in south Norfolk and north Suffolk – greens and commons tend to be large and, by the twelfth century, had usually attracted to their margins the majority of settlement in a parish. Further south, in contrast, greens and 'tyes' were usually smaller in size, were settled at a later date, and formed only one element in the matrix of dispersion. What is particularly intriguing, however, is that in northern East Anglia common-edge settlements were not confined to the boulder clays but were a prominent feature of other soil regions – of the fertile loams of north-east Norfolk, even to some extent of the light acid lands of Breckland. Here, however, the commons around which farms congregated were largely, or entirely, restricted to the flood plains of rivers and major streams.

Elsewhere in ancient countryside areas – in the Chilterns, and on the London clays, both regions which were quite sparsely populated in late Saxon times – settlements clustered around greens and commons were a less prominent feature of the medieval landscape (Hunter 1999, 99; Williamson 2000a, 189). Large commons were found where extensive spreads of acid sands and gravels occurred, as in the area around Colchester, but while their margins attracted a scatter of farms and cottages they seldom became the primary focus of settlement in a vill.

Two initial observations can be made on the basis of this evidence. The first is that the northern parts of East Anglia are distinguished from all other districts not only by the central importance of commons and common-edge settlement, but also by their ubiquity. The second is that in all districts, the majority of common-edge settlements are associated with areas of damp soils, such as those found in wet depressions in clay plateaux. Yet at the same time, they were not found in *all* such locations, being absent from most valley floors outside northern East Anglia.

It will be apparent that these features are, for the most part, difficult to square with any simple interpretation of commons as residual areas of 'waste' which came to act as magnets for settlement when reserves of grazing began to dwindle. Such an explanation works, to an extent, on the high clay interfluves of northern East Anglia, where some of the greens and commons have names suggesting woodland origins: Diss Heywood in the Norfolk parish of Diss, for example, or Allwood Green near Mellis in Suffolk. In Suffolk, moreover, the distribution of the largest woods recorded in Domesday book appears to coincide with those areas in which, later in the middle ages, the most extensive commons could be found – that is, the particularly level areas of plateau to the north of Halesworth (Rackham 1988) (although such a correlation is rather less marked in Norfolk). Edward Martin has discussed how the monks of Bury Abbey, given the choice of three different estates by a late Saxon benefactor, chose Chippenhall in Fressingfield because 'it abounded in woods' (Hervey 1925, II, 291).

> In 1066 there was wood for 160 swine at Chippenhall, which had been reduced to 100 by 1086. By the 18th century there was virtually no woodland at Chippenhall, but there was, and still is, a fine green, with the partial ghost of another green close by (Martin 2001, 6).

But any interpretation of clayland greens and commons as the last fragments of 'waste' hardly explains the numerous 'low' commons found in Norfolk and northern Suffolk, running in ribbon-fashion along the floodplains of water-courses, coinciding with extensive deposits of poorly draining peat. Moreover, fieldwalking surveys and documentary research in these districts suggest that while commons on the clay interfluves were indeed beyond the boundaries of the main areas of Saxon arable, they were by no means the only remaining unploughed areas at the time that settlement was attracted to their margins. Rather, analysis of field names, documentary references to woodland, and the distribution of stray sherds of late Saxon and early medieval pottery recovered at places like Fransham or Hales suggests that they originally lay within more extensive uncultivated zones, accompanied by other areas of woodland and grazing (Rogerson 1995). An interpretation of clayland commons simply as residual 'waste' is still more implausible in the case of the smaller greens and tyes characteristic of south Suffolk, north Essex and east Hertfordshire. Most are found on pockets of damp ground, often close to the sources of water-courses. But this cannot be because such areas represented the last vestiges of unploughed, or unploughable, ground, for many of these districts could also boast extensive areas of enclosed manorial woodland and deer parks. These generally occupied rather different locations in the landscape (woodland in particular often clustering at the margins of clay plateaux, perhaps to limit the distance which wood and timber needed to be hauled down rutted clay roads (Witney 1990)) but the three forms of land use could be found in close proximity, as for example in the south of Writtle in Essex, where a number of woods, parks and greens, interdigitated in complex ways, together occupied a single block of land in the far south of the parish (Hunter 1999, 103). All this indicates, clearly enough, that greens, tyes and other damp commons were specifically set aside to provide grazing and other resources, their boundaries consciously decided, either by the unilateral decision of a manorial lord, or by negotiation between lord and principal tenants, or perhaps – in northern East Anglia especially – by agreement between groups of free men. In this context, it is noteworthy that the term frequently used for a small common, surrounded by farms, in Essex and East Anglia – 'tye' – comes from the Old English *Teag*, 'a close, a small enclosure' (Smith 1956), suggesting land intentionally fenced off and set apart from the surrounding land, be that waste, woodland, or arable.

Meadow and pasture

It is impossible to consider the functions or significance of these damp commons without a brief examination of the character of medieval grazing resources more generally. Even in early Saxon times many areas of grazing had been largely or entirely cleared of trees – the heaths and chalk downlands, deforested in remote prehistory. But well into the late Saxon period much, perhaps most, comprised wood-pastures of the type recorded by Domesday, the use, destruction, and conversion of which – to open commons, managed woods, or parks – I have discussed in chapter 2. The most important point made there can usefully be repeated here. Domesday suggests that, on the whole, wood-pastures survived better in areas of 'ancient countryside' than in champion districts; and it was in the former that, by the thirteenth century, managed woods, commons and parks were most numerous and extensive. The precise character of non-arable land use might change over time, in other words, but its distribution in relation to champion and non-champion areas remained much the same. Yet although arable was generally more extensive in champion than in woodland clayland areas, these nevertheless carried only average, and in many cases less than average, population densities.

Pastures were areas directly grazed by livestock. Meadows, in contrast, were principally mown, for hay. In practice the distinction between the two was never entirely clear-cut for meadows were invariably grazed for some of the year, usually after the hay had been cut in mid summer, and in early medieval times it may well have been more blurred. In Bruce Campbell's words, 'Meadow and pasture existed on a continuum and in practice the distinction between them is unlikely to have been as consistently drawn as the precise terminology of the documents might imply' (Campbell 2000, 78). Nevertheless, in many districts the difference is very apparent in the high value of meadow land, compared with all other forms of land use (Rackham 1986, 337; Fox 1984, 122). Acre for acre meadow might be worth two, three or even more times as much as arable. At Sherington in north Buckinghamshire, for example, the demesne meadows were leased in 1312 for six times the amount charged for the arable (Chibnall 1965, 113). Some meadows were held in severalty, usually as part of the manorial demesne, but common meadows for the use of tenants were frequent in many districts. Sometimes tenants held strips, permanently attached to their holdings, analogous to the arable lands in open fields; alternatively the strips might be re-allocated each year, through the drawing of lots or some similar procedure (Rackham 1986, 337).

Most medieval meadows, and certainly all the larger areas, were found on the floodplains of rivers and streams. There was a simple reason for this. Grass growth is most rapid between mid-May and mid-June, when the hay was cut. But in central and eastern England, in particular, the size of the crop could be adversely affected by periods of low rainfall. Any deficiency in precipitation could, however, 'be offset by higher water tables which provide a continuously moist root range' (Robinson 1949, 256). Damp valley floors thus offered ideal conditions for hay production.

Text books often describe meadow as 'essential' to medieval farmers and meadowland is invariably listed as a standard feature of the 'typical' medieval village: hay meadows were 'almost as vital to the community as the arable' (Bennet 1937, 43). In Kerridge's words, they were 'the eyes of the land, like waterholes in the bush and artesian wells in the outback. No farmstead, no village could be built unless hard by them' (Kerridge 1973, 22–3). Hay, we are told, was essential to feed the livestock through the winter, and especially in the period from January to late March, when grass grows little, if at all. During the last century grass grew for an average of 250 days a year and while, in the comparatively warm conditions pertaining between *c.* 800 and 1300, this period may have been extended for another thirty days or so, pastures alone would be insufficient to sustain draft oxen, in particular, during the late winter, in the run-up to the vital spring ploughings (Spedding and Diekmahns 1972, 19).

Meadows have been known in England since late prehistoric times, and are mentioned in the famous law of Ine, already referred to, in terms reminiscent of later practice: 'If ceorls have a common meadow ... divided in shares ...' (Whitelock 1955, 368). They frequently appear in Anglo-Saxon charters, from all areas of England (Rackham 1986, 33). Nevertheless, the evidence suggests that the adoption of hay meadows on a large scale was gradual, and it is possible that – in early Saxon times, when population levels were low and grazing extensive – they were a relatively rare feature of the landscape. Increasing population in the course of the middle Saxon period, and the need to maintain larger numbers of draft oxen as larger ploughs came into widespread use, may well have encouraged the more intensive management of wet grassland – just as it encouraged, in some districts, the congregation of farms close to this resource. At Yarnton, on the Thames gravels outside Oxford, just outside the area studied here, the low-lying flood plain had been used as pasture in early Saxon times: but from the eighth or ninth centuries areas were enclosed with ditches and hedges, and managed as hay meadow (Hey 2001, 224). Nevertheless, for a long time meadows remained in limited supply, and many Anglo-Saxon communities survived well enough without them. As Rackham has pointed out, Domesday suggests that only around 1.2 per cent of the total land area of England consisted of meadowland at the end of the eleventh century. 'England in 1086 had at least as much arable land as in 1500, but much less meadow. Meadow had spread to every part of the country, but countless places only had an acre or two and many ... managed without it' (Rackham 1986, 334–5). Rackham's precise figures need to be treated with a measure of caution, not least because Domesday is demonstrably uneven in

FIGURE 50.
Wood-pasture at
Staverton Park, a
former medieval deer
park near Wantisden
in Suffolk.

its coverage of this resource, but it is hard to argue with his general point, that 'the practice of meadow was slow in being adopted' in early medieval England.

In part this was simply because, while reserves of wood-pasture remained extensive, there was less need for winter fodder, because the wide range of herbs and shrubs found in these environments would have provided a longer grazing season than the herbs and grasses of open pastures, which generally offer little winter sustenance. Cattle, sheep and goats will browse off dry autumn foliage, even bare twigs, and they will eat the various undershrubs, like brambles, which remain green well into the winter; sheep in particular will avidly consume evergreens like ivy and mistletoe and cattle will eat holly with enthusiasm (Figure 50). Hay meadows are labour-intensive and their management 'implies a pastoral economy where the number of animals exceeds winter pasture' (Biddick 1989, 19–21). Where 'wastes' remained extensive, in other words, there was less incentive to cut, dry and store hay. Moreover, the leaves of certain trees – including oak, ash, elm and holly – can themselves be stored as 'leafy hay', and although not well documented in southern England in medieval times this practice was ancient, occurred widely across Europe, and was maintained in some parts of England into the nineteenth century (Grieg 1988; Halstead 1988; Muir 2000, 96; Fleming 1998b, 85). Indeed, some trees were probably managed primarily with fodder in mind. Instead of being pollarded, they were *shred*: that is, the side branches were removed, in order to stimulate lateral epicormic growth. Trees like fuzzy toilet brushes can still be seen in parts of western France.

To some extent the existence of extensive wood-pastures would thus have discouraged the practice of managing flood plain land as hay meadow. But in addition, the slow development of meadows reflects the fact that their creation was not always just a matter of management: of removing animals from the areas in question in the spring, in order to allow the hay crop to grow and mature. It also, in many contexts, involved a positive act of investment and creation, for much river-valley land was too wet and water-logged in its native state to provide the right conditions for growing good-quality grass, but instead produced only coarse herbage, dominated by sedge and rushes, unpalatable to livestock and of low nutritional value. In such circumstances, the land in question needed to be drained, by cutting ditches through and round. In places, it had to be embanked against too frequent flooding from the main watercourse (Kerridge 1973, 23). It was thus only gradually, in the course of the twelfth and thirteenth centuries, that the area of meadow land was gradually extended, so that by *c.* 1250 it occupied around four per cent of the land area of England (Rackham 1986, 337).

The distribution of meadows

Yet meadows remained unevenly distributed. To judge from Bruce Campbell's exhaustive analysis of *Inquisitions Post Mortem*, even in the early fourteenth century they remained in short supply in many districts 'in the east and west of England'. By contrast, they were relatively abundant on the Midland Plain:

> From Somerset and east Devon in the south-west to the Vale of Pickering in Yorkshire's north Riding in the north-east, it was in the clay vales of this broad diagonal band of country that meadowland was most con-sistently represented. Except on the wolds, few demesnes were without at least some meadow ...' (Campbell 2000, 75–6).

There were exceptions to this broad pattern. The Lea valley in Hertfordshire and Essex, for example – well outside the Midland Plain – had substantial areas of meadow land. But for the most part comparatively small amounts are recorded on demesnes in the IPMs outside the Midland belt, and in East Anglia in particular many demesnes had tiny quantities, or none at all (Figure 51).

Domesday seems to show a similar picture, although in detail it is evidently distorted by inconsistent recording. As Figure 52 shows, the survey notes the existence of meadow in a variety of ways, depending on the 'circuit' – that

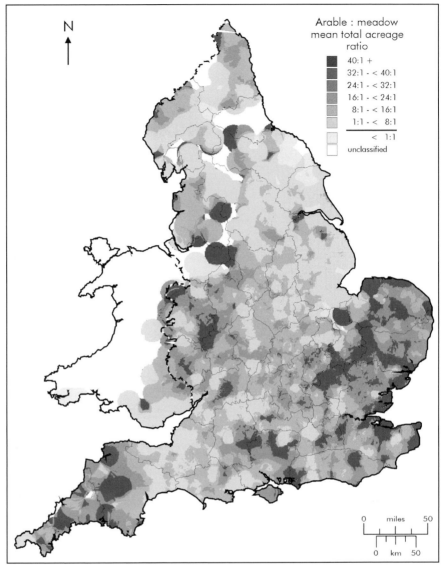

Arable : meadow
mean total acreage
ratio

- 40:1 +
- 32:1 - < 40:1
- 24:1 - < 32:1
- 16:1 - < 24:1
- 8:1 - < 16:1
- 1:1 - < 8:1
- < 1:1
- unclassified

FIGURE 51.
The ratio of arable
acreage to meadow
acreage in England
1300–49 (after
Campbell 2000).
Meadow was generally
much more abundant
in the champion
Midlands than in
areas to the south east
and west (compare
with Figure 5, p.4).

is, the group of counties overseen by a particular group of officials (Darby 1977, 5–9). The circuit which apparently included Bedfordshire, Buckingham-shire, Hertfordshire and Middlesex thus recorded meadow in terms of the numbers of plough oxen that could be supported, using the phrase *pratum x carucis* or similar. In parts of Cambridgeshire, meadow was often recorded in the same way but sometimes in terms of its acreage. Recording in acres was also the usual practice in Little Domesday, the volume of the survey embracing Norfolk, Suffolk and Essex; and in the circuit embracing the north and west of the area studied here – that is, the counties of Northamptonshire, Leicester-shire, and Oxfordshire. But there are good grounds for believing that in this case meadow land was recorded less diligently by the officials responsible, possibly because it was an abundant resource. Certainly, there is a very marked

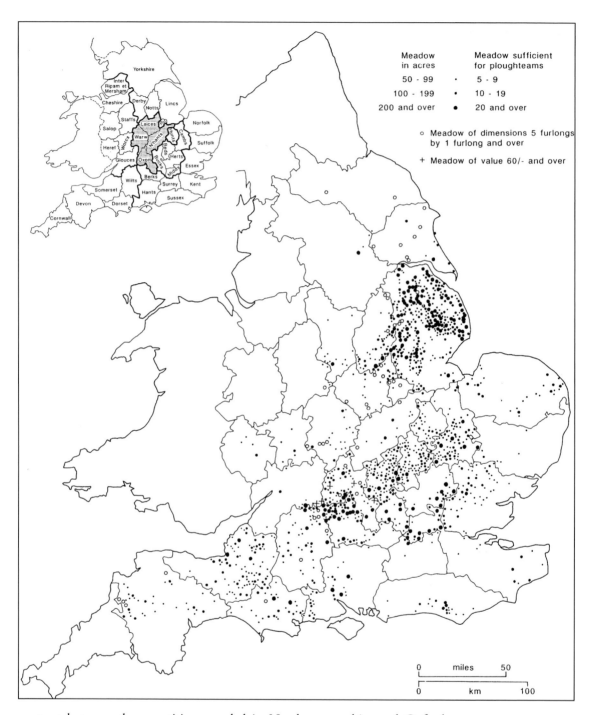

contrast between the quantities recorded in Northamptonshire and Oxfordshire, and those noted in the adjacent county of Buckinghamshire, even
allowing for the different methods of recording. The fall-off at the county
boundary is sudden and does not correlate with any obvious change in the
character of the natural topography. Allowing for this, it is evident that at the

168

time of Domesday there was also a marked concentration of meadow land in the Midlands, with only limited amounts outside it.

By late Saxon times, in other words, there was a clear correlation between districts with abundant meadow land on the one hand, and areas of nucleated villages and well-developed open-field agriculture on the other. In Rackham's words,

> We have no evidence that meadow began earlier in one type of landscape than another. But it developed more rapidly among the communal enterprise, villages, and open-field farming of the Planned Countryside. In the 'do-it-yourself' landscape of what is now Ancient Countryside, *meadow was hardly beyond the experimental stage by 1086* (Rackham 1986, 335: my italics).

What explains this intriguing pattern? One possibility, hinted at by Rackham but not further explored, is that the more communal and organised character of open-field communities in the Midlands somehow encouraged more intensive management of low-lying grassland. Alternatively, perhaps, the intensively arable character of these landscapes – the early elimination of waste, the outward expansion of ploughland to the extremities of the vill – made meadows essential at an early date. In other words, the early adoption of meadows may have been a consequence of the particular tenurial, economic and demographic development of Midland communities in later Saxon times.

FIGURE 52.
The distribution of meadow land in Domesday. Inconsistencies of recording distort the picture, but meadow land is again more abundant in Midland than in non-Midland areas. Note how meadow appears to be systematically under-recorded in the circuit embracing Northamptonshire, Leicesterhire, Warwickshire and Oxfordshire (after Darby 1977).

But another alternative also needs to be considered: that the distribution of meadow land was largely a consequence of environmental factors, and that the early development of meadows somehow encouraged the emergence of nucleated villages, rather than the other way round. In this context it is important to emphasise again that in some places meadows could be created with relative ease; in others, only with some difficulty; while in a few, they could not be created at all. As Ault put it, 'In medieval times, meadows were the gift of nature, not the work of man' (Ault 1972, 25): and while this statement certainly underestimates the extent to which the relevant environments could be modified by human agency there were whole districts in which meadows could never be brought into existence on a large scale. The light lands of western Norfolk have little meadow recorded in either Domesday or the IPMs: as Campbell noted, 'with a low rainfall, sandy soils overlying chalk, and no substantial rivers, opportunities for the establishment of meadows were mostly non-existent' (Campbell 2000, 73–5). But obvious environmental circumstances of this kind do not, superficially at least, apply to many of the other districts in which meadows remained in relatively short supply, such as the claylands of East Anglia, Hertfordshire, and Essex. Here other, more subtle circumstances retarded and restricted their development.

The crucial factor was the character of the deposits found in the floors of the principal watercourses. Where floodplains were occupied by alluvial soils, or by soils formed in some combination of alluvium and gravel, meadows often were, indeed, the 'gift of nature'. Only minor ditching, and appropriate

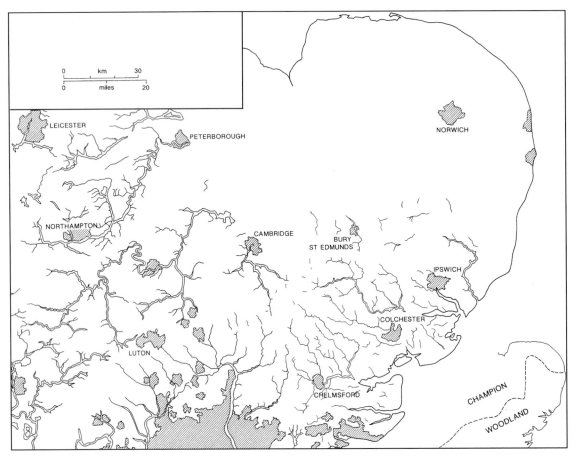

FIGURE 53.
The main areas of
alluvial soils, suitable
for the creation of hay
meadows, within the
study area. Source:
Soil Survey of
England and Wales.

livestock management, were usually required to produce good crops of hay. Where, in contrast, valley floors were filled with acid peat and drainage was impaired, coarse herbage was the natural produce and meadows of reasonable quality could only be created, if at all, by cutting more extensive and substantial networks of drains and dykes. The distribution of alluvial as opposed to peat soils, in other words, ought to provide a good guide to those areas in which meadows would have been created easiest, and earliest.

As Figure 53 indicates, the extent and configuration of alluvial deposits varied greatly across the area studied. In the west – in the champion Midlands – topography was ideal for meadow-making. The flood-plains of the Ouse, Nene, Welland, Soar, Ivel and Thame and their major tributaries are wide and filled with extensive deposits of gravel and alluvium, giving rise to a variety of seasonally waterlogged soils ideal for meadow land, principally those of the Fladbury 1 and Thames Associations – deep, clayey pelo-alluvial and pelo-calcareous alluvial gley soils respectively (Hodge *et al.* 1984, 194–6; 328–30). Not surprisingly, most champion vills in the Midlands appear, by the high middle ages, to have had between five and ten per cent of their land devoted to meadows (Fox 1984, 121). At Laxton in Nottinghamshire, for example, there were 130 acres of meadow, compared with 1,307 acres of open field land; while at Sherington in north Buckinghamshire the tenants held 858 acres in the two open fields, and 54 acres of meadow, while the demesne comprised 556 acres of land, of which 20 were meadow (Orwin and Orwin 1938, 103–4; Chibnall 1965, 92, 111–13). Even in vills located away from the principal valleys, on the high 'wolds' of Northamptonshire and Leicestershire, there was usually a sufficiency of meadow land: a late twelfth-century agreement from Preston Capes in Northamptonshire thus describes the demesne with 96 acres of arable and 9½ of meadow (Fox 1984, 89).

But moving south and east beyond the Chiltern escarpment – into 'ancient countryside' – we encounter a very different situation. Here, the valleys of the principal rivers draining the dipslope of the Chilterns contain soils which are again generally suitable for meadows – principally those of the Frome Association, formed in chalky and gravely alluvium (Hodge *et al.* 1984, 202–3). But not in great abundance. The spacing of the principal rivers is generally closer than in the Midlands but the individual floodplains are very much narrower. Moreover, tributary streams are few in number, have even narrower floodplains, and often dry out completely in the summer months. 'The absence of running water in the Chilterns away from the main valleys meant that meadows … were often scarce, or of poor quality, or both, and frequently lay in small pockets' (Reed 1979, 100). Many manors in upland locations, to judge from thirteenth- and fourteenth-century extents, had negligible quantities. A survey of Westwick manor in St Albans (Hertfordshire) for example, made in 1306, describes 801 acres of arable, 44 acres of pasture and 32 acres of woodland, but only 11.5 acres of meadow, just over one per cent of the total area of the manor (Hunn 1994, 53). Moving still further to the south, away from the Chiltern dipslope and into the area of London clay and associated Eocene deposits, the situation was generally similar. There were some extensive tracts of good meadow land in the wide valley of the river Lea – a locality which shows up as a significant concentration of meadow in Domesday – and to some extent in that of the lower Colne and the Thames. But these major valleys were widely spaced and away from them meadow land was in short supply because 'the numerous streams which cross the London Clay do not have well-developed flood plains' (Roden 1973, 341). On the Knights Hospitallers' manor of Moor Hall in Rainham, Essex, for example, there were 159 acres of arable but only one and a half of meadow. On the estates of St Albans Abbey, which extended over both the London clays and the Chiltern dip slope, there was 'comparatively little meadow land' on most manors by the thirteenth century (Levett 1938, 188–9).

Moving now north and east, into the boulder clay region of east Hertfordshire, north and central Essex and south Suffolk, the situation was different again. As in the Chilterns, the floodplains of the principal rivers are narrow. But the valleys are more closely spaced, and tributaries with well-formed, if narrow, floodplains abound. Here, in other words, there was more potential meadow land, and by the thirteenth century meadows 'occupied the floors of even the smallest valleys' (Rackham 1980b, 104). But the topography ensured that, in comparison with the Midlands, it was widely distributed in a myriad of narrow ribbons. On the demesnes of the Knights Hospitallers in this district hay was thus 'an important commodity' in the thirteenth century, but it was 'typically gathered from small allotments of meadow land'. At Great Dunmow in Essex, for example, in *c.* 1250 the single acre of meadow land which the order owned lay in two separate plots (Gervers 1996, lxxxiv). Moreover, the ratio of meadow to arable, while generally higher than on many Chiltern manors, was still normally low by Midland standards. On the demesne at Little Maplestead in 1338 there was only a single acre of meadow for every 35 of arable; at Cressing at the same date the ratio was 1:36 (Larking and Kemble 1887, 168); while at Writtle in 1328 it was 1:33 (Newton 1970, 26–7).

In all the areas so far discussed seasonally waterlogged alluvial land, suitable for making meadows, existed, albeit in varying amounts and in varying configurations. In northern East Anglia, however, the situation was different. Potential meadow land of reasonable quality was in relatively short supply. This assertion will surprise many readers, in whose mind's eye will appear images of the Norfolk Broads. Rivers like the Waveney, Yare and Bure, or the Alde and the Gipping, do indeed have wide flood plains, comparable in scale to the great rivers of the Midlands. But instead of alluvium, their floors are largely occupied by extensive areas of moist peat, or by mixtures of peat and clay, which give rise to the acid, peaty soils of the Mendham, Adventurers' 1 and 2, Altcar 2, Isleham 2 and Hanworth Associations (Hodge *et al.* 1984, 83–7, 90–2, 212–13, 231–5, 247–9). The flood plains of the many minor tributary rivers are also, to a large extent, dominated by peat, with only relatively limited pockets of alluvium. East Anglia was remarkably well-endowed with wide river valleys and other damp, low-lying land. But in its natural, undrained state the majority of this would have been occupied by rough fen vegetation.

With an effort, much of this land certainly could be converted to meadow, often for the exclusive use of demesnes, and much already had been by the time of Domesday. At Forncett in Norfolk attempts were still being made to reclaim valley-floor fens, and upgrade them to meadow, as late as 1300 (Davenport 1906, 31). Nevertheless, even in the early nineteenth century many valley floors were still occupied by common fens, and local meadow land was frequently criticised for its poor quality. As Arthur Young put it in 1804:

> No person can have been to Norfolk without quickly perceiving, that in this branch of rural economy the county has very little to boast. Nowhere are meadows and pastures worse managed: in all parts of the county we see them over-run with all sorts of spontaneous rubbish, bushes, briars, rushes; the water stagnant … (Young 1804, 370).

In Suffolk, similarly, he believed that the management of meadows could 'scarcely be worse' (Young 1813, 159). Young and other agricultural writers misunderstood the reasons for the poor quality of the region's meadows, as did those who attempted – usually in vain – to improve them in the course of the eighteenth and nineteenth centuries by instigating schemes of 'floating', or irrigation, of the kind usually associated with the chalklands of Wessex (Wade Martins and Williamson 1994). The paucity, and the poor quality, of meadow land was for centuries a defining characteristic of East Anglian agriculture.

The differences between the flood-plains of the Midland rivers, and those found in East Anglia, is even today mirrored in their vegetation. Most botanists and ecologists now employ the National Vegetation Classification scheme to describe and map plant communities in Britain (e.g. Rodwell 1991). The principal valley-floor communities of semi-natural vegetation are not evenly distributed, even in the relatively restricted region under consideration here. The two most important rich fen communities, dominated by sedge and *Schoenus* – M9 and M13 – are widespread in East Anglia but comparatively rare in the Midlands (Rodwell 1991, 88–96, 128–39). The fen-meadows M22 (*Juncus subnodulosus – Cirsium palustre* fen-meadow) and M24 (*Molinia caerula – Cirsium dissectum* fen meadow) are also more common in East Anglia, and to some extent Essex and Hertfordshire, than in Midland counties (Rodwell 1991, 227–43, 256–66). True meadow vegetation, in contrast, has a different distribution. The area occupied by the most important communities has been much reduced by modern farming methods but both MG4 – *Alopecurus pratensis – Sanguisorba officianalis* grassland – and MG5 – *Cynosurus cristatus – Centaurea nigra* grassland – are principally a feature of the valley floors in the Midlands and south of England, and are comparatively rare in the eastern counties.

Meadows and settlement

Many readers will have spotted where this argument is heading. There was a clear inverse correlation between, on the one hand, the extent and configuration of land most suitable for the creation of hay meadows and, on the other, the extent and importance of common-edge settlement. In the Midlands, where meadowland could be created with relative ease and was abundant in early medieval times, green-edge settlements were rare. In Hertfordshire and Essex, where meadow land was widely distributed but often in small parcels, small green-edge hamlets were a significant feature of the settlement pattern, but almost always a subsidiary one. In northern East Anglia, however, where meadow land was difficult to create, usually in short supply, and generally of poor quality – but where there were numerous pockets of waterlogged clay, and extensive valley-floor fens – damp commons were extensive and common-edge settlement almost ubiquitous. Even the exceptions to this broad pattern prove the rule. Thus in the Midlands the areas of 'upland' between major valleys – and, therefore, major reserves of meadow land – tend to be relatively narrow, usually no more than five to ten kilometres wide. The main exception – the high claylands between the Ouse and the Nene – is precisely the area in which, unusually for the 'champion' Midlands, greenside hamlets were a prominent feature of the medieval landscape.

But there was also a more basic, and more important, correlation between areas in which meadow was in limited supply or widely dispersed, and districts featuring dispersed settlements *of all kinds*, including isolated farms set in their own fields and hamlets strung out along the sides of roads, rather than clustered around commons. Meadow land and its management evidently encouraged nucleation of settlement; and the larger and more concentrated the area of meadow, the more nucleated the settlement pattern was likely to be.

The reasons for this are quite straightforward, and once again related to the practicalities of farming life, and in particular to the crucial 'bottlenecks' of the farming year, when labour needed to be mobilised rapidly. When first cut, grass contains around 75 per cent water, and to ensure good-quality hay this needs to be reduced to about 15 per cent before stacking. The moisture is reduced partly by the action of the wind, and partly by the sun's heat. To encourage the escape of water vapour the cut herbage has to be repeatedly turned over and shaken out to expose as large a surface as possible to the air, a very labour-intensive operation:

> The work must be carried out in such a manner that the herbage is not unduly exposed to the leaching action of rain nor yet to the bleaching action of the sun. Moreover, because the leaf of the grass plant has a higher feeding value than the stem, it is important to avoid over-drying which would cause the leaves to become brittle and liable to be broken off by the various implements used in the making and collection of the hay (Robinson 1949, 286).

Yet stacking the hay while it contains too much sap can cause heating in the stack, leading to loss of digestible protein; while stacking when actually damp can lead to mould and rot. Hay-making with traditional tools thus required good weather, abundant labour – and the careful timing of farming operations: 'make hay while the sun shines'. 'In the fickle English climate, haymaking is always a hazardous practice and the produce is always subject to serious losses in feeding values' (Robinson 1949, 286). Hay meadows, it need hardly be said, operated best when large amounts of labour could be turned on to them at short notice. Many a crop was saved by rapid carting and stacking (Figure 54). It is hardly surprising, then, that large areas of good meadow land favoured the emergence of large nucleated villages. In contrast, areas in which meadow was widely distributed in small pockets encouraged the development of a more mixed pattern, with nucleated villages in the major valleys, smaller hamlets, freehold farms and minor manors beside the thinner ribbons of meadow in tributary valleys – and green-edge settlements on the meadow-less interfluves. This was the classic settlement mix in areas like north Essex or east Hertfordshire. And where very little meadow existed, as in much of northern East Anglia, damp grazing of all kinds formed powerful magnets for settlement as population rose in late Saxon times, and in many parishes by the twelfth century the majority of farms had come to cluster on the margins of greens and commons.

FIGURE 54.
The hay harvest was
one of the key
bottlenecks in the
traditional farming
year, when a large
labour force had to be
mobilised with speed.
Haymaking at
Lockinge in
Oxfordshire in 1905.

Some greens and commons may have been cut for hay. At Diss in Norfolk for example Pennings Green was closed to grazing from May Day until Lammas: the tenements fronting on the green took it in turn to cut the hay (Blomefield 1805, 37). Some Essex greens were similarly enclosed during May and June, mown, and then thrown open for grazing (Hunter 1999, 99). But this was probably a late medieval development and the original and primary use of these areas was certainly as pasture, and they served in some sense as *alternatives* to meadow land.

A number of greens and similar commons, as we have seen, were still tree-covered at the time of Domesday but others had evidently already degenerated to open pasture (above, p. 56). Many if not most were probably selected specifically because they were good places in which to grow grass. True, the 'low' commons, in the floors of peat-filled river valleys, would never have produced good herbage but greens located on the upland clays were different. The term 'green' itself is not recorded before 1300 but it occurs in place names from the time of Domesday Book: Mangreen in Norfolk, for example, is the 'green used by everyone'. One explanation for the term is that ploughland was so extensive when the boundaries of these commons came to be defined that they were already islands of 'green' in a landscape which was, for much of the year, brown. But as we have seen, other areas of grassland and wood-pasture generally survived at this time and the term probably has other implications. One early meaning of the adjective 'green' was 'covered with a growth of herbage or foliage; verdant' (Oxford English Dictionary, 1201). It is possible that greens were 'verdant' in contrast to adjacent areas of less luxuriant grass growth, especially in late summer and autumn. The majority of greens occur in areas where droughtiness seriously restricts grass yields, and limits the duration of summer grazing. On Beccles soils, for example, 'grass growth is limited to spring and early summer' and so, in terms of modern farming, ' the land is unsuited to intensive [livestock] production' – unless it is irrigated (Hodge *et al.* 1984, 121). Greens, tyes and larger clayland commons were damp places, difficult to cultivate. But they were also, for the same reason, good places for growing grass, and in particular provided good growth late into the autumn.

Meadows served to concentrate settlement, but in a particular way. People did not necessarily need to live right next to them, but rather in places which were in easy reach, where they could assemble for work at short notice. Farmers did not each need to supervise their livestock when the land was grazed after Lammas because where the meadows were in large blocks this was more conveniently done in common, and where they were in small ribbons they were usually demesne property, and could be treated like any small pasture close. But where meadow land was limited and areas of common *grazing* were of more importance in the economy of peasant farmers it was more convenient for farms to be located right next to them. In such circumstances, farms would disperse across the landscape, forming loose girdles around damp commons, or lining the main roads leading to them.

To some extent, it appears that the more limited the area of meadow land, the greater the need to preserve such areas of common grazing from the plough – most strikingly in northern East Anglia, where vast areas of commons existed well into post-medieval times. But the situation is at once more complex, and more subtle, than this. The kind of topography which ensured that meadows were in short supply – muted terrain, wide clay tablelands, sluggish watercourses – also tended to produce large areas of land which were hard or impossible to cultivate. In regions to the south and west of the Gipping, in contrast, the more undulating terrain meant that there were fewer such unploughable areas, but also more potential meadow land. Greens in this region were thus smaller, and often less significant in the settlement pattern. Indeed, many were so small that readers might wonder whether they were of much significance to farmers. But many of the farms that clustered beside them were relatively humble establishments. More importantly, in many areas such diminutive greens represented nodal points in a more extensive web of common pasture provided by the network of hedged lanes and wide drift ways.

Within the area studied there was thus a close and understandable relationship between the character of settlement and the extent, and configuration, of meadow land. But there is another correlation, even more worthy of note. Where meadow land was extensive at an early date – in the champion Midlands – woodland and pasture were generally in short supply, to judge from the evidence of placenames and Domesday Book, reviewed in Chapter 2. Given, as we have seen, that Domesday suggests that population densities were poorly correlated with variations in the extent of pasture and woodland, the implication is that 'woodland' and 'champion' districts had simply developed different ways of managing livestock. In champion areas, abundant hay supplies meant that there was less need to retain areas of grazing ground: ploughlands could thus be greatly expanded at the expense of 'waste'. In woodland districts, in contrast – ignoring for the moment those of poor soil in the far south of the study area – the more limited availability of hay meant that the grazing season needed to be extended late into the autumn or even beyond, and there was thus more incentive to retain extensive tracts of pasture and wood-pasture. Over the two centuries following the Norman Conquest the area of meadow land was steadily extended but this essential dichotomy remained. In champion areas, the arable was now expanded to such an extent that in many vills virtually no woodland or pasture survived. In the woodland districts of East Anglia, northern and central Essex, and eastern Hertfordshire, in contrast, as the wood-pastures were replaced by arable – or converted to managed woods or deer parks – greens and commons had to be set aside, to provide adequate grazing and browse for the livestock, and especially the draught oxen, of the tenants.

Yet the widespread eradication of wood-pastures at an early date from many Midland districts may not *only* have been a consequence of the greater availability of hay here. Because farmers in this region came to live in nucleated villages, because they were obliged, by the character of the soil, to co-operate closely in ploughing, and because in other ways they were now organising their agricultural activities along communal lines, they may have been better able to agree to the expansion of the communal ploughlands (and to work together to achieve this end) than those living in the smaller and less cohesive communities characteristic of 'woodland' districts.

Life without meadows

The creation or definition of greens and commons, and the establishment of their associated settlements, had begun in the more populous 'woodland' districts of northern East Anglia before the Norman Conquest. But it accelerated in the late eleventh and twelfth centuries, not simply perhaps because of continued population growth but also because of the expropriation of large areas of 'waste' by Anglo-Norman lords to create managed woods and, in particular, deer parks. In areas like north-west Essex (Figure 38, above, p. 108) these must have consumed a high proportion of the remaining wood-pastures. Yet even though the common wood-pastures dwindled, the environment of these districts remained less degraded, more diverse than that of the champion

Midlands. It did not come to consist merely of meadow, cropped land, and fallow. This was important because the greens and commons could only ever have made a limited contribution to the sustenance of livestock, even in those districts in which they were extensive, simply because they produced little grass during the winter months, and could indeed be damaged by too much winter grazing. It was therefore fortunate that numerous sources of fodder were available in these districts which could be used to supplement hay supplies, and that other forms of grazing were available. Leafy hay thus continued to be exploited on some scale. As late as the sixteenth century the agricultural writer Thomas Tusser, an Essex man, could recommend its use as winter feed:

> If frost doo continue, this leson doth well,
> For comfort of cattell the fewell to fell;
> From eurie tree the superfluous bows
> Now prune for thy neat therupon to go browse.
>
> (Grigson 1984, 74)

The practice of shredding was still widespread at this time. A survey of the manor of Redgrave in the claylands of Suffolk, made shortly after the Dissolution, thus describes how on the 'seyd mannor and dyvers tenementes there … be growing 1,100 okes of 60, 80 and 100 yeares growth part tymber parte usually cropped and shred' (WSRO Accn 1066). Indeed, not all wood-pastures degraded rapidly to open pasture. Even in densely settled Norfolk, the great intercommoned wood-pasture to the east of Norwich only degenerated to the treeless Mousehold Heath in the course of the twelfth and thirteenth centuries (Rackham 1986, 299–303). Where population pressure was less, in south Essex or the Chilterns, many large wooded commons survived right through the medieval period. More importantly, in most of these districts there were woods, deer parks, hedges, and hedgerow trees in abundance, which could provide not only fodder but also some grazing well into the autumn, and beyond. Much herbage could be obtained from field edges and ditches, and from roadside verges, even in the depths of winter. In addition to all this, in Hertfordshire, Essex, Suffolk and Norfolk the practice of maintaining 'borders' or 'hedge greens' was widespread. The cropped area of enclosed fields frequently did not run right up to the boundary hedge but instead there was a strip, left uncultivated, on which the ploughteam could turn, and which was mown for hay, or used for grazing tethered cattle. In the eighteenth century both Young and Walker commented on the mown strips beside hedgerows as a characteristic feature of the Hertfordshire countryside (Walker 1795, 154; Young 1767, 258), and hedgerow grazing is often referred to in medieval documents (Roden 1973, 327). And, of course, grazing on the fallows and the harvest aftermath was always of vital importance, in woodland as in champion districts. It was thus perfectly possible for medieval communities to manage with relatively little meadow land. Indeed, the most populous areas of early medieval England – Norfolk and north Suffolk – were precisely those in which meadows were most limited in extent, and greens and commons most extensive.

Meadow and Green   So far I have only examined the impact which varying quantities and configurations of meadow land had upon the development of settlement in *clayland* districts. But it is likely that the character of meadows also helped structure the development of the medieval landscapes in areas of light land. In some districts – mainly along the foot of the chalk escarpment in Bedfordshire and south Cambridgeshire, but also in places in west Norfolk – alluvial soils and relatively substantial, fast-moving watercourses allowed the creation, sometimes at a relatively late date, of significant areas of meadow land, and it was probably this which encouraged the progressive enclosure and infilling of large greens and commons at places like Thriplow and Bassingbourne, as population rose and space needed to be found for houses and their associated enclosures. More intensive management of grassland, in other words, allowed the development of true nucleations from loose clusters of farms, a process which may (as I have noted) have been accompanied, or followed, by the reorganisation of field systems along more regular lines. In many districts, in contrast, meadow land remained in short supply, or was scattered in small ribbons and pockets, and here more dispersed patterns of settlement, or loosely nucleated villages, remained the norm. In all districts, and on all soils, the extent and character of meadow land was thus a powerful factor in the evolution of rural settlement, from middle Saxon through to post-medieval times.

CHAPTER EIGHT

Landscape, Society and Environment

Social change and the open fields

In the foregoing chapters some of the reasons behind the emergence of regional variations in the medieval landscape have been discussed. I have argued that not only the essential difference between 'woodland' and 'champion' regions, but also the different versions of, and hybrids between, these broad landscape types, can be explained in environmental terms: as responses to particular challenges posed or restrictions imposed by soils and topography. Certain circumstances thus encouraged the development of settlement patterns dominated by nucleated villages – an abundance of good meadow land lying in large concentrations, clay soils subject to compaction and puddling, and light, waterless land in which farms and cottages were obliged to cluster in restricted locations. But these various factors were not, in the last analysis, discrete and separate. They were all aspects of the same key developments, technological and demographic.

As population grew and settlements stabilised in the eighth and ninth centuries, and as heavier and more fertile soils were brought into cultivation, larger ploughs, drawn by large ox teams, came into widespread use. Together, perhaps, with changes in the way that property was held and resources allocated, this encouraged a concentration of settlement close to areas of damp ground, suitable for pasture. Where such areas of land were in short supply – that is, in districts of light, freely draining soils – girdles of farms emerged around their margins, leading in time to the development of nucleated villages, often as damp commons were progressively infilled and built over. This development was often made possible by the more intensive management of remaining areas of damp ground as hay meadows. On heavier land population pressure and the adoption of the new technology had rather different effects. On the difficult and intractable clay soils of the Midlands the need to assemble plough teams rapidly, together with the fact that large, compact areas suitable for management as meadow land often existed, encouraged the development from middle Saxon times of nucleated patterns of settlement. But where clay soils could be cultivated over longer periods, and where potential meadow was either distributed in smaller ribbons and/or in short supply, then settlement became increasingly dispersed as the frontiers of cultivation expanded. New farms or submanors were established beside narrow ribbons of meadow, or else continued to disperse, in traditional fashion, around the margins of damp

commons. The extent and particular character of these latter developments
varied according to time and place, depending on the ease with which, and
the extent to which, meadow land could be created.

Nucleated settlement patterns thus arose primarily from the widespread
adoption of large ploughs, and from the requirements of the large teams of
oxen that pulled them. In some places the needs of co-aration might be
dominant, in others the need to manage hay meadows, and in yet others a
desire to remain close to areas of damp pasture, suitable for summer and
autumn grazing. Whatever the precise combination of factors underlying their
development, nucleated settlement patterns were closely associated with landscapes of extensive open fields. In areas of light soil, land allotted to tenants
or repeatedly divided between co-heirs had to take the form of scattered parcels,
because there was no other way of ensuring an equitable distribution of good
and bad, near and distant land. On the heavy clays of the Midlands, in
contrast, scattering of holdings was primarily instituted to ensure equal access
to land of equivalent character during the short spring ploughing season. Over
such intermingled properties, communal rotations were imposed, sometimes
perhaps from the start, sometimes later. Their principal purpose was to facilitate
the management of livestock: in sheep-corn districts, to simplify the process
of close folding, so crucial for keeping the land in heart; in Midland townships,
to allow for the grazing of the fallows and the harvest aftermath, for in these
districts the ploughlands had often, by the eleventh or twelfth centuries,
reached the boundaries of the vill, and pasture was in short supply.

The development of such intensively arable landscapes was probably the
consequence of abundant hay supplies, which allowed a growing population
to be fed by simply expanding the arable, inexorably, at the expense of
woodland and pasture. The cohesive, co-operative character of Midland
communities made it relatively easy for farmers to agree to remove the wastes,
and to combine together to achieve this end. In 'woodland' regions, in contrast,
significant areas of wood-pasture normally survived at the time of Domesday,
and even in the thirteenth century commons, managed woodland and private
wood-pastures remained a prominent feature of the landscape, in spite of the
fact that most of these districts carried average or above-average population
densities. In some 'woodland' districts, of course, large reserves of woodland
and waste simply reflected poor soils and low population densities, although
it is worth pointing out that most such areas – like the Chiltern dipslope, or
the heavy London clays – were also deficient in good-quality meadow land,
something which may well have contributed to the slow pace of clearance and
colonisation. Either way, all these areas came to be characterised by fairly
dispersed patterns of settlement. Where meadow was limited or scattered in
a myriad of small parcels, where there were few environmental constraints on
the location of farms, and where the character of soils permitted farmers,
even when customarily combining to form common ploughs, to live apart
from one another, there was no reason why nucleated villages should be the
sole form of settlement. Conversely, as clearance of woods and pastures

proceeded, there might be good reasons why farms should disperse across the landscape, in order to be located beside narrow ribbons of meadow, or beside areas of damp ground which could provide lush grazing late into the year.

The interaction of various environmental factors thus produced a constellation of local and regional landscapes which the familiar division between 'woodland' and 'champion' serves to some extent to suppress and confuse. It is certainly clear that the development of different kinds of medieval landscape cannot be explained simply in terms of social, demographic, or economic variations, because such things as the proliferation of local lords or the rise of markets occurred throughout the region studied, and such variation as they displayed in incidence and intensity did not correspond in any clear way with the distribution of landscape types. The latter were correlated instead with particular configurations of soils, topography and climate: the principal factors moulding this landscape of peasant farmers were, not surprisingly, agricultural and environmental.

And yet I do not mean to suggest that wider social, economic and tenurial influences played no part in the shaping of these varied landscapes – in all the changes which I have outlined in the previous chapters. They did: but their impact was always mediated through local and regional environmental circumstances. The steady development of a more hierarchical society in the course of the Saxon period, with the development of 'multiple estates' and their subsequent fragmentation into a mosaic of local lordships, was perhaps the driving force in landscape change. While many of the developments in settlement and field systems occurring over this long period could have taken place simply as a consequence of technological innovation and demographic expansion, the demands of proliferating demesnes seem often to have been a key factor. In the course of the middle and later Saxon periods more and more people were drawn into the service-tenancy system – came to owe labour services to a local lord. But it was not the general increase in burdens which was critical, but rather the requirement of demesnes, in Faith's words, for 'large inputs of labour in a comparatively short time at the crucial points in the agricultural year' (Faith 1997, 110). In the Midlands, the need for rapid mobilisation of plough teams in the spring, and for rapid mobilisation of labour for the hay harvest, *might* have been enough on their own to prevent the spread of settlement away from old sites as population grew in late Saxon times. But these things could just as easily have led to the development of small hamlets – each containing enough farms (three or four, perhaps) to make a viable team – strung out along the margins of the great Midland meadows. That this did not happen was doubtless the consequence of decisions taken by demesne managers. Middle Saxon estates had usually maintained their own ploughs and teams, overseen by slaves or *geburs* living on the *inland*: but while these were enough to deal with such things as the summer ploughing of the fallows, they were insufficient to cope with the ploughing preparatory to winter and – in particular – spring sowing on these difficult soils (Ault

1972, 20–1). For this, they needed to call upon the ploughs and teams of peasants living on the outlying *warland*. As local demesnes proliferated, such services were both appropriated, and increased, by emergent local lords, and by the early twelfth century were of crucial importance in demesne economies. Ploughing services were of particular importance because they gave lords 'access to valuable draught stock which they did not need to maintain all though the year' (Faith 1997, 112–13).

Where the window of opportunity for cultivation was narrow the thegn's reeve, or the lord's steward, could not wait around while Aelfric and his oxen were sent for at his farm, several kilometres away. Aelfric needed to be close at hand. And at haymaking time, similarly, the proximity of the workforce was of critical concern for the simple reason that most demesnes had little other manpower available to cut and turn the hay. Indeed, village bylaws attest the particular concern of manorial lords for their hay, and many were evidently willing to pay a bonus for the efficient and speedy performance of these particular labour services. At Newington in Oxfordshire in the mid thirteenth century, for example, every virgator was bound

> To mow the lord's meadow once a year until it is mown. He ought to tedder and rake the grass and take it to the lord's grange. For this service he shall have a wheaten loaf sufficient for two days and cheese worth a ha'penny and the mowers shall have among themselves one of the best sheep from the lord's fold, whichever they wish. One cheese and one basin of salt when all the hay has been carried (Ault 1972, 25).

And there may well have been other reasons why, given the particular environmental circumstances and the expansion of service-tenancies, nucleated settlement patterns came to characterise Midland districts. I have already noted how, within the area studied, the *most* nucleated patterns of settlement, and the *most* regular open-field systems, were found towards the west, in Leicestershire, Northamptonshire and north Buckinghamshire – districts which, in post-medieval times, gradually became quintessential pasture-farming country, the grass 'shires'. This eventual dominance of livestock farming was in large measure the consequence of the high ploughing costs on these soils. But it also reflected low and unpredictable yields resulting from higher rainfall levels in this more westerly region, especially during the summer months: something which, in a medieval context, might spell disaster to the lord's harvest unless those owing customary services could be turned on to the fields without delay.

But the emergence of local lordship, and the wider social changes with which it was associated, had other effects on the development of champion landscapes. The services due from bond tenants, dwelling on the *inland* of large estates, may have been firmly tied to specific allotments of land since middle Saxon times but the steady increase in the proportion of the population holding by dependent tenure ensured that more and more of the arable land had to be measured and assessed. Notional assessments in virgates, bovates and the rest may have originated in systems of taxation imposed on the relatively free peasantry dwelling on the outlying *warland*, but these units were systematically adopted and adapted by local lords as part of the process of appropriating labour services, and increasing them. As standard, customary holdings were thus created, existing field systems on the Midland clays were often comprehensively reorganised in order to ensure that each virgate (or bovate) of land was spread evenly across the fields, often following a regular sequence which, as we have seen, might be mirrored in the layout of regular tofts within the village itself. Such regular assessments were probably, for the most part, imposed by the lord or lords of the villages in question. But they were perhaps designed with the interests of tenants as much as demesnes in mind. Very regular distributions of equal-sized holdings provided obvious evidence of equity of value, an important consideration when each made the same contribution in terms of labour services and the common plough. Land scattered with obsessive regularity across the landscape was land self-evidently of equal quality and – of crucial importance on soils with a short working period – equal *accessibility*. The imposition of these fixed tenurial structures was probably associated with the adoption and enforcement of customs of impartible inheritance, which became almost ubiquitous in these champion districts. Manorial lords could not allow holdings to disintegrate, or be recombined in new ways, without limitation, for this would militate against the prompt delivery of ploughing, haymaking and other services upon which the efficient functioning of demesne agriculture depended.

The reorganisation of field systems along more 'regular' lines, which continued in some areas into the post-Conquest period, was also motivated by other factors. In particular, as many scholars have argued, it was associated with the adoption of a regular two- or three-field system in place of more irregular, haphazard arrangements, a move made necessary by the eradication of pasture and the consequent need to manage more intensively the grazing offered by the harvest aftermath and the fallows. The splitting of townships between two or more manors, in the course of the tenth, eleventh or twelfth centuries, must have been a powerful encouragement for such schemes of wholesale reorganisation. In Robert Dodgshon's words, 'the radical changes of layout induced by splitting presented an opportunity to rethink – or perhaps to think for the first time – about what was a desirable or suitable layout of holdings or fields ...' (Dodgshon 1980, 140). So far as the evidence goes, most townships on the Midland clays probably thus evolved in a number of stages, and not always with the same chronology: just as most champion landscapes were eventually removed by large-scale planned enclosure, but not necessarily at the same time. Once communal forms of agriculture had come into existence, in other words, they were particularly susceptible to planned reorganisation: and such was their complexity that they could usually only be *removed*, in the course of the post-medieval period, by planned reorganisation – that is, by some kind of general enclosure, often by parliamentary act.

Yet this perhaps oversimplifies the true complexity of the relationship between lordship and the landscape, for within what we conventionally think of as the 'champion' belt the proliferation of lords and manors could sometimes encourage a movement *away* from regularity and communality, especially where the environmental factors encouraging the adoption of 'Midland' arrangements were comparatively muted. On the claylands of west Cambridgeshire, for example, increasing tenurial complexity often led to the development of new settlement foci, away from existing villages, in the course of the tenth, eleventh, and twelfth centuries.

Lordship, tenure and woodland landscapes

At first sight changing structures of lordship, and changing systems of tenurial organisation, were of less significance in moulding the various features of 'woodland' landscapes and indeed, the failure of such areas to develop along classic 'Midland' lines has sometimes been ascribed to the comparative weakness of lordship there. But as we have seen there is little in the available evidence to suggest that woodland areas were always, or even usually, associated with weak lordship. Many of these districts were in fact as heavily manorialised as the Midlands, and everywhere an abstract web of assessment was imposed upon the peasant world. But there was less attempt to regularise either the *tenementa* of East Anglia, or the virgates encountered elsewhere, in order to ensure that they were of equal area or value. This was more difficult and perhaps less necessary, given the more dispersed character of settlement, the more individualistic systems of agriculture, and the less cohesive character of local communities. Nevertheless, there are signs that, as in the champion lands, the imposition of systems of assessment, the exaction of dues and services, might on occasion be manifested in the physical landscape in the form of measured systems of land allotment. Certainly, we must be careful not to see these landscapes as entirely the product of gradual, 'do it yourself', piecemeal development, or to assume that the only planned elements found within them represent the fragmentary remains of ancient, prehistoric or Roman, systems of land allotment. In East Anglia, for example, some common-edge settlements have very regular arrangements of tofts, which certainly look planned. Most are small-scale layouts on the edge of peripheral greens, towards parish boundaries. They feature 'long narrow tenement plots of more or less equal width' (Warner 1987, 45), similar to those noted by Brown and Taylor in north Bedfordshire (above, p. 78). But some larger examples of apparent green-edge planning also occur, such as Worlingworth in Suffolk (Martin 2000). Most common-edge farms were probably established on land allocated by lords, even in 'free' East Anglia. Nevertheless, for the most part this was apparently done without the kind of large-scale landscape planning evident in some Midland districts. Commons themselves seldom have regular, rectilinear boundaries; most common-edge tofts are far from regular in layout; and while traces of small-scale early medieval planning can indeed be detected in 'ancient countryside' areas, by and large these are characterised by irregularity, in the layout both of fields and of settlements.

Yet it is possible that the hand of lordship had a rather more basic impact on the development of 'woodland' landscapes – might account to some extent for the character of their settlement patterns. Historians often attribute landscapes of scattered farms and hamlets to 'late settlement', but do not always explain *why* the two things should have been linked. The connection lies in the fact that the relationships between peasants, land and lords changed significantly during the twelfth and thirteenth centuries. Robert Dodgshon and others have emphasised the close relationship between open-field land and standard, customary tenements – assessed in virgates, *tenementa* or whatever, and held in return for services and various dues and fines: and the contrast between this and land measured in other ways, and held by free tenants in return for money rents, which was created by assarting and colonisation in the course of the later twelfth and thirteenth centuries (Dodgshon 1980, 96). The difference was in part related to a shift away from a reliance on labour services, towards the employment of labourers paid in cash, in the management of demesnes. But it may also have reflected a drift in the balance of power away from peasant communities, to manorial lords, in the wake of the Conquest. Most tenants lost the right to appeal to royal courts when in dispute with their lords, who were now increasingly able to do as they liked with the remaining 'waste' on their manors. This situation was effectively recognised by the Statute of Merton of 1236, which allowed manorial lords to over-rule even the free tenants of the vill, and enclose what land they pleased, provided the latter were left with 'sufficient' waste. In Brian Robert's words, 'the rise of the doctrine of the lord's ownership of the waste during the twelfth and thirteenth centuries, and the provision of a defence against *Novel Disseisin* by the Statute of Merton ... are key factors in explaining the swing to individual colonisation and emphasis on personal rather than communal rights' (Roberts 1973, 229). The division between assessed and non-assessed land 'was a territorial divide scarred deeply and enduringly on the face of most townships' (Dodgshon 1980, 104), and was normally expressed as a division between an inner 'core' of open-fields, and an outer penumbra of hedged or walled enclosures. It is easy to see here an important explanation for the large numbers of isolated farms, set in their own fields, encountered in 'woodland' areas of Essex, Hertfordshire, Middlesex or south Buckinghamshire. Given the survival here, into post-Conquest times, of fairly large areas of pasture and wood-pasture, there was plenty of opportunity for the creation of ring-fence farms held by free tenure, beyond the cultivated bounds of existing communities.

This argument should not be taken too far, however, not least because by late Saxon times woodland and pasture were already a dwindling resource across much of East Anglia, Essex and Hertfordshire. Moreover, while some of these outlying sites and their associated fields certainly were established as late as the thirteenth century, and some were held by free tenure (just as some were created by subinfeudation, and were separate manors), many if not most were part of the assessed structure of manors and townships: they were rated in terms of virgates or tenementa, and they owed labour services. As long ago as 1915 Gray described the 'consolidated virgate' as a typical feature of Essex peasant farming, while Roden noted how, on the central Essex boulder clays, 'virgate and half virgate holdings usually consisted of crofts and closes grouped around isolated farmsteads' (Roden 1973, 339). On the Chiltern dipslope, similarly, many virgates and half-virgate holdings consisted largely or entirely of enclosed land (Roden 1973, 333). Changes in forms of tenure may have been one factor in the proliferation of isolated farms and hamlets in the course of the twelfth and thirteenth centuries, but of more importance were the kinds of practical, agricultural factors already discussed: the need for farms and cottages to be located beside areas of meadow or pasture, as the landscape became increasingly cleared, bounded and filled with people.

Nevertheless, while lordship may not have been a key factor in moulding the basic distinction between woodland and champion landscapes – and while lords evidently played less part in the layout or planning of woodland as opposed to champion landscapes – variations in the strength and incidence of lordship may well have had a determining role in the development of different *kinds*, and varieties, of woodland countryside. One key factor here was the character of villein inheritance practices, which followed local custom, as defined by manorial courts. And custom in turn broadly reflected the strength of local lordship and, in particular, the scale and character of the labour services required by demesnes. Customary tenants were probably always keen to divide their holdings between their sons, just as they were happy to buy and sell portions of customary land as the size and wealth of families fluctuated (Harvey 1984). Where rents were primarily paid in cash this mattered little. But where they were paid in labour; where there was the greatest need for customary labour; and especially the greatest need to mobilise it quickly; this might cause problems for demesne managers. They needed to know precisely who was responsible for carrying out the work, and if holdings had fragmented into numerous portions, or had been recombined in novel ways through inheritance or sale, this could cause obvious difficulties. Where labour services were crucial to demesne economies, lords and their agents would strive to maintain the integrity of customary holdings.

I noted in Chapter 2 how northern East Anglia was characterised in the early middle ages by relatively large numbers of free men, and by a plethora of relatively small manors. The reasons for this were probably environmental and economic, as I have argued, rather than ethnic: but whatever their origins, these features had an important influence on the development of local landscapes. The large number of small manors meant that demesnes were generally small in extent, compared with the area occupied by tenanted land. This ensured that demands for labour service were relatively limited, and this in turn had a number of important effects. Firstly, as new farms were created in the post-Conquest period, these were more likely than not to be held by free tenures – especially as many were located beside upland greens and commons, at a distance from the core areas of demesne land, and therefore inconveniently sited for the exaction of labour dues. Free tenures thus tended to proliferate in these districts in the course of the twelfth and thirteenth centuries, in spite of the fact that the immediate effect of the Conquest had been the downgrading in status of many members of the free peasantry. But secondly, there was a strong tendency for both free and bond tenants to practice partible, rather than impartible inheritance, and for an active land market to develop at an early date (Dodwell 1967). This, combined with rapid population growth in a region peculiarly well suited to cereal growing, ensured the wholesale disintegration of holdings into strips, and the development in many places of extensive, if irregular, open fields. In addition, small manors and a relatively weak manorial structure ensured that the remaining tracts of wood-pasture degenerated steadily into treeless commons. Some land was enclosed by manorial lords and used for coppiced woods or deer parks, but both population pressure, and the weakness of manorial authority, meant that these were limited in numbers, and in area, compared with the situation in most other 'woodland' regions (Figure 55). Social and tenurial structures, combined with high population densities, thus ensured the development of the distinctive East Anglian version of 'woodland' countryside, with extensive but irregular open fields, large commons, and comparatively few woods and deer parks.

South and west of the Gipping, on the boulder clays of south Suffolk, northern and central Essex, and east Hertfordshire, late Saxon population densities were lower and the proportions of free men and sokemen less. Here, manorial control was generally stronger, demesnes were larger, and labour services heavier: the large demesnes, with 300 sown acres or more, were heavily reliant on peasant labour services, especially for ploughing (Campbell 2000, 86). Open fields were generally confined to the lighter soils of the principal valleys, associated with pre-Conquest settlements – villages and hamlets. Where the land was most dissected, as we have seen, the open fields could cover a large area of ground. But almost everywhere they came to be surrounded by an outer ring of enclosed land, often several kilometres wide where the interfluves were extensive. Nucleations of settlement were associated with manorial complexes, and with the main areas of meadow land. The areas of open field thus approximated to the lightest land, most in need of regular folding but, equally, relatively easy to plough, even in wet conditions. Some of these fields may have originated in the settlement of tenants around the halls of lords, others perhaps came into existence as the properties of thegns or free men disintegrated under the impact of partible inheritance. Either way, customary services owed by those dwelling close to manorial halls were generally sufficient to deal with the more immediate demands of demesne agriculture – principally hay making – and as population rose and cultivation expanded at the expense of woodland and waste onto the interfluves in the course of the twelfth and thirteenth centuries lords were happy for settlement to disperse across the landscape. Some of the new settlements were sub-manors; some were peasant farms held by free tenure, for a cash rent – indeed, the proportion holding by socage tenures increased steadily in these regions in the

FIGURE 55.
Bradfield Woods in
Suffolk. Ancient
semi-natural coppiced
woods like this are a
more common feature
of the East Anglian
landscape in the area
to the south and west,
than to the north and
east, of the river
Gipping.

post-Conquest period. But most comprised assessed land, held for labour services. With sufficient labour sited close at hand, available to service the principal bottlenecks of the farming year, demesne managers could be relaxed about this convenient dispersion of bond farms across the countryside.

Some of the assarted land was added to the fringes of existing areas of open arable and some took the form of new open fields. But most comprised enclosed land, held in severalty. Sale, exchange, and divided inheritance ensured that such fields sometimes fragmented into strips, but often only to a limited extent – often, for example, to form 'subdivided closes' (above, p. 106) rather than true open-field furlongs. Demesne managers might – given the facts that most demesne arable occupied the lighter land, available for ploughing over a long period in the spring, and that meadows formed a comparatively small element in the economy – be happy for a high proportion of dependent farms to disperse across the landscape. But in this country of large demesnes they were nevertheless reliant on regular labour services for the execution of other, less pressing tasks. They were thus keen to preserve the integrity of even the outlying customary holdings, and impartible inheritance was thus the normal custom in these districts, usually in the form of primogeniture but also, in parts of east Hertfordshire especially, ultimogeniture or 'Borough English'. It is true that there were some manors on which, by the thirteenth century, tenants practised partible inheritance; and it also true that on many manors in this district a market in customary land was well-established (Roden 1973,

357). But overall, the pressures exerted to maintain the integrity of holdings ensured that fragmentation of holdings was much less than in areas to the north and east of the Gipping. Indeed, even free holdings generally passed down the generations intact, as those holding by socage tenure generally followed the dominant local custom, laid down by manorial courts (Homans 1941, 110).

The strength of lordship in this region, compared with districts to the north – at least before the rapid growth in free tenures in the course of the twelfth and thirteenth centuries – probably accounts for a number of other important features of the landscape. In particular, it may in part explain why there were more areas of managed woodland, and more deer parks, than in the area to the north and east of the Gipping, although the greater extent of surviving wood-pastures at the time of Domesday was also presumably a factor in this (Rackham 1986, 124).

Moving south and west, onto the less fertile soils of the Chiltern dipslope and the London Clays, we see similar but more pronounced themes. Lordship was strong in late Saxon times in these areas, demesnes were large, free men and sokemen few in number. By the thirteenth century, when we see their economies clearly, these were areas of heavy labour services. Open fields were mainly limited to the easily ploughed light land of the major valleys; land, once again, in need of regular folding. It was here that most Domesday manors were located, close to narrow ribbons of meadow. Here, once again, demesne managers could deal easily with the principal bottlenecks of the agricultural year and as cultivation expanded, and the great woodlands fell to the axe, farms spread freely across the clay-covered uplands. But at the same time, strength of lordship and the large size of many demesnes ensured, as on the boulder clays to the east, that primogeniture was the usual custom, both on bond and on the increasing number of free holdings, and that the land market was relatively muted. New land was thus less likely to disintegrate into strips; enclosed fields dominated the landscape of the clay-covered interfluves, interspersed with the seigniorial woods and parks, privatised from the wastes.

A wider view

This has been a regional study, focusing on a relatively restricted – if topographically varied – area of England. Readers may be wondering whether the ideas presented here can be more widely applied, in other areas, especially as an explanation for the divergent development of 'woodland' and 'champion' landscapes. Across this rather wider stage, a far greater range of environmental and social variables was at work in moulding the medieval countryside. But in some districts at least we can discern developments similar to those discussed in the previous chapters. Thus the evolution of settlement and landscape on the chalk soils of Wessex or the South Downs – the development of champion countrysides and nucleated villages – must have occurred in similar ways to those suggested for the light lands of western East Anglia or the Chilterns.

Settlement tended to cluster in late Saxon times as a consequence of the restricted availability of water and damp grazing grounds; and in such circumstances, the development of intermixed holdings was a natural consequence of population increase, the growth in the number of farms, and the outward extension of cultivation at the expense of shared 'waste'. And here, too, both the subdivision of holdings in the form of strips, and the eventual regularisation of field systems, were doubtless encouraged by the need for intensive manuring and the organisation of the fold. The field systems of Wessex and the South Downs, however, evidently developed in similar ways to those on the chalklands of south Cambridgeshire and north Hertfordshire, rather than along East Anglian lines. In part this was because the chalk soils were relatively fertile, and population densities higher; in part it was probably because of the greater availability of meadow land. Both factors together encouraged the development of more tightly nucleated patterns of settlement, and more 'regular' field systems, than was usually the case on the sandy lands of western East Anglia.

The model I have proposed for the development of 'regular' open fields on *heavy* soils may also have a wider relevance. The critical factors were the extent of meadow land, and the length of time over which arable soils could be effectively worked, especially in spring. Thus the entire champion belt running through the middle of England – very varied in social and tenurial composition by the time of Domesday – was characterised both by an abundance of good meadow land, concentrated in large blocks, and by soils which included a high proportion of non-calcareous pelosols or pelo-stagnogleys (Ragg *et al.* 1984). Throughout this broad belt of clayland country similar processes may well have been at work: the development of cohesive communities, combining together to plough these difficult soils; the emergence of an economy geared around the exploitation of hay; the steady erosion of 'waste' and the development of extensive forms of farming. But in the 'ancient countryside' districts to the west of the champion Midlands – in Herefordshire, Shropshire, north Warwickshire, Worcestershire and south Staffordshire – the situation was rather different. At the time of Domesday these areas boasted population densities little different from those of the champion lands to the east, but in several districts the land was easier to work – especially the deep, well-drained brown earth soils found in south west Staffordshire, northern and eastern Shropshire, and southern and eastern Herefordshire. Meadow land was more scattered and in some areas comparatively sparse, for valley floors comprised either areas of peat soil or else rather thin ribbons of alluvium. Not surprisingly, these areas developed fairly dispersed patterns of settlement, and irregular field systems, similar in broad outline (although differing in a number of details) to those which emerged in the eastern areas of 'woodland' countryside (Dyer 2000, 106–10).

In other districts of heavy land, rather different combinations of environmental factors worked to discourage the development of villages and extensive, regular field systems. In the Weald of Kent, for example, we can see parallels with the situation on the poor London clays. Tenacious and acid soils and, once again, limited reserves of valley-floor meadow ensured low population densities; late colonisation again involved a plethora of isolated farms, small green-edge settlements, and the dominance of enclosed fields held in severalty.

Custom, trajectory and regional identity

The precise combination of influences moulding the development of the medieval landscape varied from place to place – and others, not noted in this discussion, were also doubtless of importance. But different forms of settlement and field system were never the simple consequence of vague 'cultural' or 'ethnic' factors, nor even a direct function of settlement chronology or tenurial structures. They were the outcome of rational adjustments to complex environmental circumstances made by farmers and managers living in a real world, structured by the rhythm of the seasons and the demands of the soil. Of course, this does not mean that tradition and custom had no part to play in the emergence and maintenance of regional variations. On the contrary: custom was the single most important articulating force in the organisation of early medieval peasant communities, and impacted on the management of the land and the structure of the landscape not only directly but also indirectly, as we have seen in the case of inheritance practices. Yet custom did not come from nowhere. Customary practices were moulded by the environment, and by the relative strengths and particular interests and needs of lords and communities – which were themselves, in large measure, probably a consequence of environmental factors. It may thus be true, as Oliver Rackham has suggested, that many open-field farmers ridged their fields simply because it was the custom to do so – it was what their neighbours did (Rackham 1986, 170). But this does not mean that ridging conferred no practical benefits – merely that it might be carried out with enthusiasm in places where it was less necessary than those in which it had first been adopted. Custom helped to smooth out, within any particular social territory or neighbourhood, variations in farming practice, in settlement patterns and field systems, making them less immediately responsive to or reflective of the details and subtleties of the local environment. Within an area in which environmental circumstances generally favoured the development of certain forms of settlement, in other words, these might appear as the normal way of living, and thus be adopted by those dwelling in particular places where – all things being equal – other arrangements might have been more convenient or agriculturally efficient. To some extent, indeed, the dominance of villages in the 'Central Province' should be viewed in this light. The specific environmental factors encouraging a nucleated pattern of settlement may not have applied in *all*, merely in *most*, cases, within this extensive zone. And at the boundaries of social territories – at major cut-off points in social interaction, such as wide rivers or high, wide interfluves – both custom, and the agrarian landscapes which it moulded, might change more dramatically than the differences in soils or topography might lead us to expect. Crossing a social boundary we would enter a district in which a different equilibrium, a different averaging out of local differences, had developed. This may explain, for example, why the contrast between the 'champion' Midlands, and the 'woodland' districts to the south east, was quite so stark, and why it corresponded so closely with one of the most important watersheds in England, running along the crest of the Chilterns and the East Anglian Heights.

Landscape change at major social boundaries was usually more subtle than this, although significant nevertheless. Throughout the Saxon period a marked cultural and political frontier ran down the line of the river Nene, separating the kingdom of East Anglia from the lands of Mercia and its satellites. The break is reflected, for example, in the sudden cut-off in the distribution of middle Saxon Ipswich Ware (Silvester 1993, 27–8). To the east of the river, on the silt soils of the Norfolk Marshland, green- and common-edge settlements were a standard feature of the medieval settlement pattern; but to the west, they were almost entirely absent (Silvester 1993, 32–3). Had settlement and field systems reflected environmental factors more closely, transitions like this would have been more gradual. Custom, by emphasising the accepted and the normal within particular social territories, served to sharpen the breaks in the landscape. Nevertheless, this does not mean that every time we find a marked change in settlement patterns or field systems, we have discovered some otherwise undocumented 'cultural frontier'. Where such breaks in landscape correspond with changes in soils or topography, it is easier and more sensible to explain them in straightforward agrarian terms.

Tradition and custom thus played their part in the formation of landscape regions, and in the practice of medieval farming. But in addition, and over a longer time period, the landscape itself – the layout of farms and fields, the pattern of settlement – could have a determining influence on the development of agrarian life. Indeed, perhaps the greatest fascination of landscape lies in the way that spatial patterns and relationships (and associated institutional forms) can persist, as an active and structuring force in social and economic organisation, long after the circumstances that engendered them have changed beyond recognition. The various landscapes of medieval England, once established, continued to mould patterns of social and economic organisation for half a millennium or more.

The rapid demographic growth which had been a major factor in most of the developments discussed in this book ground to a halt in the fourteenth century, with the onset of the Black Death and other disasters; and from the fifteenth century, open fields began to be enclosed on some scale. There were fewer people, but real wages were higher and rents lower. Farms became larger and, as living standards increased, farmers began to specialise in the production of some particular commodity, or group of commodities. These developments were not simply a consequence of demographic change, but were part of wider changes in the character of society, associated with the emergence of a capitalist, market-orientated economy: and they continued even when population growth

picked up again in the sixteenth century. In some areas arable crops continued to be the most important product, but in others cattle farming or sheep grazing increased in significance and by the sixteenth century a number of distinct farming regions had developed. Their pattern was complicated: Figure 57, based on the work of Joan Thirsk, represents a very simplified schedule (Thirsk 1987).

For farmers wanting to specialise in rearing, fattening, or dairying the narrow, intermixed, unhedged strips of the open fields were a nuisance and an impediment. Pastoral pursuits developed earliest where common pastures were extensive, but also where, as in 'ancient countryside' districts, the majority of land lay in hedged fields or in open fields which could be enclosed with relative ease. The 'irregular' open fields in woodland districts were particularly susceptible to informal, piecemeal enclosure because the strips of any cultivator were usually clustered in the area close to his farm – rather than being widely scattered across the whole of a parish – so that each man generally had few neighbours (Williamson 2000b, 64–6) (Figure 56).

It was thus a comparatively easy matter to gather together, through purchase or exchange, a group of contiguous strips, and enclose them. Moreover, there was little opposition to such a process, as communal organisation of agriculture was generally often less deeply entrenched in these districts, with their scattered farms and hamlets, than it was in the champion lands, while the abundance of commons reduced the economic importance of fallow grazing. By the

FIGURE 56.
Billingford, Norfolk. There were extensive areas of irregular open fields in the parish in medieval times but by the nineteenth century these had entirely disappeared as a consequence of piecemeal enclosure. The glebe land, however, was not so easily consolidated by this method – the incumbent was, in effect, a tenant rather than an owner – and thus continued to take the form of scattered strips, although now embedded within enclosed fields.

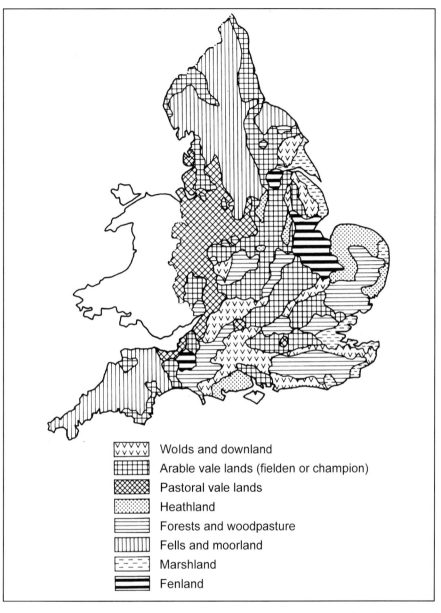

FIGURE 57.
Farming regions in
early-modern England,
after Joan Thirsk. In
the sixteenth and
seventeenth centuries
some areas of lowland
England continued to
specialise in arable
production – the
sheep-corn districts of
'wold and downland'
and 'heathland', and
the 'arable vale lands',
largely concentrated in
the champion
Midlands. Elsewhere,
in the 'pastoral vale
lands' and the 'forests
and woodpastures',
livestock rearing in
enclosed landscapes
predominated.

Wolds and downland
Arable vale lands (fielden or champion)
Pastoral vale lands
Heathland
Forests and woodpasture
Fells and moorland
Marshland
Fenland

middle of the seventeenth century few open fields existed on the claylands of
East Anglia or the Home Counties, or in the Welsh Marches and the West
Country, although large areas of common grazing often survived in these
districts. As a consequence, the division between woodland and champion
became sharper than ever before. It became manifest as a clear and simple
distinction between landscapes of open fields and communal farming, and
landscapes in severalty; and also, though to a lesser extent, between landscapes
which were primarily pastoral, and those which were essentially arable in
character. Some historians and archaeologists still write as if this was always
the main distinction between the 'two countrysides' (Johnson 1996, 25–8).

But it was only its early-modern manifestation, and even in the seventeenth century the correspondence between 'woodland' areas, and pastoral farming, was only ever partial, with some (such as the Chilterns) continuing for the most part to specialise in arable husbandry.

Custom, tradition and the physical structures of landscape were thus powerful factors in the creation and perpetuation of regional differences in late medieval and post-medieval times. But so too were the kinds of subtle environmental factors which, as I have explained, had structured those more basic patterns of landscape which emerged in the Saxon period. In particular, the shortage of good-quality meadow continued to be a major influence on the development of farming practice in a number of regions, affecting, for example, the speed with which horses replaced oxen as the main draft animals in the course of the twelfth and thirteenth centuries. Horses were faster and more adaptable than oxen but, as Walter of Henley argued, they were more expensive to keep, for they were fed on oats as well as hay, whereas oxen were, for the most part, fed on hay alone (Langdon 1986, 159). Langdon has suggested that in areas with little pasture, livestock were fed a higher proportion of grain and this favoured the adoption of horses, as they benefited more than oxen from a grain-rich diet (Langdon 1986, 160). But oxen remained the dominant plough beasts in the champion Midlands, where very little pasture existed by the twelfth century, and a more important factor was probably the extent of good-quality meadow land. Where hay was scarce, it would make sense to devote a portion of the arable to legumes or oats, and use horses for traction. Indeed, those areas with the *greatest* shortage of meadow – Norfolk and north Suffolk – were precisely those in which 'horse ploughing was introduced earliest and proceeded furthest' (Campbell 2000, 129). The only other regions of England where horse ploughing made such headway in the twelfth and thirteenth centuries were likewise ones in which meadows were in very limited supply – the Chilterns, the Yorkshire Wolds, and north Kent (Campbell 2000, 131). But what is also striking is that similar patterns in farming practice appear again at a much later date. The curious paradox of East Anglian agriculture – soils and climate ideally suited to the cultivation of grain crops, yet a marked shortage of good-quality meadow land – may be one reason why the key agricultural developments of the late seventeenth and eighteenth centuries first occurred here – the cultivation of turnips and clover as livestock fodder. Once again, the other districts which contemporaries believed were at the vanguard of the 'new husbandry' included the Wolds and the Chilterns (Williamson 2002). In these and other ways, quite subtle environmental factors combined to mould major variations in agrarian practices, and in the life of the countryside, into comparatively recent times.

Conclusion

The widespread adoption of turnips and clover was one aspect of a wider package of change which transformed English farming in the eighteenth and early nineteenth centuries, the period of the so-called 'agricultural revolution'. Parliamentary enclosure removed vast tracts of common grazing and all but a few fragments of the old open fields; while marling, the under-drainage of arable land, and the systematic reclamation of fens together created a new geography of farming in England, much like that of today (Williamson 2002). Essex, East Anglia, the Fens, and the eastern seaboard were now the prime arable areas. The Midlands and west became the principal livestock-farming and dairying districts. But in innumerable ways the ancient divisions in the landscape, between 'woodland' and 'champion' areas, remained and still remain. The old ploughridges, fossilised by conversion to pasture in the Midland shires, are steadily disappearing but the contrast between 'village England' and the landscape of isolated farms and greenside hamlets is still very evident, structuring even the character of the 'natural' environment. Hedges in ancient countryside areas are generally more species-rich than those in former champion lands, and many contain a range of slow-colonising plants only rarely found in Midland hedges (Figures 58 and 59). The high water mark of champion agriculture effectively wiped clean the environmental slate, removing all habitats except arable fields and meadows.

The Midland open fields must have been environmental disaster areas, and even from the perspective of agricultural efficiency they compared poorly with districts of more irregular field systems and enclosed fields. In these, the survival of woods and pastures ensured recurrent inputs of nutrients from outside the

FIGURE 58.
Species-poor hawthorn hedge at Warham in north Norfolk, typical of those created by parliamentary enclosure.

FIGURE 59.
Species-rich hedge at
Littlebury Green in
north-west Essex, full
of dogwood, spindle,
hazel and wayfaring
tree.

NATIONAL TRUST

arable fields themselves, while the more flexible attitude towards cropping and
rotations allowed, in many areas, a variety of innovations (Campbell 1983).
The Midland system, in contrast, 'embodied strong institutional restraints
upon any radical alteration and was founded upon the virtual elimination of
'natural' grazings, a trend difficult to reverse under conditions of population
pressure' (Fox 1984, 146). Midland farmers used their one great advantage –
abundant hay supplies – to cope with population growth in the simplest
possible way – by making the ploughlands as extensive as possible. But in so
doing they locked themselves into a system in which levels of production
would always be limited.

Some readers may have found this book an uncongenial read, especially in
its use of models, often with little supporting evidence, to explain early
landscape development; and, above all, in its strongly environmental, 'cow
and plough' approach to early medieval societies. I would plead guilty on both
charges, but would neither apologise nor recant. Models and guesswork are
indispensable when direct evidence is in short supply. And as for the role of
the environment, I can do no better than quote W. G. Hoskins:

> Ecology is that branch of science which treats of plants and animals in
> relation to the environment in which they live. Human beings ought
> to be studied in this way ... We should be studying living human

communities and their reaction to their environment, and to changes in that environment, over the past 2,000 years ... (Hoskins 1966, 21–2).

Unquestionably, many of the arguments advanced in this book will not stand the test of time. But its essential message may prove more durable – that the character of fields and settlement patterns cannot be understood in isolation from the practice of farming, and that farming can only be understood in the context of the environment. The fact that any other approach is acceptable to historians merely highlights the extent to which modern urban, industrial society has become dangerously divorced from the realities of food production and the natural world.

Bibliography

Abels, R. (1996) 'Sheriffs, lord-seeking and the Norman settlement of the south-east Midlands', *Anglo-Norman Studies* **19**, 19–50.

Addington, S. (1982) 'Landscape and settlements in south Norfolk', *Norfolk Archaeology* **28**, 97–139.

Allen, R. C. (1992) *Enclosure and the Yeoman: The Agricultural Development of the South Midlands 1450–1850*, Oxford.

Allison, K. J. (1957) 'The sheep-corn husbandry of Norfolk in the sixteenth and seventeenth Centuries', *Agricultural History Review* **5**, 12–30.

Arnold, C. and Wardle, P. (1981) 'Early medieval settlement patterns in England', *Medieval Archaeology* **25**, 145–9.

Ault, W. O. (1972) *Open-field Farming in Medieval England: A Study of Village By-laws*, London.

Avery, B. W., Findlay, D. C., and Mackney, D. (1974) *Soil Map of England and Wales*, Soil Survey, Harpenden.

Bailey, M. (1989) *A Marginal Economy? East Anglian Breckland in the Later Middle Ages*, Cambridge.

Bailey, M. (1990) 'Sand into gold: the evolution of the foldcourse system in west Suffolk, 1200–1600', *Agricultural History Review* **38**, 40–57.

Bailey, M. (ed.) (1998) *The Hertfordshire Lay Subsidy Rolls 1307 and 1334*, Hertford.

Baker, A. R. H. (1973) 'Field systems of south-east England'. In A. H. R. Baker and R. A. Butlin (eds.) *Studies of Field Systems in the British Isles*, Cambridge, 377–429.

Baker, A. R. H. (1973) 'Changes in the late Middle Ages'. In H. C. Darby (ed.) *A New Historical Geography of England*, Cambridge, 186–247.

Baker, A. R. H. and Butlin, R. A. (1973) 'Conclusion: problems and perspectives'. In A. H. R. Baker and R. A. Butlin (eds.) *Studies of Field Systems in the British Isles*, Cambridge, 619–656.

Barker, D., Birch, S., Hunt, J., Hurst, V. and Williams, K. 'Settlement patterns in Guilden Morden', *The South-West Cambridgeshire Project: Interim Report, 1999–2000*, 17–27.

Barton, P. (1981) *Medieval Economy and Society in Shenley: A Hertfordshire Manor in the Thirteenth and Fourteenth Centuries*, Hertford.

Bassett, S. J. (1982) *Saffron Walden: Excavation and Research 1972–80*. CBA Research Report **45**, Chelmsford.

Basset, S. J. (1989) 'In Search of the Origins of Anglo-Saxon Kingdoms'. In S. J. Bassett (ed.) *The Origins of Anglo-Saxon Kingdoms*, Leicester, 3–27.

Bassett, S. (1997) 'Continuity and fission in the Anglo-Saxon landscape: the origins of the Rodings (Essex)', *Landscape History* **19**, 25–42.

Bath, B. H. Slicher van, (1963) *The Agrarian History of Western Europe AD 500–1850*, London.

Bedingfeld, A. L. (1966) *A Cartulary of Creake Abbey*, Norfolk Record Society, Norwich.

Bell, M. (1981) 'Sediments and environmental changes'. In M. Jones and G. Dimbleby (eds.) *The Environment of Man: the Iron Age to the Anglo-Saxon period*, British Archaeological Report **87**, Oxford, 75–91.

Bennett, H. S. (1937) *Life on the English Manor*, Cambridge.

Biddick, K. (1989) *The Other Economy: Pastoral Husbandry on a Medieval Estate*, Berkeley.

Birch, W. de Grey (1885–99) *Cartularium Saxonicum*, London.

Bibliography

Bishop, T. A. M. (1935) 'Assarting and the growth of the open fields', *Economic History Review* **6**, 26–40.

Blair, J. (1988) 'Minster churches in the landscape'. In D. Hooke (ed.) *Anglo-Saxon Settlements*, Oxford.

Blomefield, F. (1805) *An Essay Towards a Topographic History of the County of Norfolk: Vol. 1: Diss Hundred*, Norwich.

Brannigan, K. (1967) 'Romano-British rural settlement in the western Chilterns', *Archaeological Journal* **124**, 129–159.

Brannigan, K. (1971) *Latimer: A Belgic, Roman, Dark Age and Early Modern Farm*, London.

Brannigan, K. (1973) *Town and Country: The archaeology of Verulamium and the Roman Chilterns*, London.

Bridbury, A. R. (1992) *The English Economy from Bede to the Reformation*, Woodbridge.

Broad, J. (1980) 'Alternate husbandry and permanent pasture in the Midlands, 1650–1800', *Agricultural History Review* **28**, 77–89.

Brown, A. E. and Taylor, C. (1989) 'The origins of dispersed settlement: some results from Bedfordshire', *Landscape History* **11**, 61–81.

Brown, T. and Foard, G. (1998) 'The Saxon landscape: a regional perspective. In P. Everson and T. Williamson (eds.) *The Archaeology of Landscape: Studies Presented to Christopher Taylor*, Manchester, 67–94.

Brunt, L. (1997) *Nature or Nurture? Explaining English Wheat Yields in the Agricultural Revolution*, University of Oxford Discussion Papers in Economic and Social History No. 19, Oxford.

Bryant, S., Perry, B. and Williamson, T. in press *A Relict Landscape in South-East Hertfordshire: Archaeological and Topographic Investigations in the Wormley Woods Area*.

Burrell, E. D. R. (1960) *Historical Geography of the Sandlings of Suffolk, 1600 to 1850*. Unpublished MSc thesis, University of London.

Caird, J. (1852) *English Agriculture 1851–52*, London.

Campbell, B. M. S. (1981a) 'Commonfield origins – the regional dimension'. In T. Rowley (ed.) *The Origins of Open-Field Agriculture*, London, 112–29.

Campbell, B. M. S. (1981b) 'The extent and layout of commonfields in east Norfolk', *Norfolk Archaeology* **28**, 5–32.

Campbell, B. M. S. (1983) 'Agricultural progress in medieval England: some evidence from East Norfolk', *Economic History Review* Second Series **36**, 26–46.

Campbell, B. M. S. (2000) *English Seigniorial Agriculture, 1250–1450*, Cambridge.

Campbell, B. M. S. and Overton, M. (1993) 'A new perspective in medieval and early modern agriculture: six centuries of Norfolk farming, *c.* 1250–1850', *Past and Present* **141**, 38–105.

Chambers, J. D. and Mingay, G. E. (1966) *The Agricultural Revolution 1750–1880*, London.

Chatwin, C. P. (1961) *British Regional Geology: East Anglia and Adjoining Areas*, London.

Chibnall, A. C. (1965) *Sherington: Fiefs and Fields of a Buckinghamshire Village*, Cambridge.

Cook, H. (1999) 'Soil water management: principles and purposes'. In H. Cook and T. Williamson (eds.) *Water Management in the English landscape: Field, Marsh and Meadow*, Edinburgh, 15–27.

Cromarty, D. (1966) *The Fields of Saffron Walden*, Chelmsford.

Cunliffe, B. (1978) 'Settlement and population in the British Iron Age: some facts, figures, and fantasies'. In B. Cunliffe and T. Rowley (eds.) *Lowland Iron Age Communities in Europe*, British Archaeological Reports **48**, Oxford.

Cunliffe, B. (1995) *Iron Age Britain*, London.

Darby, H. C. (1940) *The Medieval Fenland*, Cambridge.

Darby, H. C. (1971) *The Domesday Geography of Eastern England*, Cambridge.

Darby, H. C. (1977) *Domesday England*, Cambridge.

Davenport, F. G. (1906) *The Economic Development of a Norfolk Manor*, London.

Davies, W. and Vierck, H. (1974) 'The contexts of the tribal hidage: social aggregates and settlement patterns', *Fruhmittelalterliche Studia* **8**, 223–93.

Davis, R. H. C. (ed.) (1954) *The Kalendar of Abbot Sampson of Bury St Edmunds and Related Documents*, Camden Third Series, LXXXIV, London.

Davis, R. H. C. (1955) 'East Anglia and the Danes', *Transactions of the Royal Historical Society* **5**, 23–39

Davison, A. (1990) *The Evolution of Settlement in Three Parishes in South East Norfolk* (Published as: *East Anglian Archaeology* **49**).

Davison, A. (1994) 'The field archaeology of Bodney, and the Stanta Extension', *Norfolk Archaeology* **42**, 57–79.

Davison, A. and Cushion, B. (1999) 'The Archaeology of the Hargham Estate', *Norfolk Archaeology* **53**, 257–274.

Dimbleby, G. W. (1962) *The Development of British Heathlands and their Soils*, Oxford.

Dodgshon, R. (1980) *The Origins of British Field Systems: An Interpretation*, London.

Dodwell, B. (1941) 'The free peasantry of East Anglia in Domesday', *Norfolk Archaeology* **27**, 145–57.

Dodwell, B. (1967) 'Holdings and inheritance in medieval East Anglia', *Economic History Review* **20**, 53–66.

Dyer, C. (1996) 'Rural settlements in medieval Warwickshire', *Transactions of the Birmingham and Warwickshire Archaeological Society* **100**, 117–32.

Dyer, C. (2000) 'Woodlands and wood-pasture in the west of England'. In J. Thirsk (ed.) *The English Rural Landscape*, Oxford, 97–121.

Emery, F. (1974) *The Oxfordshire Landscape*, London.

Everitt, A. (1977) 'River and wold: reflections on the historical origins of regions and *pays*', *Journal of Historical Geography* **3**, 1–19.

Eyre, S. R. (1955) 'The curving ploughland strip and its historical implications', *Agricultural History Review* **3**, 80–94.

Faith, R. (1997) *The English Peasantry and the Growth of Lordship*, Leicester.

Fisher, D. J. V. (1973) *The Anglo-Saxon Age*, London.

Fleming, A. (1988) *The Dartmoor Reaves*, London.

Fleming, A. (1998) 'Prehistoric landscapes and the quest for territorial pattern'. In P. Everson and T. Williamson (eds.) *The Archaeology of Landscape: Studies Presented to Christopher Taylor*, Manchester, 42–67.

Fleming, A. (1998b) *Swaledale: Valley of the Wild River*, Edinburgh.

Fleming, R. (1991) *Kings and Lords in Conquest England*, London.

Foard, G. (1978) 'Systematic fieldwalking and the investigation of Saxon settlement in Northamptonshire', *World Archaeology* **9**.

Ford, W. J. (1976) 'Some settlement patterns in the central region of the Warwickshire Avon'. In P. Sawyer (ed.) *English Medieval Settlement*, London, 274–94.

Folkingham, W. (1610) *Feudographica*, London.

Fowler, P. J. and Taylor, C. (1978) 'Roman fields into medieval furlongs'. In H. C. Bowen and P. J. Fowler (eds.) *Early Land Allotment in the British Isles*, British Archaeological Reports 48, Oxford, 159–62.

Fox, H. S. A. (1981) 'Approaches to the adoption of the midland system'. In T. Rowley (ed.) *The Origins of Open-Field Agriculture*, London, 64–111.

Fox, H. S. A. (1983) 'Contraction: desertion and dwindling of dispersed settlement in a Devon parish', *Medieval Village Research Group Annual Report* **31**, 40–2.

Fox, H. S. A. (1984) 'Some ecological dimensions of English medieval field systems'. In K. Biddick (ed.) *Archaeological Approaches to Medieval Europe*, Kalamazoo, 129–158.

Fox, H. S. A. (1989) 'The people of the wolds'. In M. Aston, D. Austin, and C. Dyer (eds.) *The Rural Settlements of Medieval England: Studies Presented to Maurice Beresford and John Hurst*, Oxford, 77–104.

Friel, I. (1982) 'The *Hicce* – an Anglo-Saxon tribe of the Hitchin area', *Hertfordshire's Past* **13**, 2–18.

Gardner, H. W. (1967) *A Survey of the Agriculture of Hertfordshire*, Royal Agricultural Society County Survey **5**, London.

Gelling, M. (1984) *Place Names in the Landscape*, London.

Gelling, M. (1992) *The West Midlands in the Early Middle Ages*, London.

Gervers, M. (ed.) (1982) *The Cartulary of the Knights of St John of Jerusalem in England, Part 1: Secunda Camera, Essex*, Records of Social and Economic History New Series 6, Oxford.

Gervers, M. (ed.) (1996) *The Cartulary of the Knights of St John of Jerusalem in England Part 2: Primara Camera, Essex*, Records of Social and Economic History New Series 23, Oxford.

Gomme, G. L. (1890) *The Village Community*, London.

Gover, J. E. B., Mawer, A. and Stenton, F. M. (1938) *The Place-names of Hertfordshire*, Cambridge.

Gray, H. L. (1915) *English Field Systems*, Cambridge, Mass.

Grieg, J. (1988) 'Plant resources'. In G. Astill and A. Grant (eds.) *The Countryside of Medieval England*, Oxford, 108–27.

Grigson, G. (ed.) (1984) *Thomas Tusser: The Five Hundred Points of Good Husbandry (1580 Edition)*, Oxford.

Hadley, D. (1996) '"And they proceeded to plough and to support themselves": the Scandinavian settlement of England', *Anglo-Norman Studies* 19, 69–96.

Hains, B. A. and Horton, A. (1969) *British Regional Geology: Central England*, London.

Hall, D. (1981) 'The origins of open-field agriculture: the archaeological fieldwork evidence'. In T. Rowley (ed.) *The Origins of Open-Field Agriculture*, London, 22–38.

Hall, D. (1982) *Medieval Fields*, Aylesbury.

Hall, D. (1989) 'Field systems and township structure'. In M. Aston, D. Austin, and C. Dyer (eds.) *The Rural Settlements of Medieval England*, Oxford, 191–206.

Hall, D. (1995) *The Open Fields of Northamptonshire*, Northamptonshire Record Society 38, Northampton.

Hall, D. (1999) 'The drainage of arable land in medieval England'. In H. Cook and T. Williamson (eds.) *Water Management in the English Landscape: Field, Marsh and Meadow*, Edinburgh, 28–40.

Halstead, P. (1998) 'Ask the fellows who lop the hay: leaf-fodder in the mountains of northwest Greece', *Rural History* 9, 2, 211–234.

Hamerow, H. (1991) 'Settlement mobility and the "Middle Saxon Shift": rural settlements and settlement patterns in Anglo-Saxon England', *Anglo-Saxon England* 20, 1–17.

Hamerow, H. (1993) *Excavations at Mucking, Vol. 2: The Anglo-Saxon Settlement*, London.

Hammond, J. (1984) 'Gnatingdon: DMV or mislaid manor?, *Norfolk Archaeological Research Group News* 37, 10–15.

Hanley, J. A. (1951) *Progressive Farming*, London.

Hardy, M. (1989) 'The Waveney Valley survey', *Current Archaeology* 115, 266–9.

Hardy, M. and Martin, E. (1986) 'Archaeological fieldwork: South Elmham St Cross and South Elmham St James', *Proceedings of the Suffolk Institute of Archaeology and History* 36, 147–50.

Hardy, M. and Martin, E. (1987) 'Archaeological fieldwork: South Elmham St Margaret, All Saints and St Nicholas', *Proceedings of the Suffolk Institute of Archaeology and History* 36, 231–35.

Harrison, M. J., Mead, W. R., and Pannett, D. J. (1965) 'A midland ridge and furrow map', *Geographical Journal* 131, 366–9.

Harrison, S. (2002) 'Open fields and earlier landscapes: six parishes in south-east Cambridgeshire', LANDSCAPES 3, 1, 35–54.

Hart, C. (1966) *The Early Charters of Eastern England*, London.

Harvey, M. (1981) 'The origin of planned field systems in Holderness, Yorkshire'. In T. Rowley (ed.) *The Origins of Open-Field Agriculture*, London, 184–201.

Harvey, P. D. A. (1984) 'Introduction'. In P. D. A. Harvey (ed.) *The Peasant Land Market in England*, Oxford, 1–30.

Harvey, S. (1976) 'The knight and the knight's fee in England'. In R. H. Hilton (ed.) *Peasants, Knights and Heretics: Studies in Medieval English Social History*, Cambridge, 133–73.

Harvey, S. (1988) 'Domesday England'. In H. E. Hallam (ed.) *The Agrarian History of England and Wales Volume II: 1042–1350*, Cambridge, 45–137.

Hervey, F. (ed.) (1925) *The Pinchbeck Register*, Brighton.

Hesse, M. (1992) 'Fields, tracks and boundaries in the Creakes, North Norfolk', *Norfolk Archaeology* **41**, 305–324.

Hesse, M. (1998) 'Medieval field systems and land tenure in South Creake, Norfolk', *Norfolk Archaeology* **43**, 79–97.

Hesse, M. (2000) 'Field systems of south-west Cambridgeshire: Abington Piggots, Litlington and the Mile Ditches', *Proceedings of the Cambridge Antiquarian Society* **89**, 49–58.

Hey, G. (2001) 'Yarnton', *Current Archaeology* **173**, 216–24.

Higham, N. J. (1990) 'Settlement, land use and Domesday ploughlands', *Landscape History* **12**, 33–44.

Hill, D. (2000) '*Sulh* – the Anglo-Saxon plough *c.* 1000 AD', *Landscape History* **22**, 7–19

Hilton, R. H. (1973) *Bond Men Made Free*, London.

Hilton, R. H. and Sawyer, P. H. (1963) 'Technical determinism: the stirrup and the plough', *Past and Present* **24**, 90–100.

Hodge, C., Burton, R., Corbett, W., Evans, R., and Scale, R. (1984) *Soils and their Uses in Eastern England*, Harpenden.

Hodges, R. (1989) *The Anglo-Saxon Achievement: Archaeology and the Beginnings of English Society*, London.

Homans, G. C. (1941) *English Villagers of the Thirteenth Century*, Cambridge, Massachusetts.

Homans, G. C. (1969) 'The explanation of English regional differences', *Past and Present* **42**, 18–34.

Hooke, D. (1998) *The Landscape of Anglo-Saxon England*, Leicester.

Hoskins, W. G. (1949) 'The Leicestershire crop returns of 1801'. In W. G. Hoskins (ed.) *Studies in Leicestershire Agricultural History*, Leicester.

Hoskins, W. G. (1955) *The Making of the English Landscape*, London.

Hoskins, W. G. (1966) *English Local History: The Past and the Future*, Leicester.

Hoskins, W. G. and Stamp, L. Dudley (1966) *The Common Lands of England and Wales*, London.

Hudspith, R. E. T. (1995) 'Fieldwalking in South Bedfordshire'. In R. Holgate (ed.) *Chiltern Archaeology: Recent Work*, Dunstable, 131–39.

Hunn, J. (1994) *Reconstruction and Measurement of Landscape Change*, British Archaeological Report 236, Oxford.

Hunn, J. (1995) 'The Romano-British landscape of the Chiltern Dipslope: a study of settlement around Verulamium'. In R. Holgate (ed.) *Chiltern Archaeology: Recent Work*, Dunstable, 76–91.

Hunn, J. (1996) *Settlement Patterns in Hertfordshire: A Review of the Typology and Function of Enclosures in the Iron Age and Roman Landscape*, British Archaeological Report **249**, Oxford.

Hunter, J. (1999) *The Essex Landscape: A Study of its Form and History*, Chelmsford.

Jewell, H. (1972) *English Local Administration in the Middle Ages*, Newton Abbot.

Johnson, M. (1996) *An Archaeology of Capitalism*, Oxford.

Jones, G. R. J. (1971) 'The multiple estate as a model framework for tracing early stages in the evolution of rural settlement'. In F. Dussart (ed.) *L'Habitat et les Paysages Ruraux d'Europe*, Liege.

Jones, G. R. J. (1976) 'Multiple estates and early settlement'. In P. H. Sawyer (ed.) *Medieval Settlement: Continuity and Change,* London, 15–40.

Jones, G. R. J. (1981) 'Early customary tenures in Wales and open-field agriculture'. In T. Rowley (ed.) *The Origins of Open-Field Agriculture*, London, 202–225.

Kerridge, E. (1967) *The Agricultural Revolution*, London.

Kerridge, E. (1973) *The Farmers of Old England*, London.

Kerridge, E. (1969) *Agrarian Problems in the Sixteenth Century and After*, London.

Kerridge, E. (1992) *The Common Fields of England*, Manchester.

Kissock, J. (1992) 'The origins of the midland village: discussion session at the Economic History Society's Conference 1992', *Medieval Settlement Research Group Annual Report* 6, 14.

Langdon, J. (1986) *Horses, Oxen, and Technological Innovation*, Cambridge.

Larking, L. B. and Kemble, J. M. (eds.) (1857) *The Knights Hospitallers in England: Being the Report of Prior Philip de Thame to the Grand Master, Elyan de Villanova, for AD 1338*, London.

Lennard, R. (1946) 'The economic position of the Domesday *villani*', *Economic Journal* 56, 244–64.

Levett, A. E. (1938) *Studies in Manorial History*, Oxford.

Lewis, C., Mitchell-Fox, P. and Dyer, C. (1997 and 2002) *Village, Hamlet and Field: Changing Medieval Settlements in Central England*, Manchester and Macclesfield.

Liddiard, R. (1999) 'The distribution of ridge and furrow in Norfolk: ploughing practice and subsequent land use', *Agricultural History Review* 47, 1–6.

Liddle, P. (1994) 'The Melbourne area survey'. In M. Parker Pearson and R. T. Schadla-Hall (eds.) *Looking at the Land: Archeological Landscapes in Eastern England*, Leicester, 34–7.

Liebermann, F. (1935) *Die Gesetze der Anelsachsen*, Leipzig.

Maine, H. S. (1881) *Village Communities in the East and West*, London.

Maitland, F. W. (1881) *Domesday Book and Beyond*, London.

Margeson, S. (1996) 'Viking settlement in Norfolk: a study of new evidence'. In S. Margeson, B. Ayers and S. Heywood (eds.) *A Festival of Norfolk Archaeology*, Norwich, 47–57.

Martin, E. (1988) 'Greens, commons and tyes'. In D. Dymond and E. Martin (eds.) *An Historical Atlas of Suffolk*, Ipswich, 48–9.

Martin, E. (1995) 'Greens, commons and tyes in Suffolk'. In A. Longcroft and R. Joby (eds.) *East Anglian Studies: essays presented to J. C. Barringer*, Norwich, 167–78.

Martin, E. (1999) 'Suffolk in the Iron Age'. In J. Davies and T. Williamson (eds.) *Land of the Iceni: The Iron Age in Northern East Anglia*, Norwich.

Martin, E. (2001) 'Rural settlement patterns in medieval Suffolk', *Annual Report of the Medieval Settlement Research Group* 15, 5–7.

Mathew, W. (1993) 'Marling in British agriculture: a case of partial identity', *Agricultural History Review* 41, 97–110.

Medlycott, M. and Germany, M. (1994) 'Archaeological fieldwalking in Essex, 1985–1993: interim results', *Essex Archaeology and History* 25, 14–27.

Millar, F. G. (1926) *English Illuminated Manuscripts from the Xth to the XIIIth Centuries*, Paris and Brussels.

Miller, E. (1957) *The Abbey and Bishopric of Ely: A Social History of an Ecclesiastical Estate from the Tenth Century to the Early Fourteenth Century*, Cambridge.

Miller, E. and Hatcher, J. (1978) *Medieval England: Rural Society and Economic Change 1086–1348*, London.

Monteith, D. (1957) *Saffron Walden and its Environs: A Study in the Development of a Landscape*, unpublished MA thesis, University of London.

Morris, M. and Wainwright, A. (1995) 'Iron Age and Romano-British settlement and economy in the Upper Bulbourne Valley, Hertfordshire'. In R. Holgate (ed.) *Chiltern Archaeology: Recent Work*, Dunstable, 68–75.

Morris, R. (1989) *Churches in the Landscape*, London.

Mosby, J. E. G. (1938) *The Land of Britain: Norfolk (Land Utilisation Survey, Part 70)*, London.

Muir, R. (2000) 'Pollards in Nidderdale: a landscape history', *Rural History: Economy, Society, Culture* 11,1, 95–111.

Munby, L. M. (1977) *The Hertfordshire Landscape*, London.

Newman, J. (2001) 'A landscape of dispersed settlement – change and growth in south-east Suffolk', *Medieval Settlement Research Group Annual Report* 15, 7–8.

Newton, K. C. (1960) *Thaxted in the Fourteenth Century*, Chelmsford.

Newton, K. C. (1970) *The Manor of Writtle: The Development of a Royal Manor in Essex, c. 1086–1500*, Chichester.

Niblett, R. (1995) *Roman Hertfordshire*, Wimbourne.

Oosthuizen, S. (1994) 'Saxon commons in south Cambridgeshire', *Proceedings of the Cambridge Antiquarian Society* **82**, 93–100.

Oosthuizen, S. (1997) 'Prehistoric fields into medieval furlongs?: evidence from Caxton, south Cambridgeshire', *Proceedings of the Cambridge Antiquarian Society* **86**, 145–52.

Oosthuizen, S. and Hesse, M. (2000) 'Summary report, 1999–2000', *The South-West Cambridgeshire project: Interim Report, 1999–2000*, 1–2.

Orwin, C. S. and Orwin, C. S. (1938) *The Open Fields*, Oxford.

Oschinsky, D. (1971) *Walter of Henley and Other Treatises on Estate Management and Accounting*, Oxford.

Partridge, C. (1989) *Foxholes Farm: a Multi-period Gravel Site*, Hertford.

Payne, F. G. (1957) 'The British plough: some stages in its development', *Agricultural History Review* **5**, 74–84.

Pelham, R. A. (1936) 'Fourteenth-century England'. In H. C. Darby (ed.) *An Historical Geography of England Before AD 1800*, Cambridge.

Pettit, P. A. (1968) *The Royal Forests of Northamptonshire: A Study of their Economy 1558–1714*, Northamptonshire Record Society Vol. 23, Northampton.

Phythian Adams, C. (1987) *Rethinking English Local History*, Leicester.

Phythian Adams, C. (1993) *Societies, Culture and Kinship 1500–1850: Cultural Provinces in English Local History*, Leicester.

Pitt, W. (1813) *General View of the Agriculture of the County of Northampton*, London.

Pollock, F. and Maitland, F. W. (1895) *The History of English Law*, Cambridge.

Postan, M. M. (1973) 'The chronology of labour services'. In M. M. Postan, *Essays on Medieval Agriculture and General Problems of the Medieval Economy*, Cambridge, 89–106.

Postgate, M. R. (1962) 'The field systems of Breckland', *Agricultural History Review* **10**, 80–101.

Postgate, M. R. (1964) *The Open Fields of Cambridgeshire*, unpublished PhD thesis, University of Cambridge.

Postgate, M. R. (1973) 'Field systems of East Anglia'. In R. A. Baker and A. R. H. Butlin (eds.), *Studies of Field Systems in the British Isles*, Cambridge, 281–324.

Prince, H. (1964) 'The origins of pits and depressions in Norfolk', *Geography* **49**, 15–32.

Rackham, O. (1976) *Trees and Woodlands in the British Landscape*, London.

Rackham, O. (1980a) *Ancient Woodland*, London.

Rackham, O. (1980b) 'The Medieval Landscape of Essex'. In D.Buckley (ed.) *The Archaeology of Essex to AD 1500*, London, 103–107.

Rackham, O. (1986) *The History of the Countryside*, London.

Rackham, O. (1988) 'Medieval woods'. In D. Dymond and E. Martin (eds.) *An Historical Atlas of Suffolk*, Ipswich, 50–1.

Ragg, J. M., Beard, G. R., George, H., Heaven, F. W., Hollis, J. M., Jones, R. J. A., Palmer, R. C., Reeve, M. J., Robson, J. D., and Whitfield, W. A. D. (1984) *Soils and their Uses in Midland and Western England*, Harpenden.

Reaney, P. H. (1935) *The Place Names of Essex*, Cambridge.

Reed, M. (1979) *The Buckinghamshire Landscape*, London.

Reed, M. (1983) 'Enclosure in north Buckinghamshire, 1500–1750', *Agricultural History Review* **31**, 104–42.

Richardson, H. G. (1942) 'The medieval plough-team', *History* **26**, 287–96.

Ridgard, J. (1988) 'The structure of a medieval manor'. In D. Dymond and E. Martin (eds.) *An Historical Atlas of Suffolk*, Ipswich, 70–1.

Riley, H. T. (ed.) (1867) *Gesta Abbatum Monasterii S. Albani* **1**, London.

Rippon, S. (1991) 'Early planned landscapes in south-east Essex', *Essex Archaeology and History* **22**, 46–60.

Ritchie, J. T. (1984) 'Validation of the CERES wheat model in diverse environments'. In W. Day and R. H. Atkin (eds.) *Wheat Growth and Modelling*, Bristol.

Roberts, B. K. (1977) *Rural Settlement in Britain*, Folkestone.

Roberts, B. K. (1973) 'Field systems of the west Midlands'. In A. R. H. Baker and R. A. Butlin (eds.) *Studies of Field Systems in the British Isles*, Cambridge, 195–205.

Roberts, B. K. and Wrathmell, S. (1998) 'Dispersed settlement in England: a national view'. In P. Everson and T. Williamson (eds.) *The Archaeology of Landscape: Studies Presented to Christopher Taylor*, Manchester, 95–116.

Roberts, B. K. and Wrathmell, S. (2000a) 'Peoples of wood and plain: an exploration of national and local regional contrasts'. In D. Hooke (ed.) *Landscape: The Richest Historical Record*, London, 85–96.

Roberts, B. K. and Wrathmell, S. (2000b) *An Atlas of Rural Settlement in England*, London.

Robinson, D. H. (1949) *Fream's Elements of Agriculture*, 13th edn., London.

Robinson, E. and Powell, D. (1984) *The Oxford Authors: John Clare*, Oxford.

Roden, D. (1973) 'Field systems of the Chiltern Hills and their environs'. In A. H. R. Baker and R. A. Butlin (eds.) *Studies of Field Systems in the British Isles*, Cambridge, 325–374.

Rodwell, W. J. and Rodwell, K. A. (1986) *Rivenhall: Investigations of a Villa, Church and Village, 1950–1977*, CBA Research Report 55, London.

Rodwell, K. A. (1988) *The Prehistoric and Roman Settlement at Kelvedon, Essex*, CBA Research Report 63, Chelmsford.

Rodwell, J. S. (ed.) (1991) *British Plant Communities Vol 2: Mires and Heaths*, Cambridge.

Rogerson, A. (1995) *Fransham: An Archaeological and Historical Study of a Parish on the Norfolk Boulder Clay*, unpublished PhD thesis, Centre of East Anglian Studies, University of East Anglia.

Rogerson, A. (1997) 'An archaeological and historical survey of the parish of Barton Bendish'. In A. Rogerson, A. Davison, D. Pritchard and R. Silvester, *Barton Bendish and Caldecote: Fieldwork in South-west Norfolk*. Published as *East Anglian Archaeology* 80, East Dereham.

Rowley, R. T. (1981) *The Origins of Open-Field Agriculture*, London.

Royal Commission on Historical Monuments, England. (1968) *An Inventory of the Historical Monuments in the County of Cambridge, Vol. 1: West Cambridgeshire*, London.

Royal Commission on Historical Monuments, England. (1979) *An Inventory of the Historical Monuments in the County of Northamptonshire, Vol. 2: Archaeological Sites in Central Northamptonshire*, London.

Royal Commission on Historical Monuments, England. (1981) *An Inventory of the Historical Monuments in the County of Northamptonshire, Vol. 3: Archaeological Sites in North-West Northamptonshire*, London.

Royal Commission on Historical Monuments, England. (1982) *An Inventory of the Historical Monuments in the County of Northamptonshire, Vol. 4: Archaeological Sites in South-West Northamptonshire*, London.

Sawyer, P. (1957) 'The density of Danish settlement in England', *University of Birmingham Journal* 6, 1, 1–17.

Sawyer, P. (1979) 'Medieval English settlement: new interpretations'. In P. Sawyer (ed.) *English Medieval Settlement*, London, 1–8.

Seebohm, F. (1890) *The English Village Community*, London.

Seymour, J. (1975) *The Complete Book of Self-Sufficiency*, London.

Sheppard, J. (1974) 'Metrological analysis of regular village plans in Yorkshire', *Agricultural History Review* 22, 118–35.

Sherlock, R. L. (1962) *British Regional Geology: London and the Thames Valley*, London.

Silvester, R. (1988) *The Fenland Project, No. 3: Norfolk Survey, Marshland and the Nar Valley* (published as: *East Anglian Archaeology* 45).

Silvester, R. (1993) 'The addition of more-or-less undifferentiated dots to a distribution map: the Fenland Survey in retrospect'. In J. Gardiner (ed.) *Flatlands and Wetlands: Current Themes in East Anglian Archaeology, East Anglian Archaeology Vol.* 50, Norwich, 24–39.

Silvester, R. (1999) 'Medieval reclamation of marsh and fen'. In H. Cook and T. Williamson (eds.) *Water Management in the English Landscape: Field, Marsh and Meadow*, Edinburgh, 122–40.

Skipper, K. (1989) *Wood-pasture: The Landscape of the Norfolk Claylands in the Early Modern Period*, unpublished MA thesis, Centre of East Anglian Studies, University of East Anglia.

Smith, A. H. (1956) *English Place Name Elements, Part 2*, Cambridge.

Smith, L. P (1967) *Potential Transpiration*, Technical Bulletin, Min. Ag. No. 16., London.

Smith, L. P and Trafford, B. D. (1978) *Climate and Drainage*, Technical Bulletin, Min. Ag. No. 34., London.

Smith, J. T. (1982) 'Villa plans and social structure in Britain and Gaul', *Bulletin de l'Institute Latines et de Centre de Recherches A. Piganiol* **17**, 321–36.

Spedding, C. R. and Diekmans, E. C. (1972) *Grass and Legumes in British Agriculture*, Farnham.

Stamp, L. Dudley (1950) *The Land of Britain: Its Use and Misuse*, London.

Steane, J. (1974) *The Northamptonshire Landscape*, London.

Stenton, F. M. (1942) 'The historical bearing of place name studies: the Danish settlement of eastern England', *Transactions of the Royal Historical Society* **24**, 1–24.

Stenton, F. M. (1947) *Anglo-Saxon England*, Oxford.

Stenton, F. M. (1961) *The First Century of English Feudalism, 1066–1166*, Oxford.

Taylor, C. (1973) *The Cambridgeshire Landscape*, London.

Taylor, C. (1975) 'Roman Settlements in the Nene valley: the impact of recent archaeology'. In P. J. Fowler (ed.) *Recent Work in Rural Archaeology*, Bradford on Avon, 107–19.

Taylor, C. (1981) 'Archaeology and the origins of open-field agriculture'. In T. Rowley (ed.) *The Origins of Open-Field Agriculture*, London, 13–22.

Taylor, C. (1983) *Village and Farmstead: A History of Rural Settlement in England*, London.

Taylor, C. (1995) 'Dispersed settlements in nucleated areas', *Landscape History* **17**, 27–34.

Taylor, C. and Oosthuizen, S. (2000) 'The morphology of Bassingbourne, Cambridgeshire', *The South-West Cambridgeshire Project: Interim Report, 1999–2000*, 38–43.

Thirsk, J. (1964) 'The common fields', *Past and Present* **29**, 3–29.

Thirsk, J. (1966) 'The origins of the common fields', *Past and Present* **33**, 142–7

Thirsk, J. (1987) *England's Agricultural Regions and Agrarian History 1500–1750*, London.

Thomasson, A. J. (1961) 'Some aspects of the drift deposits and geomorphology of south-east Hertfordshire', *Proceedings of the Geological Society* **72**, 287–302.

Thomasson, A. J. (1969) *Soils of the Saffron Walden District*, Harpenden.

Thomasson, A. J. (1975) *Soils and Field Drainage: Soil Survey Technical Monograph* **7**, Harpenden.

Turner, M. E. (1981) 'Arable in England and Wales: estimates from the 1801 Crop Return', *Journal of Historical Geography* **7**, 291–302.

Turner, M. E. (1982) *Volume 190: Home Office Acreage Returns HO67: List and Analysis*. Three parts, London.

Tyler, S. (1996) 'Early Saxon Essex AD *c.* 400–700'. In O. Bedwin (ed.) *The Archaeology of Essex: Proceedings of the Whittle Conference*, Chelmsford, 108–16.

Vancouver, C. (1813b) *General View of the Agriculture of Essex*, London.

Vinogradoff, P. (1892) *Villeinage in England*, Oxford.

Wade, K. (1980) 'A settlement site at Bonhunt Farm, Wicken Bonhunt, Essex'. In D. Buckley (ed.) *The Archaeology of Essex to AD 1500*, London, 96–102.

Wade, K. (1983) 'The early Anglo-Saxon period'. In A. J. Lawson (ed.) *The Archaeology of Witton, Near North Walsham, Norfolk*, published as *East Anglian Archaeology* **18**, 50–69.

Wade-Martins, P. (1980a) *Excavations in North Elmham Park, 1967–72, Vol 1. East Anglian Archaeology Report No. 9*, East Dereham.

Wade-Martins, P. (1980b) *Village Sites in the Launditch Hundred, East Anglian Archaeology* **10**, East Dereham.

Wade Martins, S. and Williamson, T. (1994) 'Floated water-meadows in Norfolk: a misplaced innovation', *Agricultural History Review* **42**, 20–37.

Bibliography

Wade Martins, S. and Williamson, T. (1999a) *Roots of Change: Farming and the Landscape in East Anglia 1700–1870*, Exeter.

Walker, D. (1795) *General View of the Agriculture of Hertfordshire*, London.

Wallis, S. and Waughman, M. (1998) *Archaeology and the Landscape in the Lower Blackwater Valley*. Published as *East Anglian Archaeology* **82**, Chelmsford.

Warner, P. (1986) 'Shared churchyards, free men church builders, and the development of parishes in eleventh-century East Anglia', *Landscape History* **8**, 39–52.

Warner, P. (1987) *Greens, Commons and Clayland Colonisation*, Leicester.

West, S. (1985) *West Stow: the Anglo-Saxon Village, Vol. 1: East Anglian Archaeology Report* **24**, Ipswich.

Whitelock, D. (1955) *English Historical Documents, Vol. 1: 500–1042*, London.

Whitelock, D. (1968) *The Will of Æthelgifu*, Oxford.

Williamson, J. (1984) 'Norfolk: the thirteenth century'. In P. D. A. Harvey (ed.) *The Peasant Land Market in England*, Oxford, 31–106.

Williamson, T. (1984) *Roman and Medieval Settlement in North-West Essex*, unpublished PhD thesis, University of Cambridge.

Williamson, T. (1986) 'The development of settlement in north-west Essex: the results of a recent field survey', *Essex Archaeology and History* **17**, 120–32.

Williamson, T. (1987) 'Early co-axial field systems on the East Anglian boulder clays', *Proceedings of the Prehistoric Society* **53**, 419–31.

Williamson, T. (1988) 'Explaining regional landscapes: woodland and champion in the south and east of England', *Landscape History* **10**, 5–13.

Williamson, T. (1993) *The Origins of Norfolk*, Manchester.

Williamson, T. (1998) 'The "Scole-Dickleburgh field system" revisited', *Landscape History* **20**, 19–28.

Williamson, T. (1999) 'Post-medieval field drainage'. In H. Cook and T. Williamson (eds.) *Water Management in the English Landscape: Field, Marsh and Meadow*, Edinburgh, 41–52.

Williamson, T. (2000a) *The Origins of Hertfordshire*, Manchester.

Williamson, T. (2000b), 'Understanding Enclosure', *Landscapes* **1.1**, 56–79.

Williamson, T. (2002) *The Transformation of Rural England: Farming and the Landscape 1700–1870*, Exeter.

Wilson, D. M. (1962) 'Anglo-Saxon rural economy: a survey of the archaeological evidence and a suggestion', *Agricultural History Review* **10**, 65–79.

Winchester, A. (1990) *Discovering Parish Boundaries*, Aylesbury.

Wingfield, C. (1995) 'The Anglo-Saxon settlement of Bedfordshire and Hertfordshire: the archaeological view'. In R. Holgate (ed.) *Chiltern Archaeology: Recent Work*, Dunstable, 31–43.

Witney, K. P. (1990) 'The woodland economy of Kent, 1066–1348', *Agricultural History Review* **38**, 20–39.

Yelling, J. A. (1977) *Common Field and Enclosure in England 1450–1850*, London.

Young, A. (1804) *General View of the Agriculture of Norfolk*, London.

Young, A. (1813) *General View of the Agriculture of Suffolk*, London.

Youngs, S. M., Gaimster, D. R. M., and Barry, T. 'Medieval Britain and Ireland in 1987', *Medieval Archaeology* **32** (1988), 265.

Index

211